re Notes in Computer Science

by G. Goos, J. Hartmanis and J. van Leeuwen

...pringer
...erlin
...eidelberg
...ew York
...rcelona
...ong Kong
...ndon
...ilan
...ris
...ngapore
...kyo

G. Feitelson   Larry Rudolph   (Eds.)

Scheduling Strategies
Parallel Processing

S 2000 Workshop, JSSPP 2000
ın, Mexico, May 1, 2000
edings

Springer

Series Editors

Gerhard Goos, Karlsruhe University, Germany
Juris Hartmanis, Cornell University, NY, USA
Jan van Leeuwen, Utrecht University, The Netherlands

Volume Editors

Dror G. Feitelson
The Hebrew University
School of Computer Science and Engineering
91904 Jerusalem, Israel
E-mail: feit@cs.huji.ac.il

Larry Rudolph
Massachusetts Institute of Technology
Laboratory for Computer Science
Cambridge, MA 02139, USA
E-mail: rudolph@lcs.mit.edu

Cataloging-in-Publication Data applied for

Die Deutsche Bibliothek - CIP-Einheitsaufnahme

Job scheduling strategies for parallel processing : proceedings /
JSPPS 2000 workshop, JSSPP 2000, Cancun, Mexico, May 1, 2000.
Dror G. Feitelson ; Larry Rudolph (ed.). - Berlin ; Heidelberg ; New York ;
Barcelona ; Hong Kong ; London ; Milan ; Paris ; Singapore ; Tokyo :
Springer, 2000
    (Lecture notes in computer science ; Vol. 1911)
    ISBN 3-540-41120-8

CR Subject Classification (1998): D.4, D.1.3, F.2.2., C.1.2, B.2.1, B.6, F.1.2

ISSN 0302-9743
ISBN 3-540-41120-8 Springer-Verlag Berlin Heidelberg New York

Springer-Verlag Berlin Heidelberg New York
a member of BertelsmannSpringer Science+Business Media GmbH
© Springer-Verlag Berlin Heidelberg 2000
Printed in Germany

Typesetting: Camera-ready by author, data conversion by Steingräber Satztechnik GmbH, Heidelberg
Printed on acid-free paper   SPIN: 10722727   06/3142   5 4 3 2 1 0

Preface

This volume contains the papers presented at the sixth workshop on Job Scheduling Strategies for Parallel Processing, which was held in conjunction with the IPDPS 2000 Conference in Cancun, Mexico, on 1 May 2000. The papers have been through a complete refereeing process, with the full version being read and evaluated by five to seven members of the program committee. We would like to take this opportunity to thank the program committee, Andrea Arpaci-Dusseau, Fran Berman, Steve Chapin, Allen Downey, Allan Gottlieb, Atsushi Hori, Phil Krueger, Richard Lagerstrom, Virginia Lo, Reagan Moore, Bill Nitzberg, Uwe Schwiegelshohn, and Mark Squillante, for an excellent job. Thanks are also due to the authors for their submissions, presentations, and final revisions for this volume. Finally, we would like to thank the MIT Laboratory for Computer Science and the Computer Science Institute at the Hebrew University for the use of their facilities in the preparation of these proceedings.

This was the sixth annual workshop in this series, which reflects the continued interest in this field. The previous five were held in conjunction with IPPS'95 through IPPS/SPDP'99. Their proceedings are available from Springer-Verlag as volumes 949, 1162, 1291, 1459, and 1659 of the Lecture Notes in Computer Science series. The last two are also available on-line from Springer LINK.

In addition to papers on traditional core areas of the workshop, such as gang scheduling and the effect of workload characteristics on performance, we experienced a return to basics. This was manifested in two recurring topics. One was the issue of system valuation (as in *value*), which included a report on the ASCI valuation project, a paper on the ESP system-level benchmark proposal, and a lively discussion that forced us to rearrange the division of papers into sessions. The other was advance reservations for meta-scheduling, which is similar to ideas such as backfilling on MPPs, but different enough to require new ideas, mechanisms, and policies.

We hope you find these papers interesting and useful.

June 2000

Dror Feitelson
Larry Rudolph

Table of Contents

Effect of Job Size Characteristics
on Job Scheduling Performance

Kento Aida

Department of Computational Intelligence and Systems Science,
Tokyo Institute of Technology
4259, Nagatsuta, Midori-ku, Yokohama-shi 226-8502, Japan
aida@dis.titech.ac.jp

Abstract. A workload characteristic on a parallel computer depends on
an administration policy or a user community for the computer system.
An administrator of a parallel computer system needs to select an appropriate scheduling algorithm that schedules multiple jobs on the computer
system efficiently. The goal of the work presented in this paper is to investigate mechanisms how job size characteristics affect job scheduling
performance. For this goal, this paper evaluates the performance of job
scheduling algorithms under various workload models, each of which has
a certain characteristic related to the number of processors requested by
a job, and analyzes the mechanism for job size characteristics that affect
job scheduling performance significantly in the evaluation. The results
showed that: (1) most scheduling algorithms classified into the first-fit
scheduling showed best performance and were not affected by job size
characteristics, (2) certain job size characteristics affected performance of
priority scheduling significantly. The analysis of the results showed that
the LJF algorithm, which dispatched the largest job first, would perfectly
pack jobs to idle processors at high load, where all jobs requested power-
of-two processors and the number of processors on a parallel computer
was power-of-two.

1 Introduction

Space sharing is one of the job scheduling strategies that are often used on
large-scale parallel computers. For instance, in pure space sharing among rigid
jobs, a submitted job requests a certain number of processors, and a job scheduler
dispatches the job to idle processors. Here, the number of processors that execute
the job is the same as that requested by the job. A job scheduler needs to
select a job to dispatch in appropriate order so as to execute multiple jobs
efficiently. Many job scheduling algorithms, *e.g.* conventional FCFS (First Come
First Served), LJF[1], Backfilling [2,3], Scan[4], etc., have been proposed, and
performance of these algorithms have been evaluated.

Many previous performance evaluation works assumed that characteristics
of parallel jobs, or a parallel workload, followed a simple mathematical model.
However, recent analysis of real workload logs, which are collected from many

D.G. Feitelson and L. Rudolph (Eds.): JSSPP 2000, LNCS 1911, pp. 1–17, 2000.

large-scale parallel computers in production use, shows that a real parallel workload has more complicated characteristics [5,6,7,8]. For instance, (1) a percentage of *small jobs*, which request small number of processors, is higher than that of *large jobs*, which request a large number of processors, (2) a percentage of jobs that request power-of-two processors is high, etc.

These job characteristics seem to affect job scheduling performance. Particularly, the effect of job size characteristics seems to be strong in pure space sharing among rigid jobs. Many researchers investigated performance of job scheduling algorithms under more realistic workloads, which have above job size characteristics [5,6,7,9]. For instance, Lo, Mache and Windisch compared performance of job scheduling algorithms under various workload models. They showed that the ScanUp algorithm [4] performed well, or increased processor utilization, as the proportion of jobs requesting power-of-two processors in the workload increased. However, mechanisms how the job size characteristics affect performance of job scheduling algorithms have not yet been discussed well.

This paper presents performance evaluation of job scheduling algorithms under various workload models, each of which has a certain characteristic related to the number of processors requested by a job. The goal of the work presented in this paper is to investigate mechanisms how the job size characteristics affect job scheduling performance. For this goal, this paper also analyzes the result in which job size characteristics affected job scheduling performance significantly. First, this paper shows five workload models used in the performance evaluation. Each model has a single characteristic for job size. For instance, a percentage of small jobs is high in one workload model, and all jobs request power-of-two processors in the other one. Because a real workload has a combination of the multiple characteristics, the workload models in this paper are not suitable to investigate practical performance of job scheduling algorithms. However, it is meaningful to investigate the effect by the individual characteristic on job scheduling performance in order to investigate the mechanisms how the job size characteristics affect job scheduling performance. Next, the paper classifies job scheduling algorithms into three groups by techniques mainly used in the algorithms. These groups are FCFS, priority scheduling and first-fit scheduling. Finally, the paper shows performance evaluation results by simulation and analyzes the result that showed most significant change. The evaluation results showed that: (1) most scheduling algorithms classified into the first-fit scheduling showed best performance and were not affected by job size characteristics, (2) certain job size characteristics affected performance of priority scheduling significantly. The analysis of the results showed that the LJF algorithm, which dispatched the largest job [1] first, would perfectly pack jobs to idle processors at high load, where all jobs requested power-of-two processors and the number of processors on a parallel computer was power-of-two.

Generally, a workload characteristic on a parallel computer depends on an administration policy or a user community. An administrator of a parallel computer needs to select an appropriate scheduling algorithm that schedules multiple jobs

---

[1] The largest job indicates the job that requests the largest number of processors.

on the computer efficiently. The results in this paper will be useful information for administrators of parallel computers.

The rest of the paper is organized as follows. Section 2 gives a job scheduling model including workload models assumed in this paper. Section 3 describes job scheduling algorithms evaluated in the paper. Section 4 presents and discusses performance evaluation results. Finally, Sect. 5 presents conclusions and future work.

2   Job Scheduling Model

This section gives a job scheduling model including workload models assumed in this paper.

2.1   Parallel Computer

A parallel computer assumed in this paper is a multiprocessor system that consists of m processors. The processors are connected equally by a crossbar switch network or a multistage interconnection network. Thus, this paper assumes that locations of processors that execute a single job affect the execution time of the job negligibly, and that the locations of other jobs executed on the computer affect the execution time of the job negligibly too.

2.2   Job Scheduler

Figure 1 illustrates a model of a job scheduler assumed in this paper. In the figure, a job submitted by a user arrives at the shared job queue, and the job scheduler obtains the number of processors requested by the job (job size) [2]. No other information is given to the job scheduler.

The job scheduler gathers status of processors, idle or busy, and dispatches a job in the shared job queue to idle processors. Here, there are two policies to execute a job. In the first policy, a job scheduler dispatches a job to S processors and guarantee the job to be executed on S processors until its completion. Here, S denotes job size. In the second policy, a job scheduler does not guarantee the job to be executed on S processors, that is, the number of processors to execute the job depends on a congestion level of jobs on the parallel computer. A job executed in the first policy is called a rigid job [10]. In this paper, all jobs that arrive at the shared job queue will be executed as rigid jobs.

2.3   Workloads

A job assumed in this paper has three parameters: (1) the number of processors that a job requests, or job size, (2) execution time and (3) arrival time.

---

[2] This paper assumes that job size is specified by a user.

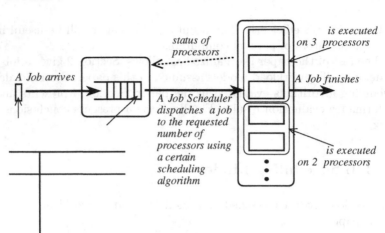

Fig. 1. A Model for a Job Scheduler

Job Size Recent analyses of real workload logs, which are collected from many large-scale parallel computers in production use, show that job size in real parallel workloads has following characteristics [5,6,7,8]:

(1) A percentage of small jobs, which request a small number of processors, is higher than that of large jobs, which request a large number of processors.
(2) A percentage of jobs that request power-of-two processors is high.
(3) A percentage of jobs that request square of n processors is high.
(4) A percentage of jobs that request multiples of 10 processors is high.

In order to discuss an effect of each characteristic on job scheduling performance, this paper uses following workload models in the performance evaluation. Each model is distinguished from others by distribution of job size. These models except the Uniform model were created from the Feitelson 1996 Model[5,8].

(a) Uniform model
    Job size is an integer that follows the Uniform distribution within the range $[1,m]$. This model is a very simple synthetic model that used in many previous performance evaluation works.
(b) Harmonic model
    Job size is an integer that follows the Harmonic distribution within the range $[1,m]$. The probability that $jobsize = n$ is proportional to $1/n^{1.5}$. This model represents the job size characteristic (1) in the above.
(c) Power2 model
    Job size is an integer that is calculated by 2^k within the range $[1,m]$. (k is an integer.) The probability of each value is uniform. This model represents the job size characteristic (2).
(d) Square model
    Job size is an integer that is calculated by k^2 within the range $[1,m]$. (k is

an integer.) The probability of each value is uniform. This model represents the job size characteristic (3).

(e) Multi10 model

Job size is an integer that is calculated by $10 \cdot k$ within the range $[1,m]$. (k is an integer.) The probability of each value is uniform. This model represents the job size characteristic (4).

Execution Time Execution time of a job follows the 3 Stage Hyper-exponential Distribution, which is defined in the Feitelson 1996 Model, in all workload models.

Arrival Time Job arrival is assumed to be Poisson in all workload models. This paper represents a congestion level of jobs on a parallel computer by *load*, which is defined by (1).

$$load = \frac{\lambda \cdot p}{m \cdot \mu} \tag{1}$$

Here, λ denotes an arrival rate of a job, and μ indicates mean service rate on a parallel computer, that is, $1/\mu$ represents mean execution time of a job. Also, p and m denote mean job size in a workload and the number of processors on a parallel computer respectively.

3 Job Scheduling Algorithm

This section describes job scheduling algorithms evaluated in this paper. This paper classifies job scheduling algorithms into three groups by techniques mainly used in the algorithms. These groups are FCFS, priority scheduling and first-fit scheduling. Table 1 summarizes classification of the algorithms, and details of the algorithms are as follows.

Table 1. A Summary of Job Scheduling Algorithms

algorithm	technique	
	priority	first-fit
FCFS	*no*	*no*
LJF	*yes*	*no*
SJF	*yes*	*no*
FCFS/First-Fit	*no*	*yes*
LJF/First-Fit	*yes*	*yes*
SJF/First-Fit	*yes*	*yes*

3.1 FCFS

FCFS (First Come First Served) is a simple and conventional algorithm. In the FCFS scheduling, a job scheduler dispatches a job at the top of a shared job queue to idle processors whenever enough idle processors to execute the job are available.

3.2 Priority Scheduling

Scheduling algorithms classified into the priority scheduling give a certain priority to each job in a shared job queue and dispatches the job with the highest priority to idle processors. This paper evaluates two algorithms classified into this groups: LJF (Largest Job First) and SJF (Smallest Job First). Both algorithms give each job a priority that is calculated by the job size. From an implementation point of view, a job scheduler sorts jobs in a shared job queue by the job size, and then dispatches a job at the top of the shared job queue to idle processors whenever enough idle processors to execute the job are available. The LJF sorts jobs to the non-increasing order, that is a job scheduler dispatches *the largest job*, the job with the largest job size, first. On the other hand, the SJF sorts jobs to the non-decreasing order, or a job scheduler dispatches *the smallest job* first.

LJF[1], Scan[4] and Subhlok96[6] can be classified into this group, because a job scheduler dispatches the largest/smallest job first in these algorithms.

3.3 First-Fit Scheduling

Scheduling algorithms classified into the first-fit scheduling dispatch jobs in a *first-fit* manner, or a job scheduler searches jobs in a shared job queue and dispatches the first job for which enough idle processors are available. This paper evaluates three algorithms classified into this group: FCFS/First-Fit, LJF/First-Fit and SJF/First-Fit. In the FCFS/First-Fit, a job scheduler searches jobs in a shared job queue from the top to the bottom, and dispatches the first job with job size that is not greater than the number of idle processors.

The LJF/First-Fit and the SJF/First-Fit use techniques both in the priority scheduling and in the first-fit scheduling. In the LJF/First-Fit, a job scheduler sorts jobs in a shared job queue to the non-increasing order of job size, and then dispatches jobs in the same way as FCFS/First-Fit. The SJF/First-Fit dispatches job in the same way as the LJF/First-Fit except that a job scheduler sorts jobs to the non-decreasing order of job size.

Backfilling[2,3], FCFS-fill[11], LSF-RTC[2] and FPFS[12] can be classified into this group.

4   Performance Evaluation

This section shows simulation results to evaluate performance of job scheduling algorithms under the workload models described in Sect. 2. The simulation model

follows the model described in Sect. 2. Here, the number of processors on a parallel computer, or m, is 128, and maximum execution time of a job is limited to 12 hours. Scheduling overhead is assumed to be negligible.

Performance of job scheduling algorithms is measured by two metrics: processor utilization and slowdown ratio. Processor utilization is the percentage that processors are busy over entire simulation. Slowdown ratio, SR, shows normalized data for mean response time, and it is derived by (2)[9].

$$SR = \frac{T_{\text{mean\_response}}}{T_{\text{mean\_execution}}} \tag{2}$$

Here, $T_{\text{mean\_response}}$ and $T_{\text{mean\_execution}}$ denote mean response time of a job and mean execution time of a job respectively. For instance, let us suppose that 10000 jobs were executed in an experiment. The mean response time of these 10000 jobs was 5 hours, and their mean execution time on processors was 2 hours. Then, the slowdown ratio is 2.5.

Job scheduling algorithms evaluated by the simulation are those in Table 1 and Backfilling[2,3]. The Backfilling is a similar algorithm to the FCFS/First-Fit except that it dispatches jobs in a more conservative way. In the Backfilling, a job scheduler estimates the time when a job waiting at the top of a shared job queue will be dispatched, and then dispatches other waiting jobs for which enough idle processors are available, so long as they do not delay the start time of the waiting job at the top of the shared job queue [3]. The Backfilling can not be performed in the job scheduling model described in Sect. 2 because a job scheduler needs to obtain execution time of each job in advance [4]. However, this paper assumes that a job scheduler under the Backfilling obtains execution time of each job when a job arrives, and shows results for the Backfilling in order to see difference between the performance of the Backfilling and that of the FCFS/First-Fit. The performance of the Backfilling will be affected by the accuracy of estimated job execution time. This paper assumes that the job scheduler obtain the exact execution time. In other words, the evaluation results will show the best performance of the Backfilling. In addition, scheduling performed by the SJF/First-Fit is same as that by the SJF. Thus, results of the SJF/First-Fit are omitted from the paper.

Results shown in this section represent the average of 100 experiments, each of which runs 10000 jobs. The *load* does not vary during the experiment. The results have confidence intervals of ±10% or less at 95% confidence level. Performance evaluation results under each job model described in Sect. 2 are as follows:

4.1 Uniform

Figure 2 and Fig. 3 show processor utilization and slowdown ratio respectively under the Uniform model. Both for processor utilization and for slowdown ratio,

---

[3] There are variations of the Backfilling. The algorithm used in this paper is called aggressive backfilling [13].

[4] Recall that information that a job scheduler obtains from a job is only the job size in this model.

algorithms both in the priority scheduling and in the first-fit scheduling showed better performance as compared with the FCFS, except that the LJF slightly degraded slowdown ratio. In the priority scheduling algorithms, the LJF showed better processor utilization than the SJF. The maximum improvement by the LJF on the FCFS was 16% [5]. The algorithm that showed the best performance in the first-fit scheduling was the LJF/First-Fit, and it improved processor utilization compared with the FCFS by 34% maximum.

When job size of a job at the top of a shared job queue is larger than the number of idle processors, the FCFS *blocks* dispatch of other jobs even when there are enough idle processors for other jobs in the shared job queue. This paper calls this situation *blocking*. The reason for low performance of the FCFS is that frequent blocking left many processors to be idle, that is, a job scheduler wasted many processor resources. In other words, the reason why the priority scheduling and the first-fit scheduling showed better performance than the FCFS is that they avoided wasting processor resources by sorting jobs or by searching jobs. The rest of this section discusses these reasons in detail.

First, this section discusses performance of the LJF. A scheduling problem discussed here can be regarded as the one-dimensional bin-packing problem, in which a job scheduler attempts to pack jobs into the idle processor space [6]. In the one-dimensional bin-packing problem, it is proved that waste of space in a bin is reduced by putting items into the non-increasing order of the item's size[14]. The LJF improved processor utilization because of this nature of the one-dimensional bin-packing problem. On the other hand, the LJF blocks dispatch of many small jobs by giving priority to larger jobs. Consequently, the LJF made response time of many small jobs longer, and then slowdown ratio under the LJF was slightly higher than that under the FCFS

Next, the reason why the SJF showed better performance compared with the FCFS is that the SJF reduced the occurrence of blocking. Blocking is caused by the situation that a larger job at the top of a shared job queue waits for dispatch while smaller jobs, for which enough idle processors are available, exist in the queue. In the SJF, a job scheduler gave a higher priority to smaller jobs, and it prevented that a larger job blocked dispatch of many smaller jobs. For this reason, the SJF improved processor utilization. Also, the reason why slowdown ratio under the SJF was much lower than those both under the FCFS and under the LJF is that a large number of smaller jobs were dispatched prior to a small number of larger jobs.

Job scheduling algorithms in the first-fit scheduling including the Backfilling showed best performance under the Uniform model. The reason for this best performance is that they prevented the occurrence of blocking efficiently by searching jobs in a shared job queue and dispatching a job for which enough idle processors are available. Although the priority scheduling also improved perfor-

---

[5] The improvement indicated by "%" means $\frac{higher\ utilization - lower\ utilization}{lower\ utilization}$ [%] in this paper.

[6] This paper use the term "idle processor space" to refer to a bin that has capacity of the number of idle processors.

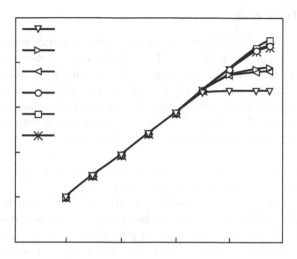

Fig. 2. Processor Utilization (Uniform)

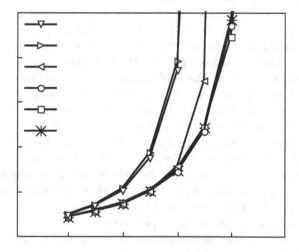

Fig. 3. Slowdown Ratio (Uniform)

mance, they could not prevent blocking as sufficiently as the first-fit scheduling. For further analysis for performance of the first-fit scheduling under the Uniform model, see[12].

4.2 Harmonic

Figure 4 and Fig. 5 show processor utilization and slowdown ratio respectively under the Harmonic model. There are several differences between results under the Uniform model and those under the Harmonic model. The major difference is observed in performance of the SJF. Processor utilization by the SJF under the Harmonic model was higher than that under the Uniform model. It showed better performance than the LJF. The SJF improved processor utilization compared with FCFS by 32% maximum, while the improvement under the Uniform model was 13%.

The reason for the performance difference is as follows: In order to improve processor utilization, it is effective to pack multiple jobs efficiently and to execute them concurrently, e.g. packing a large job with multiple small jobs, packing multiple small jobs and etc., so that waste of processor resources will be reduced. In the Uniform model, job size of jobs that arrive at a shared job queue follows the uniform distribution. A job scheduler dispatches small jobs prior to large jobs. Consequently, when the job scheduler dispatches a large job that remains in the shared job queue, there are not enough small jobs to be packed with the large job in the queue. On the other hand, under the Harmonic model, an arrival rate of small jobs is much higher than that of large jobs. It means that the probability that small jobs arrive soon after the job scheduler dispatches a large job is much higher. Thus, these small jobs will be packed with the large job. For this reason, the SJF under the Harmonic model packed multiple jobs more efficiently compared with that under the Uniform model.

In addition, slowdown ratio by the SJF under the Harmonic model was much lower than that under the Uniform model. It was close to slowdown ratio by the FCFS/First-Fit and the LJF/First-Fit, which were also much lower than that under Uniform Model. Their slowdown ratio remained small at higher *load*, e.g. lower than six at *load* = 0.9, while their slowdown ratio under the Uniform model went to infinity at *load* > 0.8. The reason why these scheduling algorithms showed lower slowdown ratio is that these dispatched a large number of small jobs prior to a small number of large jobs, where the number of small jobs under the Harmonic model was much greater than that under the Uniform model. For instance, 90% of jobs requested 16 processors or less and 58% of jobs requested two processors or less in the experiment.

The next major difference observed in the results is performance of the Backfilling. While the Backfilling showed almost same performance as other algorithms in the first-fit scheduling under the Uniform Model, the performance of the Backfilling was lower than the others under the Harmonic model. For instance, the Backfilling improved processor utilization compared with the FCFS by 31% maximum, while the improvement by the FCFS/First-Fit was 40%. It is supposed that the reason is due to the conservative way to dispatch jobs in the Backfilling. Further discussion about this reason is required but it will be the author's future work.

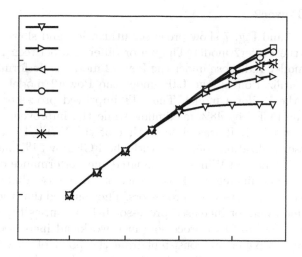

Fig. 4. Processor Utilization (Harmonic)

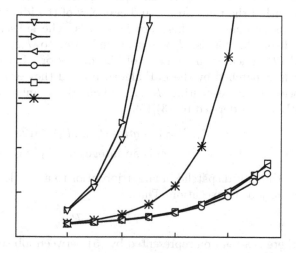

Fig. 5. Slowdown Ratio (Harmonic)

4.3   Power2

Figure 6 and Fig. 7 show processor utilization and slowdown ratio respectively under the Power2 model. The major difference between results under the Uniform model and those under the Power2 model is performance of the LJF. Processor utilization by the LJF under the Power2 model was higher than that under the Uniform model. The LJF improved processor utilization compared with the FCFS by 48% maximum, while the improvement under the Uniform model was 16%. It was close to that of the FCFS/First-Fit, which improved processor utilization compared with the FCFS by 51% maximum.

Lo, Mache and Windisch compared the performance of job scheduling algorithms under different workloads, each of which has a different proportion of jobs that request power-of-two processors. They showed that the ScanUp algorithm[4] performed well, or increased processor utilization, as the proportion of jobs requesting power-of-two processors in a workload increased. Both results by Lo and by this paper are consistent from the point of view that a job scheduling algorithm performs well under the workload in which the proportion of jobs requesting power-of-two jobs is high.

The reason for the high processor utilization by the LJF under the Power2 model is that the LJF packed jobs very efficiently. In order to show the reasons more precisely, this paper regards the scheduling problem discussed here as the one-dimensional bin-packing problem again. The goal is to pack items, or jobs, into the bin, or the idle processor space, efficiently. Here, job size is 2^n (n is an integer within the range [0,7]), and capacity of the idle processor space is 2^7.

Let us assume that there are jobs, J_i's. The subscript denotes the order of the dispatch, that is, J_i is dispatched prior to J_{i+1}. P_i denotes job size of J_i, and IP indicates the number of idle processors. Let us suppose that s jobs has been dispatched by the LJF algorithm and they are still in execution, that is, processors are executing $J_1...J_s$. Then, the number of processors that are currently idle is derived by (3)[15].

$$IP = c_1 \cdot min(P_1, ..., P_s) \leq 128 \tag{3}$$
$$c_1 \text{ is an integer and } c_1 \geq 0$$

Because the LJF dispatches a larger job prior to a smaller job, J_s is the smallest job among jobs in execution. Thus,

$$IP = c_1 \cdot P_s. \tag{4}$$

Here, there is a relation represented by (5) between job size of the job at the top of a shared job queue, namely P_{s+1}, and job size of J_s, or P_s.

$$P_s = 2^{c_2} \cdot P_{s+1} \leq 128 \tag{5}$$
$$c_2 \text{ is an integer and } c_1 \geq 0$$

Therefore, (6) is derived from both (4) and (5).

$$IP = c \cdot P_{s+1} \leq 128 \tag{6}$$
$$c = c_1 \cdot 2^{c_2}$$

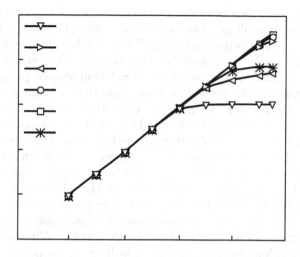

Fig. 6. Processor Utilization (Power2)

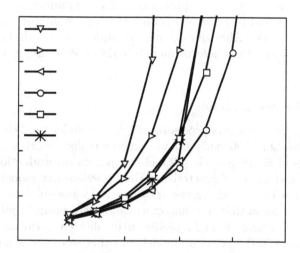

Fig. 7. Slowdown Ratio (Power2)

Equation (6) indicates that the number of idle processors will always be an integer multiple (possibly zero) of job size of the job at the top of a shared job queue, when the LJF performs job scheduling. Consequently, while enough number of jobs wait in a shared job queue, the LJF will pack jobs so as to fill idle processors perfectly.

The discussion mentioned above is valid for off-line bin-packing, or the assumption that all jobs have arrived at a shared job queue before a job scheduler starts to perform the scheduling. The job scheduling model in this paper could not be regarded as the off-line bin-packing. However, simulation log indicated that scheduling performed in the simulation showed partially same behavior as the discussion above when *load* was high, that is, many jobs were dispatched like off-line bin-packing at high *load*. Thus, the reason why processor utilization by LJF under the Power2 model was high can be explained by the above discussion.

While processor utilization by the LJF was high, slowdown ratio was not so good. The reason is same as that under the Uniform model, that is, the LJF blocked dispatch of many small jobs by giving a higher priority to larger jobs. Also, the reason why slowdown ratio by the LJF/First-Fit was worse than that by the FCFS/First-Fit is the same as the previous reason.

In addition, as the results under the Harmonic model, performance of the Backfilling was also lower than the FCFS/First-Fit under the Power2 model. The Backfilling improved processor utilization compared with the FCFS by 28% maximum, while the improvement by the FCFS/First-Fit was 51%.

4.4   Square and Multi10

Figure 8 and Fig. 9 show processor utilization under the Square model and the Multi10 model respectively. Both results were almost same as that under the Uniform model. Also, slowdown ratio under these both models were also similar to that under the Uniform model. This paper omits graphs for the slowdown ratio.

4.5   Feitelson Model

Finally, Fig. 10 shows processor utilization under the Feitelson 1996 model[5,8]. The Feitelson 1996 model is a well-known realistic workload model that is created by logs of six large-scale parallel computers in production use. A workload in this model has all characteristics that previous five models have.

Under this model, processor utilization was similar to that under the Power2 model. It mean that the characteristic, a percentage of jobs that request power-of-two processors is high, significantly affected performance of job scheduling algorithms in the Feitelson model. In other words, it seems that the proportion of jobs requesting power-of-two processors has strong effect on job scheduling performance in the real workload.

5   Conclusions

The goal of the work presented in this paper is to investigate mechanisms how job size characteristics affect job scheduling performance. This paper presented overall performance evaluation to show effect of an individual job size characteristic on job scheduling performance, and analyzed the evaluation result that showed most significant change.

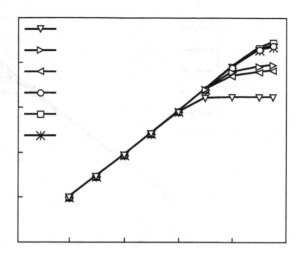

Fig. 8. Processor Utilization (Squares)

The evaluation results showed that:

(1) The first-fit scheduling except the Backfilling showed best performance and were not affected by job size characteristics.
(2) Job size characteristics modeled by the Harmonic model and that by the Power2 model affected performance of priority scheduling significantly. Particularly, the effect of the job size characteristic under the Power2 model on the LJF performance was most significant among the results. It improved processor utilization compared with the FCFS by 48% maximum, while the improvement under the Uniform model was 16%.
(3) The analysis of scheduling performed by the LJF under the Power2 model showed that the LJF would perfectly pack jobs to idle processors at high load, where all jobs requested power-of-two processors and the number of processors on a parallel computer was power-of-two.

The analysis for the results in this paper has not yet been complete in order to achieve the goal. There are results that need more precise analysis, e.g. the effect on performance of the Backfilling. Furthermore, Scheduling algorithms evaluated in this paper, except the FCFS and the Backfilling, are not starvation-free. Thus, these scheduling algorithms need to be performed with some aging technique in order to improve practicability. However, the aging may affect performance of the job scheduling algorithms. It seems that this is a reason why the Backfilling showed lower performance than the FCFS/First-Fit. The author has evaluated the effect of an aging technique on the performance of the FCFS/First-Fit[12].

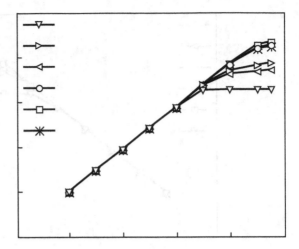

Fig. 9. Processor Utilization (Multi10)

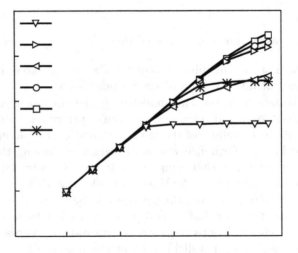

Fig. 10. Processor Utilization (Feitelson)

In this FCFS/First-Fit with aging, a job scheduler suppress to search jobs in a shared job queue when there exists a job waiting for long time (more than the pre-defined threshold), and dispatches this job first. The results showed that processor utilization of the FCFS/First-Fit with aging was degraded compared with that without aging. There are many aging techniques[4,12] for job scheduling algorithms, and effects of the aging techniques on job scheduling performance seems to be various. Discussion about the effects is the author's future work.

References

1. K. Li and K. Cheng. Job Scheduling in a Partitionable Mesh Using a Two-Dimensional Buddy System Partitioning Scheme. *IEEE Trans. on Parallel and Distributed Systems*, 2(4):413–422, 1991.
2. D. A. Lifka. The ANL/IBM SP Scheduling System. In *Job Scheduling Strategies for Parallel Processing, Lecture Notes in Computer Science 949*, pages 295–303. Springer-Verlag, 1995.
3. J. S. Skovira, W. Chan, and H. Zhou. The EASY - LoadLeveler API Project. In *Job Scheduling Strategies for Parallel Processing, Lecture Notes in Computer Science 1162*, pages 41–47. Springer-Verlag, 1996.
4. P. Krueger, T. Lai, and V. A. Dixit-Radiya. Job Scheduling Is More Important than Processor Allocation for Hypercube Computers. *IEEE Trans. on Parallel and Distributed Systems*, 5(5):488–497, 1994.
5. D. G. Feitelson. Packing Scheme for Gang Scheduling. In *Job Scheduling Strategies for Parallel Processing, Lecture Notes in Computer Science 1162*, pages 89–110. Springer-Verlag, 1996.
6. J. Subhlok, T. Gross, and T Suzuoka. Impact of Job Mix on Optimizations for Space Sharing Scheduler. In *Proc. of Supercomputing '96*, 1996.
7. A. B. Downey. A parallel workload model and its implications for processor allocation. In *Proc. the 6th International Symposium of High Performance Distributed Computing*, pages 112–123, 1997.
8. Parallel Workloads Archive. http://www.cs.huji.ac.il/labs/parallel/workload/.
9. V. Lo, J. Mache, and K. Windisch. A Comparative Study of Real Workload Traces and Synthetic Workload. In *Job Scheduling Strategies for Parallel Processing, Lecture Notes in Computer Science 1459*, pages 25–46. Springer-Verlag, 1998.
10. D. G. Feitelson and L. Rudolph. Toward Convergence in Job Schedulers for Parallel Supercomputers. In *Job Scheduling Strategies for Parallel Processing, Lecture Notes in Computer Science 1162*, pages 1–26. Springer-Verlag, 1996.
11. R. Gibbons. A Historical Application Profiler for Use by Parallel Schedulers. In *Job Scheduling Strategies for Parallel Processing, Lecture Notes in Computer Science 1291*, pages 58–77. Springer-Verlag, 1997.
12. K. Aida, H. Kasahara, and S. Narita. Job Scheduling Scheme for Pure Space Sharing Among Rigid Jobs. In *Job Scheduling Strategies for Parallel Processing, Lecture Notes in Computer Science 1459*, pages 98–121, 1998.
13. H. Franke, J. Jann, J. E. Moreira, P. Pattnaik, and M. A. Jette. An Evaluation of Parallel Job Scheduling for ASCI Blue-Pacific. In *Proc. SC99*, 1999.
14. E. G. Coffman, M. R. Garey, and D. S. Johnson. Approximation Algorithms for Bin-packing - An Updated Survey. In *Algorithm Design for Computer System Design*, pages 49–106. Springer-Verlag, 1984.
15. E. G. Coffman, M. R. Garey, and D. S. Johnson. Bin Packing with Divisible Item Sizes. *Journal of Complexity*, 3:406–428, 1987.

Improving Parallel Job Scheduling
Using Runtime Measurements

Fabricio Alves Barbosa da Silva[1] and Isaac D. Scherson[1,2]

[1] Université Pierre et Marie Curie, Laboratoire ASIM, LIP6, Paris, France.
fabricio.silva@lip6.fr
[2] Information and Comp. Science, University of California, Irvine, CA 92697 U.S.A.
isaac@uci.edu

Abstract. We investigate the use of runtime measurements to improve job scheduling on a parallel machine. Emphasis is on gang scheduling based strategies. With the information gathered at runtime, we define a task classification scheme based on fuzzy logic and Bayesian estimators. The resulting local task classification is used to provide better service to I/O bound and interactive jobs under gang scheduling. This is achieved through the use of idle times and also by controlling the spinning time of a task in the spin block mechanism depending on the node's workload. Simulation results show considerable improvements, in particular for I/O bound workloads, in both throughput and machine utilization for a gang scheduler using runtime information compared with gang schedulers for which this type of information is not available.

1 Introduction

We analyze the utilization of runtime information in parallel job scheduling to improve throughput and utilization on a parallel computer. Our objective is to use certain job and/or architecture dependent parameters to cluster tasks into classes. Parameters may include number of I/O calls, duration of I/O calls, number of messages sent/received. It will be seen that the task classification is done using fuzzy sets and Bayesian estimators. Observe that the classification of a task may change over time, since we consider, as in [2], that characteristics of jobs may change during execution.

We will deal with gang scheduling based strategies. Gang scheduling can be defined as follows: Given a job composed of N tasks, in gang scheduling these N tasks compose a process working set[22], and all tasks belonging to this process working set are scheduled simultaneously in different processors, i.e., gang scheduling is the class of algorithms that schedule on the basis of whole process working sets. Gang scheduling allows both the time sharing as well as the space sharing of the machine, and was originally introduced by Ousterhout[22]. Performance benefits of gang scheduling the set of tasks of a job has been extensively analyzed in [16,10,13,30] Packing schemes for Gang scheduling were analyzed in [9].

D.G. Feitelson and L. Rudolph (Eds.): JSSPP 2000, LNCS 1911, pp. 18–39, 2000.

Some possible uses for the task classification information are to decide which task to schedule next, to decide what to do in the case of an idle slot in gang scheduling, or to define spinning time of a task in the spin block mechanism[1,8] depending on the total workload on a processor. In the spin block mechanism, a task spins for some time before blocking while waiting for an incoming message. The idea is to vary this spinning time of a task depending on the workload at a given time. Our objective is to give better service to I/O bound and interactive tasks. Another possibility is to use task classification to identify I/O bound tasks in order to reschedule them in idle slots or if a gang scheduled task blocks itself. This approach is different from the one proposed in Lee et al. [20] since it does not interrupt running jobs.

This paper is organized as follows: in section 2 we discuss some previous work in parallel/distributed job scheduling that considers the use of runtime information to modify scheduling-related parameters at runtime. Section 3 presents the task classification mechanism based on runtime information we use in this paper. How to use this information to improve throughput and utilization in parallel job scheduling through a priority computation mechanism is discussed at section 4. Section 5 discusses the utilization of task classification information to control spin time in the spin-block mechanism in order to give better service to I/O bound and interactive jobs in gang scheduling. Our experimental results are presented and discussed in section 6 and section 7 contains our final remarks.

2   Previous Work

In [1], Arpaci-Dusseau, Culler and Mainwaring use information available at run time (in this case the number of incoming messages) to decide if a task should continue to spin or block in the pairwise cost benefit analysis in the implicit coscheduling algorithm.

In [14], Feitelson and Rudolph used runtime information to identify activity working sets, i.e. the set of activities (tasks) that should be scheduled together, through the monitoring of the utilization pattern of *communication objects* by the activities. Their work can be considered complementary to ours in the sense that our objective here is not to identify activity working sets at runtime but to improve throughput and utilization of parallel machines for different scheduling strategies using such runtime information.

In [20], Lee et al., along with an analysis of I/O implications for gang scheduled workloads, presented a method for runtime identification of gangedness, through the analysis of messaging statistics. It differs from our work in the sense that our objective is not to explicitly identify gangedness, but to provide a task classification, which may vary over time depending on the application, which can also be used to verify the gangedness of an application at a given time among other possibilities.

This paper is an extension of some of our previous work [25,26] where we describe the Concurrent Gang scheduling algorithm. Here we present a more robust task classification scheme and we investigate new ways of providing better service to I/O and interactive applications in gang scheduling. This is achieved by using idle slots and idle time due to blocked tasks and also by the variation of the spinning time of a task. In the determination of the spin time of a task we take into account runtime information about other tasks in the same PE.

3   Task Classification Using Runtime information

As described in the introduction, our objective is the utilization of various runtime measurements, such as I/O access rates and communication rates, to improve the utilization and throughput in parallel job scheduling. This is achieved through a task classification scheme using runtime information. In this section we detail the task classification made by the operating system based on runtime measurements using fuzzy logic theory. A discussion of the utilization of Bayesian estimators to increase the robustness of the first scheme based on fuzzy logic follows, and a "fuzzy" variation of the Bayesian estimator is presented.

3.1   Task Classification

We will use the information gathered at runtime to allow each PE to classify each one of its allocated tasks into a number of previously defined classes. Examples of such classes are: I/O intensive, communication intensive, and computation intensive. Each one of these classes is represented by a fuzzy set [31]. A fuzzy set is characterized by a membership function $f_A(x)$ with associates each task T to a real number in the interval [0,1], with the value of $f_A(T)$ representing the "grade of membership"[31] of T in A. Thus, the nearer the value of $F_A(T)$ to unity, the higher the grade of membership of T in A, that is, the degree to which a task belongs to a given class. For instance, consider the class of I/O intensive tasks, with its respective characteristic function $f_{IO}(T)$. A value of $f_{IO}(T) = 1$ indicates that the task T belongs to the class I/O intensive with maximum degree 1, while a value of $f_{IO}(x) = 0$ indicates that the task T has executed no I/O statement at all. Observe the deterministic nature of grade of membership associations. It is also worth noting that the actual number of classes used on a system depends on the architecture of the machine.

The information related to a task is gathered during system calls and context switches. Information that can be used to compute the grade of membership are the type, number and time spent on system calls, number and destination of messages sent by a task, number and origin of received messages, and other system dependent data. These informations can be stored, for instance, by the operating system on the internal data structure related to the task.

When applying fuzzy sets to task classification, the value of $f(T)$ for a class is computed by the PE on a regular basis, at the preemption of the related task. As an example, let's consider the I/O intensive class. On each I/O related system call, the operating system will store information related to the call on the internal data structure associated to the task, and at the end of the time slice, the scheduler computes the time spent on I/O calls in the previous slice.

One possible way of computing the grade of membership of a task to the class I/O intensive is to consider an average of the time spent in I/O that is made over the last N times where the task was scheduled. As many jobs proceed in phases, the reason for using an average over the last N times a task was scheduled is detection of phase change. If a task changes from a I/O intensive phase to a computation intensive phase, this change should be detected by the scheduler. In this case, the average time spent in I/O statements will reduce while the average time spent in computational statements will increase. The grades of membership for the classes I/O intensive and computation intensive will follow this variation.

In general, the computation of the degree of membership of a task to the class I/O intensive will always depend on the number and/or duration of the I/O system calls made by the task. The same is valid for the communication intensive class; the number and/or duration of communication statements will define the grade of membership of a task to this class. For the class computing intensive, grade of membership will also be a function of system calls and communication statements, but in another sense: for a smaller the number of system calls and communications there is a increase of the grade of membership of a given task to the class computing intensive.

In the subsection 3.3 we present a more robust way for computing the grade of membership of a task related to a class than the average over N slices presented in this subsection, through the use of Bayesian estimators. Then a practical example for task classification computation is presented in subsection 3.4 along with an overhead analysis of the process. In the next subsection we further develop the concept of classes as fuzzy sets.

3.2   Classes as Points

Fuzzy sets can be better visualized using the geometric representation shown in figure 1[18]. A fuzzy set is represented by a point in the cube. The set of all fuzzy subsets equals the unit hypercube $I^n = [0, 1]$. A fuzzy set is any point in the cube I. So (X, I^n) defines the fundamental measurable space of finite fuzzy theory.

Now consider the fuzzy subsets of X. We can view the fuzzy subset B=(1/3, 2/3) (which in our case is equal to a class) as one of the continuum many continuous valued membership function $M_A : X \longrightarrow [0, 1]$. Indeed this corresponds to the classical Zadeh sets as functions definition of fuzzy sets. In this example element t_1 belongs to, or fits in, subset B to degree 1/3. Element t_2 has a membership of 2/3. Analogous to the bit vector representation of finite countable sets, we say that the fit vector (1/3, 2/3) represents B. The element $m_B(x_i)$ equals the *ith* fit or or fuzzy unit value. The sets as points view the geometrically represents the fuzzy subset B as a point in the I^2, the unit square, as in figure 1

Viewing a class as a fuzzy sets corresponds to associate them to a point in a n-dimensional space, with n being the number of tasks allocated to a processor at time T. That is, given a class B, it can be described at a given time T as B(T) = $(f_B(t_1), f_B(t_2), f_B(t_3), ..., f_B(t_n))$ for tasks $t_1, t_2, t_3, ..., t_n$.

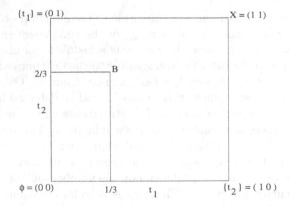

Fig. 1. Sets as points. The class B (which is also a fuzzy subset) is a point in the unit 2-cube with coordinates of fit values (1/3,2/3), considering a processing element with two tasks. The first task t_1 fits or belongs to B to degree 1/3, the task t_2 to degree 2/3. The cube consists of all possible fuzzy sets of two elements t_1, t_2.

3.3   Task Classification Using Bayesian Estimators

In this section we introduce a more robust task classification mechanism than the one described in section 3.1, which is a average of the last N measurements, using elements of Bayesian decision theory. Bayesian decision theory is a formal mathematical structure which guides a decision maker in choosing a course of action in the face of uncertainty about the consequences of that choice[17]. In particular we will be interested in this section in defining a task classifier using a Bayesian estimator adapted to the fuzzy theory.

A Bayesian model is a statistical description of an estimation problem which has two main components. The first component, the prior model $p(u)$ (this probability function is also known as prior probability distribution) is a probabilistic description of the world or its properties before any sense data is collected. The second component, the sensor model $p(d|u)$, is a description of the noisy or stochastic process that relate the original (unknown) state u to the sampled input image or sensor values d. These two probabilistic models can be combined to obtain a posterior model, $p(u|d)$ (posterior probability distribution), which is the probabilistic description of the current estimate of u given the data d. To compute the posterior model we use Bayes' rule:

$$p(u|d) = \frac{p(d|u)p(u)}{p(d)} \qquad (1)$$

where

$$p(d) = \sum_u p(d|u)p(u) \qquad (2)$$

The fuzzy version of equation 1 to compute the grade membership of a task T to a class i as a function of measurement E can be written as[19]:

$$S_E(i) = \frac{S_i(E)f_i(T)}{\sum_1^k S_j(E)f_j(T)} \tag{3}$$

Where $S_j(k)$ represents subsethood between two fuzzy sets j and k. In our case $S_i(E)$ is the subsethood between the two fuzzy sets represented by measurement E on task T and class i. Therefore, $S_i(E)$ is the grade of membership of task T relative to class i considering only the data gathered at measurement E. $f_i(T)$ is the grade of membership of task T relative to class i before measurement E. $S_E(i)$ represents the grade of membership of task T relative to class i after the measurement E. It becomes $f_i(T)$ in the next interval computation.

3.4   Overhead Analysis of Information Gathering

It is possible to compute the grade of membership of a task using equation 3 with very low overhead and a small amount of stored information based on the number of executed statements related to a task. This can be done, for instance, as follows: at initialization the grade of membership $(f_i(T))$ of a task related to each class is equal to 1/2, as well as the measurement related to each class $(S_i(E))$. The measurement related to a time slice is described below. In the following, we consider three classes: I/O intensive, computation intensive and communication intensive.

- If the task is blocked due to an I/O call in that time slice, the measurement of the grade of membership of the class I/O bound is equal to 1/2. Otherwise is equal to zero.
- If the task executes a number N of communication statements in a time slice, the measurement of the grade of membership of the class communication intensive is equal to 1/2. Otherwise is equal to zero. If a task blocks due to I/O and, before blocking, executes N or more communication statements, we can consider two cases. First, both measurements related to the classes I/O intensive and communication intensive are equal to 1/2. Second, only the measurement related to the class communication intensive is equal to 1/2, with the measurement related to the class I/O intensive being equal to zero. Which strategy to choose depends on the use made by the scheduler of the task classification information.
- If the task is not blocked due to an I/O call and executes less than N communication statements, the measurement of the grade of membership of the class computation intensive for that time slice is equal to 1/2. Otherwise is equal to zero.

The measurement for an interval is then summed to the previous total measurement multiplied by 1/2, becoming the new total measurement for a given class. Observe that the total measurement related to each class is a real number between]0,1[. Having the total measurement for all classes and the grade of membership of a task to all predefined classes, it is possible to compute equation 3. Note that the result of equation 3 becomes the new grade of membership of a task T to a class C. Observe that the only overhead associated with measurement is to count the number of executed statements that are associated with a class in a time slice. In the case of an I/O statement, as the task will block anyway, there is no overhead associated with the measure.

4   Scheduling Using Runtime Measurements

Here we will illustrate one possible use of task classification to improve scheduling in parallel machines. Our emphasis here is to improve throughput and utilization of gang schedulers. Observe that the strategies described in this section can be applied to a large number of gang scheduler implementations, including traditional gang schedulers[3,15] and distributed hierarchical control schedulers [11,12].

We may consider two types of parallel tasks in a gang scheduler: Those that should be scheduled as a gang with other tasks in other processors and those for which gang scheduling is not mandatory. Examples of the first class are tasks that compose a job with fine grain synchronization interactions [13] and communication intensive jobs[8]. Second class task examples are local tasks or tasks that compose an I/O bound parallel job. On the other hand a traditional UNIX scheduler does a good job in scheduling I/O bound tasks since it gives high priority to I/O blocked tasks when data become available from disk. As those tasks typically run for a small amount of time and then block again, giving them high priority means running the task that will take the least amount of time before blocking. This behavior is coherent to the theory of uniprocessors scheduling where the best scheduling strategy possible under the sum of completion times is Shortest Job First [21](in [21] authors define the sum of completion times as total completion time). Another example of jobs where gang scheduling is not mandatory are embarrassingly parallel jobs. As the number of iterations among tasks belonging to this class of jobs are small, the basic requirement for scheduling an embarrassingly parallel job is to give those jobs the greater possible fraction of CPU time, even in an uncoordinated manner.

Differentiation among tasks that should be gang scheduled and those for which a more flexible scheduler is better is made using the grade of membership information computed by each PE (as explained in the last subsection) for each task allocated to a processor. The grade of membership of the task currently scheduled is computed at the next preemption of the task. This information is used to decide if gang scheduling is mandatory or not for a specific task.

When using task classification information, the local task scheduler on each PE computes a priority for each task allocated to the PE. This priority defines if a task T is a good candidate for being rescheduled if another task blocks or in case of a idle slot. The priority of each task is defined based on the grade of membership of a task to each one of the major classes described before. As an example of the computation of the priority of a task T in a PE we have:

$$Pr(T) = max(\alpha \times f_{IO}, f_{COMP}) \qquad (4)$$

Where f_{IO}, f_{COMP} are the grade for membership of task T to the classes I/O intensive and Computation intensive. The objective of the parameter α is to give greater priority to I/O bound tasks ($\alpha > 1$). The choices made in equation 4 intend to give high priority to I/O intensive tasks and computation intensive tasks, since such tasks can benefit the most from uncoordinated scheduling. The multiplication factor α for the class I/O intensive gives higher priority to I/O bound tasks over computation intensive tasks. The reason is that I/O bound tasks have a greater probably to block when scheduled than computing intensive tasks. By other side, communication and synchronization intensive tasks have low priority since they require coordinated scheduling to achieve efficient execution and machine utilization[13,8]. A communication intensive phase will reflect negatively over the grade of membership of the class computation intensive, reducing the possibility of a task be scheduled by the local task scheduler. Among a set of tasks of the same priority, the local task scheduler uses a round robin strategy. The local task scheduler also defines a minimum priority β. If no parallel task has priority larger than β, the local task scheduler considers that all tasks in the PE do intensive communication and or synchronization, thus requiring coordinated scheduling. Observe that there is no starvation of communication intensive tasks, as they will be scheduled in a regular basis by the gang scheduler itself, regardless of the decisions made by the local task schedulers.

Observe that the parameters α and β define the bounds of the variation of the priority of a task in order to it be considered to rescheduling, as stated in the next proposition.

Proposition 1. $\alpha \leq Pr(T) \leq \beta$, in order to a task be considered for rescheduling.

Proof. β is the lower bound by definition. For the upper bound, observe that $f_{IO}^{max} = 1$. So, as $\alpha > 1$, the upper bound is $\alpha \times 1 = \alpha$

Simulations in [26] of a scheduling algorithm (Concurrent Gang) that uses a simpler version of the priority mechanism/task classification described here have shown that the priority computation has better performance than round robin for choosing the task that run next in case of task blocking.

Interactive tasks can be regarded as a special type of I/O intensive task, where the task waits for a input from the user at regular intervals of time. These tasks also suffer under gang scheduling, and should have priority as I/O intensive tasks.

5   Adjusting Spinning Time
as a Function of the Workload

Another parameter that can be adjusted in order to improve throughput of I/O bounds and interactive jobs in gang scheduling is the spinning time of a task in the spin block mechanism. Our objective is to make changes not only depending on the runtime measurements of the related job, but also considering other jobs where tasks are allocated to the same processor. We consider that a typical workload will be composed of a mix of jobs of different types and it is important to achieve a compromise in order to give a good response for all types of jobs.

The anticipated blocking of a job performing synchronization or communication can benefit those jobs that do not need coordinated scheduling, such as I/O intensive and embarrassingly parallel. So the idea is to determine the spinning time of a task depending on the workload allocated in a processor. For instance, in a given moment of time if a processor has many I/O intensive jobs allocated to it, this would have a negative impact in spinning time duration. As described in [1], a minimum spin time should be guaranteed in order to insure that processes stay coordinated if already in such a state (baseline spin time). This minimum amount of time ensures the completion of the communication operation when all involved processes are scheduled and there is no load imbalance among tasks of the same job.

Considering gang scheduling the spinning time of a task may vary between a baseline spin time and a spin only state with no blocking. The main external factor that will have influence in the variation of the spin time is the number of interactive and I/O bound tasks in the workload allocated to one processor. A large number of these tasks would imply a smaller spinning time. The additional remaining time until the next global preemption will be used to provide better service to I/O bound and interactive tasks. The algorithm we propose to set up the spinning time as a function of the workload on a given PE for a gang scheduling based algorithm is as follows: If there is one or more tasks in a PE classified as I/O intensive or interactive, a task doing communication will block just after the baseline spin time if the two following conditions are satisfied:

- At least one of the tasks classified as interactive or I/O bound is ready
- There is a minimum amount of time δ between the end of baseline and the next context switch epoch.

If any of the two conditions are not satisfied the task doing communication will spin until receiving the waited response. The δ time is a function of the context switch time of the machine. Given γ, the context switch time of the machine, it is clear that $\delta > \gamma$. We can define that $\delta > 2 \times \gamma$, in order to give the job at least the same amount of CPU time that the system will spend in context switch. In our experiments we empirically define it as being 4 times the average amount of time required for a context switch.

If both conditions are satisfied, the tasks will spin for a time corresponding to the baseline spin time, and if no message is received the task blocks and the I/O bound or interactive task can be scheduled. The reason of minimizing the spinning time is the need of I/O and interactive tasks to receive better service in gang scheduling. Observe that in gang scheduling tasks are coordinated due to the scheduling strategy itself; so an application with no load imbalances would need only the time corresponding the baseline to complete the communication.

The control of spin time using task classification information is another mechanism available to the scheduler to provide better service to I/O bound and interactive jobs under gang scheduling. Observe that the spin time control depending on the workload is always used in conjunction with the priority mechanism described in section 4.

6   Experimental Results

We present some simulation results that compares the performance of a gang scheduler that uses the algorithms described in sections 4 and 5 with another gang scheduler without such mechanisms. The packing strategy used is first fit without thread migration in all cases. The implementation of gang scheduler used in this section is a simple one, since our objective is to measure the benefits of using runtime measurements. We compared a gang scheduler that makes use of runtime information with another one that does not consider it. First we describe our simulation methodology, and then we present and comment the results obtained in our simulations.

6.1   Simulation Methodology

To perform the actual experiments we used a general purpose event driven simulator being developed by our research group for studying a variety of problems (e.g., dynamic scheduling, load balancing, etc). This simulation was first described in [24]. For the experiments of this section we used an improved version that supports the change of the spinning time of a task during a simulation.

We have modeled in our simulations a network of workstations connected by a network characterized by LogP[6,5] parameters. The LogP parameters corresponds to those of a Myrinet network, and they were the similar to the ones used in [1], with Latency being equal to 10 μs, and overhead to 8.75 μs. We defined the baseline spin time as being equal to a request-response message pair, which in the LogP model is equal to 2L+4o. Therefore, the baseline time is equal to 55 μs. The number of processors considered were 8 and 16. I/O requests of a job were directed to the local disk of each workstation, and consecutive requests were executed on a first come first serve basis. Quantum size is fixed as being equal to 200 ms and context switch time equal to 200 μs.

The values of the α and β parameters used for simulations were $\alpha = 2$ and $\beta = 0.3$. As stated in proposition 1 the priority should vary inside the bounds defined by α and β in order to a task be considered to reschedule.

For defining job inter arrival, time, job size and job duration we used a statistical model proposed in [7]. This is model of the workload observed on a 322-node partition of the Cornell Theory Center's IBM SP2 from June 25, 1996 to September 12,1996. The model is based on finding Hyper-Erlang distributions of common order that match the first three moments of the observed distributions. As the characteristics of jobs with different degrees of parallelism differ, the full range of degrees of parallelism is first divided into subranges. This is done based on powers of two. A separate model of the inter arrival times and the service times (runtimes) is found for each range. The defined ranges are 1, 2, 3-4, 5-8, 9-16, 17-32, 33-64, 65-128, 129-256 and 257-322. For the simulations for a 16 processors machine we used 5 ranges, and for a 8 processors machine 4 ranges. The time unit of the parameters found in [7] was seconds, and the duration of all simulations was defined as being equal to 50000 seconds. A number of jobs are submitted during this period in function of the inter arrival time, but not necessarily all submitted jobs are completed by the end of simulation. A long time was chosen in order to minimize the influence of start-up effects.

In order to avoid the saturation of the machine, we limited the number of tasks that can be allocated to a node at a given moment of time to 10. If a job arrives and there is no set of processors available with less than 10 tasks allocated to them, the task waits until the required number of processors become available.

The algorithm used to make the measurements related to a task and to compute the grade of membership of the same task is the one described in subsection 3.4.

We use a mix of four types of synthetic applications in our experiments:

- *I/O* - This job type is composed of bursts of local computations followed by bursts of I/O commands, as represented in figure 2. This pattern reflects the I/O properties of many parallel programs, where execution behavior can be naturally partitioned into disjoint intervals. Each interval consists of a single burst of I/O with a minimal amount of computation followed by a single burst of computation with a minimal amount of I/O [23]. The interval composed of a computation burst followed by an I/O burst are know as phases, and a sequence of consecutive phases that are statistically identical are defined as a working set. The execution behavior of an I/O bound program is therefore comprised as a sequence of I/O working sets. This general model of program behavior is consistent with results from measurement studies [27,28]. The time duration of the I/O burst was equal to 100 *ms* in average. The ratio of the I/O working set used in simulations was 1/1, that is, for a burst of 100 *ms* of I/O there was a burst of 100 *ms* of computation in average. Observe that I/O requests from different jobs to the same disk are queued and served by arrival order.

- *Embarrassingly parallel* - In this kind of application constituent processes work independently with a small amount or no communication at all among them. Embarrassingly parallel applications require fair scheduling of the constituent processes, with no need for explicit coordinated scheduling.

- *Msg* - In this type of synthetic application we model message passing jobs, where messages are exchanged between two processes chosen at random. Each process sends or receives a message every 10 *ms* in average. The communication semantics used here were the same of the PVM system[4], that is, asynchronous sends and blocking receives. For the modified version of gang scheduler, the one that incorporates spin control and priority computation, the spinning time of the receive call will be defined by the spin control mechanism described in section 5. The pure gang scheduler only implements the spin only mechanism, since the original gang schedulers do not know what to do if a task blocks.

– *BSP* - This type of application models Bulk Synchronous Parallel (BSP) style jobs[29]. A BSP job is a sequence of supersteps, each superstep being composed by a mix of computation/communication statements, with all processes being synchronized between two supersteps. In this type of applications, there is a synchronization call every 50 *ms* (in average). All communication/computation generated previous to the barrier call is completed before the job proceeds in the next computation /communication superstep. Again, there is a spin time associated with the barrier and communication calls.

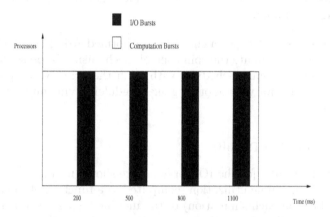

Fig. 2. I/O bound job with one I/O working set

In all simulations, the same sequence of jobs were submitted to both a Gang scheduler with the priority computation and spin time control mechanisms described in section 4 and 5 and another gang scheduler without such mechanisms. A different sequence is generated for each experiment. The packing strategy was first fit without thread migration. Each workload was composed of a mix of the 4 types of jobs previously defined:

– *IO*- This workload was composed of I/O bound jobs only. As I/O bound jobs suffer under gang scheduling, this workload was simulated in order to evaluate the performance impact of the modified gang scheduler if compared to a traditional gang scheduler.
– *IO/Msg* - This workload was composed of a mix of IO and Msg jobs. At each job arrival, the job type was chosen according with a uniform distribution, with a probability of 0.5 to both jobs
– *IO/BSP* - As in the previous workload, both job types had the same probability of being chosen at each job arrival.
– *IO/Msg/Embarrassingly* - Since the priority mechanisms intends to give better service to I/O bound and Compute intensive bounds, we included the Embarrassingly parallel type in the IO/Msg workload. Our objective is to

verify if there is any improvements in throughput due to the inclusion of computing intensive jobs.
- *IO/BSP/Embarrassingly* - Same case for the IO/BSP workload. As in previous cases, at each job arrival all three job types have equal probability to be chosen.
- *Emb/Msg and Emb/BSP* - These workloads were added to evaluate the impact of the priority mechanism over workloads that do not include I/O bound jobs. They are composed of Embarrassingly parallel jobs with Msg and BSP job types respectively. In this case the spin control is not activated since it is conceived to provide better service to I/O bound and interactive tasks only, as these are the type of jobs that have poor performance under gang scheduling.

A second set of experiments were performed using the workloads IO/BSP and IO/Msg to evaluate the spin control mechanism. To do so, we compared the performance of a gang scheduler with both the priority computation and spin control mechanisms with another gang scheduler having only the priority control mechanism.

6.2   Simulation Results

Simulations results for the IO workload are shown in figure 3. In the utilization column, the machine utilization (computed as a function of the total idle time of the machine on each simulation) of the modified gang scheduler was divided by the machine utilization of the non-modified version of the gang scheduler. In the throughput column, the throughput of the modified gang scheduler (The number of jobs completed until the end of the simulation, 50000 seconds) is divided by the throughput in the original gang. We can see a very significant improvement of the modified gang over the original gang scheduler, due to the priority mechanism. To explain the reason of such improvement, tables 1 and 2 show the actual results of simulations for 8 and 16 processors machines under the I/O bound workload. In [23] , Rosti et al. suggest that that the overlapping of the I/O demands of some jobs with the computational demands of other jobs may offer a potential improvement in performance. The improvement shown in figure 3 is due to this overlapping. The detection of I/O intensive tasks and the immediate scheduling of one of these tasks when another task doing I/O blocks results in a more efficient utilization of both disk and CPU resources. As we consider an I/O working set composed by a burst of 100 ms of computation followed by another burst of 100 ms of I/O, the scheduler implementing the priority mechanism always tries to overlap the I/O phase of a job with the computation phase of another, which explains the results obtained. In the ideal case, the scheduling strategy will be able to interleave the execution of applications such that the ratio of the per-phase computation and I/O requirements is maintained very close to 1, thus achieving a total overlapping of computation and I/O. For this workload, since the utilization of the machine is doubled by using runtime information, we can conclude that the overlap of I/O phase is almost 100%, since the duration of the I/O phase is in average equal to the duration of the computation phase. The utilization obtained for the gang scheduler without runtime information is due only to the computation phase. The differences between throughput and utilization are due to I/O contention, which is considered in the simulations. Another interesting point is that, in both machines, about half of the completed jobs were 1 task jobs, since a large amount of jobs generated by the workload model were 1 task jobs.

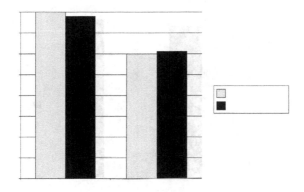

Fig. 3. I/O bound workload with one I/O working set

Table 1. Experimental results - I/O intensive workload - 8 Processors

8 Processors	Jobs Completed	Utilization (%)
With Runtime Information.	60	84
Without Runtime Information	40	42

Table 2. Experimental results - I/O intensive workload - 16 Processors

16 Processors	Jobs Completed	Utilization (%)
With Runtime Information.	55	84
Without Runtime Information	36	43

For the IO/Msg workload, results are shown in figure 4. Again, the modified gang achieved better results for both throughput and utilization. Since Gang schedulers have good performance for communication bound jobs, the improvement due the utilization of runtime measurements and task classification is smaller if compared to the results obtained for the IO workload. This can be explained by the fact that machine utilization of the gang scheduler without runtime information is better in this case if compared to the results related to the previous workload. Tables 3 and 4 show the absolute machine utilization for the experiments using the IO/Msg workload. As the machine utilization for the regular gang scheduler is around 60%, an improvement in utilization as observed with the IO workload is no longer possible.

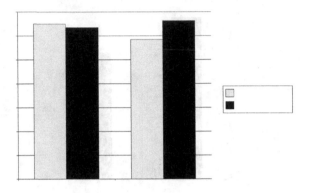

Fig. 4. IO/Msg workload

Table 3. Experimental results - IO/Msg workload - 8 Processors

8 Processors	Jobs Completed	Utilization (%)
With Runtime Information.	50	82
Without Runtime Information	43	63

Table 4. Experimental results - IO/Msg workload - 16 Processors

16 Processors	Jobs Completed	Utilization (%)
With Runtime Information.	53	79
Without Runtime Information	40	62

Results for the IO/Msg/Emb workload are shown in figure 5. The greater flexibility of the modified gang algorithm to deal with I/O intensive and embarrassingly parallel jobs results in an increase in throughput and utilization. It is worth noting, however, that the influence of idle time due to I/O bound jobs is

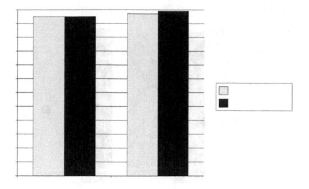

Fig. 5. IO/Msg/Emb workload

reduced. Observe that the regular gang scheduler having even better machine utilization if compared to results for the IO/Msg workload, as shown in tables 5 and 6.

Table 5. Experimental results - I0/Msg/Emb workload - 8 Processors

8 Processors	Jobs Completed	Utilization (%)
With Runtime Information.	47	83
Without Runtime Information	40	72

Table 6. Experimental results - IO/Msg/Emb workload - 16 Processors

16 Processors	Jobs Completed	Utilization (%)
With Runtime Information.	61	81
Without Runtime Information	51	70

When we substitute the Msg workload for the BSP workload in the previous experiments, results are similar in both relative and absolute values. The reason is that both types of jobs are communication/synchronization intensive, taking advantage of the gang scheduling strategy. Results for IO/BSP and IO/BSP/Emb workloads are shown in figures 6 and 7 respectively. As in previous cases, there is improvement over the gang scheduler without the priority computation and spin control mechanisms in both utilization and throughput. Again, the combination of the priority and spin control mechanisms explains the better results obtained by the scheduler using runtime measurements for both workloads.

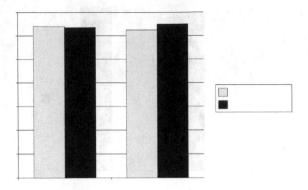

Fig. 6. IO/BSP workload

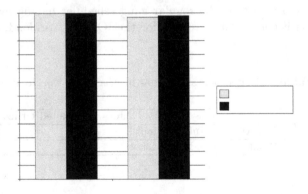

Fig. 7. IO/BSP/Emb workload

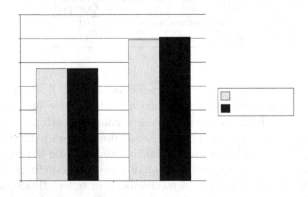

Fig. 8. Evaluation of the spin control mechanism - IO/BSP workload

To evaluate the impact of the spin control mechanism in the total performance of the modified gang scheduler, we compared the performance between a modified gang with both the priority and spin control mechanisms and other version of the modified gang where only the priority computation was active. Results for workloads IO/BSP and IO/Msg are shown in figures 8 and 9 respectively. In figures 8 and 9 the performance of the scheduler with spin control and priority mechanism is divided by the performance of the gang scheduler with the priority computation only. The gain in throughput is due to the better service provided to I/O bound jobs, while in utilization gang scheduling with only the priority mechanism has slightly better performance. This can be explained by the fact the I/O bound jobs run for some time and then block again, while BSP and Msg jobs keep spinning and runs again after receiving the message. As said before, the objective of the spin control mechanism is to achieve a compromise in order to have a better performance for I/O intensive tasks, because these tasks suffer under gang scheduling. In gang scheduling with spin control and priority, this compromise is achieved by given a better a service to I/O bound jobs through the reduction in the spin time of synchronization/communication intensive tasks.

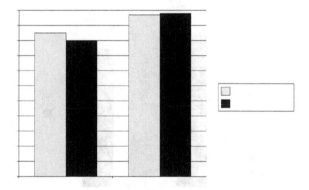

Fig. 9. Evaluation of the spin control mechanism - IO/Msg Workload

To evaluate the performance impact for workloads with no I/O intensive jobs, we have simulated two workloads composed of embarrassingly parallel jobs with Msg and BSP jobs respectively. Comparative results are displayed in figures 10 and 11. Since gang scheduling has a good performance for both synchronization and communication intensive jobs, the improvement is reduced if compared to the previous workloads. Observe that the performances of both the regular gang scheduler and the gang scheduler using runtime information are quite similar. The main improvement in these cases is in utilization. This improvement is due mainly to the scheduling of tasks belonging to embarrassingly parallel jobs on idle slots in the Ousterhout matrix[22], that is, those time slices where a processor do not has a parallel task to schedule.

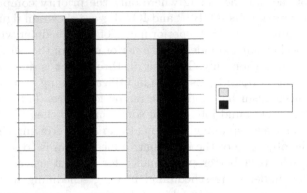

Fig. 10. Emb/Msg workload

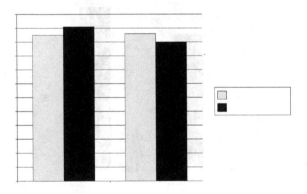

Fig. 11. Emb/BSP workload

7   Conclusion

In this paper we present some possible uses of runtime measurements for improving throughput and utilization in parallel job scheduling. We believe that incorporating such information in parallel schedulers is a step in the right direction, since with more information available about running jobs in a given moment of time a scheduler will be able to do a intelligent choice about a number of events in parallel task scheduling. The events explored on this paper are the task blocking in gang scheduling and the control of spin time in a spin-blocking based communication. The increase in throughput and utilization is confirmed by the experimental results we obtained.

However, there a number of possibilities not explored in this paper that are subject of our current and future research. For instance, questions that we are investigating are the use of runtime information and task classification to improve parallel/distributed scheduling without explicit coordination, the effects of the utilization of runtime measurements on other implementations of gang scheduling such as the distributed hierarchical control algorithm, the utilization of task classification to identify gangedness of an application, and other ways of using task classification information to improve parallel job scheduling.

Acknowledgments

The first author is supported by Capes, Brazilian Government, grant number 1897/95-11. The second author is supported in part by the Irvine Research Unit in Advanced Computing and NASA under grant #NAG5-3692.

References

1. A. C. Arpaci-Dusseau, D. E. Culler, and A. M. Mainwaring. Scheduling with Implicit Information in Distributed Systems. In *Proceedings of ACM SIGMET-RICS'98*, pages 233–243, 1998.
2. J. Edmonds, D.D. Chinn, T. Brecht, and X. Deng. Non-Clairvoyant Multiprocessor Scheduling of Jobs with Changing Execution Characteristics (extended abstract). In *Proceedings of the 1997 ACM Symposium of Theory of Computing*, pages 120–129, 1997.
3. A. Hori et al. Implementation of Gang Scheduling on Workstation Cluster. *Job Scheduling Strategies for Parallel Processing*, LNCS 1162:126–139, 1996.
4. Al Geist et al. *PVM : Parallel Virtual Machine - A User's guide and tutorial for networked parallel computing*. The MIT Press, 1994.
5. D. Culler et al. LogP: Towards a Realistic Model of Parallel Computation. In *Proceedings of 4th ACM SIGPLAN Symposium on Principles an Practice of Parallel Programming*, pages 1–12, 1993.
6. D. Culler et al. A Practical Model of Parallel Computation. *Communication of the ACM*, 93(11):78–85, 1996.
7. J. Jann et al. Modeling of Workloads in MPP. *Job Scheduling Strategies for Parallel Processing*, LNCS 1291:95–116, 1997.
8. Patrick G. Solbalvarro et al. Dynamic Coscheduling on Workstation Clusters. *Job Scheduling Strategies for Parallel Processing*, LNCS 1459:231–256, 1998.
9. D. Feitelson. Packing Schemes for Gang Scheduling. *Job Scheduling Strategies for Parallel Processing*, LNCS 1162:89–110, 1996.
10. D. Feitelson and M. A.Jette. Improved Utilization and Responsiveness with Gang Scheduling. *Job Scheduling Strategies for Parallel Processing*, LNCS 1291:238–261, 1997.
11. D. Feitelson and L. Rudolph. Distributed Hierarchical Control for Parallel Processing. *IEEE Computer*, pages 65–77, May 1990.

12. D Feitelson and L. Rudolph. Mapping and Scheduling in a Shared Parallel Environment Using Distributed Hiearchical Control. In *Proceedings of the 1990 International Conference on Parallel Processing*, 1990.
13. D. Feitelson and L. Rudolph. Gang Scheduling Performance Benefits for Fine-Grain Synchronization. *Journal of Parallel and Distributed Computing*, 16:306–318, 1992.
14. D. Feitelson and L. Rudolph. Coscheduling Based on Runtime Identification of Activity Working Sets. *International Journal of Parallel Programming*, 23(2):135–160, 1995.
15. A. Hori, H. Tezuka, and Y. Ishikawa. Overhead Analysis of Preemptive Gang Scheduling. *Job Scheduling Strategies for Parallel Processing*, LNCS 1459:217–230, 1998.
16. M. A. Jette. Performance Characteristics of Gang Scheduling In Multiprogrammed Environments. In *Proceedings of SC'97*, 1997.
17. J.J.Martin. *Bayesian Decison Problems and Markov Chains*. John Wiley and Sons Inc., New York, N.Y., 1967.
18. B. Kosko. Fuzziness vs. Probability. *International Jounal of General Systems*, 17(2-3), 1990.
19. B. Kosko. *Neural Networks and Fuzzy Systems: A Dynamical Systems Approach for Machine Intelligence*. Prentice Hall, Inc., 1992.
20. W. Lee, M. Frank, V. Lee, K. Mackenzie, and L. Rudolph. Implications of I/O for Gang Scheduled Workloads. *Job Scheduling Strategies for Parallel Processing*, LNCS 1291:215–237, 1997.
21. R. Motwani, S. Phillips, and E. Torng. Non-clairvoyant scheduling. *Theoretical Computer Science*, 130(1):17–47, 1994.
22. J.K. Ousterhout. Scheduling Techniques for Concurrent Systems. In *Proceedings of the 3rd International Conference on Distributed Comp. Systems*, pages 22–30, 1982.
23. E. Rosti, G. Serazzi, E. Smirni, and M. S. Squillante. The Impact of I/O on Program Behavior and Parallel Scheduling. In *Proceedings of ACM SIGMETRICS'98*, pages 56–64, 1998.
24. F.A.B. Silva, L.M. Campos, and I.D. Scherson. A Lower Bound for Dynamic Scheduling of Data Parallel Programs. In *Proceedings EUROPAR'98*, 1998.
25. F.A.B. Silva and I.D. Scherson. Towards Flexibility and Scalability in Parallel Job Scheduling. In *Proceedings of the 1999 IASTED Conference on Parallel and Distributed Computing Systems*, 1999.
26. F.A.B. Silva and I.D. Scherson. Improving Throughput and Utilization on Parallel Machines Through Concurrent Gang. In *Proceedings of the IEEE International Parallel and Distributed Processing Symposium 2000*, 2000.
27. E. Smirni, R. A. Aydt, A. A. Chien, and D. A. Reed. I/O Requirements of scientific aplications: an evolutionary view. In *Proceedings of the IEEE international Symposium of High Performance Distributed Computing*, pages 49–59, 1996.
28. E. Smirni and D. A. Reed. Lessons from characterizing the input/output behavior of parallel scientific applications. *Performance Evaluation*, 33:27–44, 1998.
29. L. G. Valiant. A bridging model for parallel computations. *Communications of the ACM*, 33(8):103 – 111, 1990.
30. F. Wang, M. Papaefthymiou, and M. S. Squillante. Performance Evaluation of Gang Scheduling for Parallel and Distributed Multiprogramming. *Job Scheduling Strategies for Parallel Processing*, LNCS 1291:277–298, 1997.
31. L. A. Zadeh. Fuzzy Sets. *Information and Control*, 8:338–353, 1965.

Valuation of Ultra-scale Computing Systems

Larry Rudolph[1] and Paul H. Smith[2]

[1] MIT Laboratory for Computer Science
545 Technology Square
Cambridge, MA 02139
rudolph@lcs.mit.edu
[2] Veridian Information Solutions
10560 Arrowhead Drive
Fairfax, Virginia 22030
phsmith@mrj.com

Abstract. The goal of the Ultra-Scale Computing Valuation Project is to understand utilization issues for both users and managers of the largest scientific computing systems and to begin developing appropriate metrics and models for such system. This paper describes a few aspects of the project.

1 Introduction

Ultra-scale computers are general-purpose computers in actual use, whose computing power (the combination of aggregate processor speed, memory size, and I/O speeds) is about an order of magnitude larger than the highest performance machine available. These ultra-scale computers, normally outside the area of focus of the commercial market forces, enable much larger and more complex computations than can be performed presently on more conventionally available platforms. However, one is never fully outside of commercial market forces nor can one completely ignore practical realities; it is important to measure the value of ultra-scale computers.

To this end, the Ultra-Scale Computing Valuation Project was undertaken to see how to evaluate the efficient use of these computers (the full version of the report is available at www.dp.doe.gov/valuation). The bottom line is that the value provided by an ultra-scale machine can only truly be measured, in the long run, by the scientific output produced by using it. But, in the short run there is much that can be done to improve the utilization of these expensive resources.

The valuation project included experts from universities, the federal government, national laboratories, and the computing industry. Several meetings were held, operational data were analyzed, and many discussions took place to arrive at the conclusions and recommendations. Participants were able to identify several operational similarities at the Ultra-scale computing centers while recognizing that there are very few general practices for measuring use and assessing value that will hold across all sites. What is needed, therefore, is a sufficiently

D.G. Feitelson and L. Rudolph (Eds.): JSSPP 2000, LNCS 1911, pp. 39–55, 2000.

flexible and graded approach that can be used by each site to measure the contributions of advanced computing systems to scientific thinking and meeting programmatic objectives. Such an approach recognizes that the first-of-their-kind status of ultra-scale platforms directly impacts initial utilization.

What cannot be measured cannot be managed, and what cannot be managed cannot be improved. Assessing the overall value of a highly sophisticated resource dedicated to pushing the forefront of knowledge requires complicated analysis and calculation. Ultimately, the value of the ultra-scale computing platform must be defined and measured in terms of usefulness to the user and the return on investment (ROI) provided to the stakeholder. The original needs of the program must be assessed. Why was the platform purchased in the first place? Are the original objectives being met? Are the numbers of projects and users served meeting expectations? To determine ROI, the value of returns must first be assessed and understood, and then it must be assigned an overall, aggregate, weighted value. ROI is not measured in dollars alone, but in value to the users and the stakeholders. This means the dimensions of value, such as the following, must initially be acknowledged, then measured:

	ASCI	NERSC	NCSA	NPACI
Availability	5	5	4	4
Capability	5	5	5	5
Response	3	3	3	3
Throughput	2	2	2	2
Allocation	2	5	3	3

Fig. 1. Value Dimensions for Ultra-Scale Computer Systems by Site. A scale of 1 to 5 is used with 5 being the most important.

- Availability: Are enough system resources available to support mission critical applications in some acceptable manner? Are users able to achieve objectives on priority jobs?
- Capability: Was enabling capability jobs a reason the platform was purchased in the first place? Can an important task be performed overnight? Can the resources required to accomplish the necessary simulations be reasonably acquired?
- Response time: Do the simulations enabled by the resources exhibit a demonstrable decrease in turnaround time, as expected by users? For specific classes of applications or users, is the response time appropriate?
- Throughput: Is the throughput (number of jobs) meeting expectations?
- Allocation: Is the system sufficiently agile to meet diverse user needs? Are the numbers of projects and users served meeting expectations?

To assess the dimensions of "value," focus should be placed on these areas. Each site performed a self-assessment on the dimension of "value," using a scale of 1-5 with 5 being the highest value (see Figure 1). As expected, there were variations in the assessment of the value of the selected parameters.

Accelerated development computers are purchased to shorten the time to develop critical new software, create new capabilities, perform key new calculations, increase the productivity of key scientists and engineers, and decrease time to market. For simulations performed on highly parallel platforms, this means advancing parallel simulation software, which in turn requires experimentation for a full range of problem sizes up to and including use of the largest system sizes available.

A very large, accelerated development computer would be considered fully utilized if adding more work to the queue of jobs awaiting execution serves only to increase the average delay for jobs in the waiting queue without increasing the throughput. Note that this definition makes no reference to the utilization rate for any of a computer's many sub-system components such as memory, disks, or processors. It does assume that when a job is assigned to a particular node (set of tightly coupled processors, memory, disks, etc.) within a parallel computer, all of those resources are unavailable for use by other jobs, and therefore are considered utilized. The peak theoretical utilization would then be achieved when jobs were assigned to all nodes all of the time.

2   Utilization as a Metric

Utilizition is the most natural metric for a computing facility. But what is meant by *utilization*? There are at least two commonly accepted definitions: One is the fraction of node hours used out of the total time the advanced computing platform is available for use. Another is the fraction of time the platform is in use regardless of its availability. The distinction between these two definitions is relevant mostly for new machines where the machine is unavailable for significant periods of time and, as a machine matures, there is less down time and the two definitions converge. According to either definition, a computer would be considered fully utilized if adding more jobs to the queue of jobs awaiting execution serves only to increase the average delay for jobs.

Neither of these definitions refer to the utilization rate for any of a computer's sub-systems such as memory, disks, or processors. Rather, it assumes that when a job is assigned to a particular node (set of tightly coupled processors, memory, disks, etc.) within a parallel computer, all of those resources are unavailable for use by other jobs and therefore are considered utilized. Theoretically, peak utilization would be achieved when jobs were assigned to all nodes all of the time.

A serious problem with utilization as a metric is that driving utilization to too high a level almost always results in an overall slowdown in system performance. When the slowdown is significant, the effect of achieving very high utilization is a counter-productive decrease in the ability of the system to support the applications for which its acquisition was justified. Another and more subtle weakness with utilization is that it does not measure the capability quality of the machine. In fact, the replacement of many capacity jobs by any capability job requiring the same total amount of resource can only decrease the utilization. Utilization as a measure penalizes exactly those capability jobs that are the driving rationale for the creation of large, integrated, ultra-scale machines.

Historically, managers of advanced computing platforms have used a variety of approaches to assess system utilization. The NASA Numerical Aerospace Simulation (NAS) Facility, for example, has operated parallel supercomputers for the past 11 years, including the Cray C-90, Intel iPSC/860, Intel Paragon, Thinking Machines CM-5, IBM SP-2, and SGI Origin 2000. The variability of the Available Node Utilization of some of those machines is shown in Figure 2. In last year's workshop (*Job Scheduling Strategies for Parallel Processing*, D.G. Feitelson and L. Rudolph (Eds.), Lecture Notes in Computer Science, Vol 1659, Springer-Verlag, 1999), James Jones and Bill Nitzberg presented a historical perspective of achievable utilization. Recognizing the range of machine architectures, a time span of more than six years, large numbers of different users, and thousands of minor configurations and policy changes, they show that the utilization of these machines reveal three general trends (see Figure 2):

- scheduling using a naive first-in, first-out, first-fit policy results in 40-60% utilization
- switching to the more sophisticated dynamic backfilling scheduling algorithm improves utilization by about 15 percentage points (yielding up to about 70% utilization)
- reducing the maximum allowable job size further increases utilization This last policy however defeats one of the purposes for buying ultra-scale machines, namely to gain new capability. Most surprising is the consistency of these trends across different platforms and user communities.

2.1   Experience with a New System

One example of the process a major facility must go through in placing a new ultrascale capability into service is demonstrated in Figure 3. In 1997, NERSC at Lawrence Berkeley National Laboratory (LBL) transitioned its primary production computing capability to a massively parallel ultra-scale computer by placing into service a large, early delivery Cray T3E. At the time of introduction, this system was the largest unclassified supercomputer in the US and represented a 20-fold increase in raw computing power to the 2,500 scientists who use NERSC. NERSC, working closely with Cray Research, was able to improve utilization through the gradual introduction and exploitation of major system software functionality such as job migration and system initiated checkpoint/restart. During the first 18 months in service, the T3E utilization increased from approximately 55% to over 90% while still focusing most of the system resources on large jobs. This represents almost a factor of two in price performance increase for the system or the equivalent (in 1999 costs) of $10.25M. At the same time the system was improving, T3E users were making improvements in applications to better utilize the system and improve its scientific output.

It is unfortunate that this scenario must be repeated for every new architecture delivered. But rapid changes in the high performance computing industry make it virtually inevitable that each new type system will experience the same learning curve. This is partly due to the facility's and its users' needs to learn how best to implement, tune, and run the new system and applications. But it is also due to the fact that few of the basic system software capabilities are transportable to the general system or can be shared among vendors. High performance computing vendors have little incentive to invest and maintain advanced system software capabilities since, until recently, there has not been a reward structure for creating a system that is more effective rather than yielding faster performance.

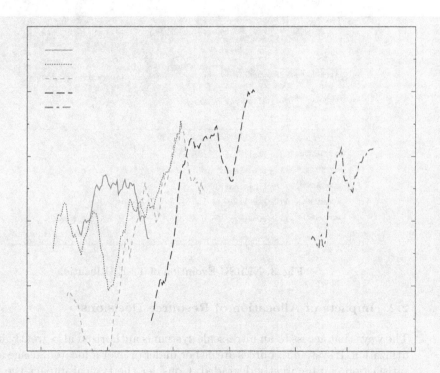

Fig. 2. NASA Overall Comparison of Parallel Supercomputer Utilization

Generally, ultra-scale computing platform managers assign preference to large jobs to ensure there are sufficient resources to run and there is a trade-off between quick turnaround for development jobs and maximum efficiency for production jobs. This trade-off translates into decisions that must be made between asynchronous, interactive user behavior and using a batch queue system to provide sustained loading over longer time versus peak loading to maximize interactivity over shorter time periods.

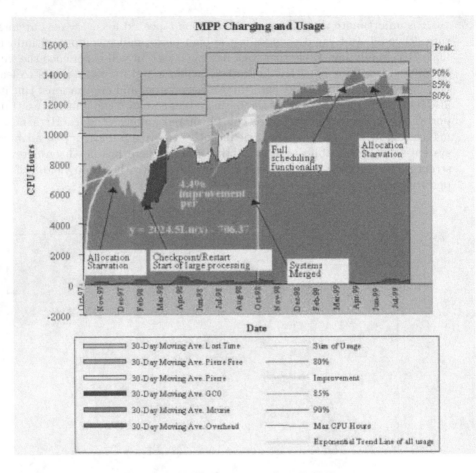

Fig. 3. NERSC Evolution of T3-E Utilization

2.2   Impacts of Allocation of Resource Decisions

The ways that access to an ultra-scale system is authorized also greatly influences utilization. If system resources are either under or over allocated, usage and client satisfaction can be greatly degraded. Consider the typical impact the following allocation methods can have on utilization:

1. Exact division of resources (typically CPU time and storage) and strict enforcement of limits subdivide the resources of the system on some priority basis. By exactly cutting up the total resources and limiting users to their share, a system can easily become underutilized. There is a "feast or famine" mentality that causes users to hoard time early in the allocation period. If enough users hoard time, then utilization is low early in the period because there are not enough jobs to keep the system busy all the time. Later, when everyone tries to use their time, they may not be able to use it completely. The results are underutilized resources AND degradation of quality of service.

2. Some sites mitigate the previous impact by periodically taking time away from users who have not used it and redistributing it to users who are short on time. Since time lost due to idle processors cannot be recreated, this typically results in a scarcity of work early in the period and a severe backlog late in the period. It also is often cumbersome to implement and manage. If the recapture of time is done too frequently, it results in several mini feasts and famines throughout the allocation period.

3. Another way to address the concern of underutilization is to oversubscribe the system by allocating more resources than it can possibly deliver. This is done in one of two ways. If there is too much oversubscription, users expect to be able to do more work than the system can perform. If enough users attempt this, the system will be clogged with work and users. More resources will be needed to manage the overload and the system loses efficiency as the quality of service degrades even though it may appear to be using all the CPU time. The second way to overallocate system resources is to institute a priority system, so that a user can submit work at a lower priority, risking expanded run times, while being charged less. Alternatively, a user can ask for higher priority and "pay" more. While this typically yields higher utilization, it also extends the slowdown factors of the system sometimes to the extent that it takes so long to run a job the scientists do not even bother to try. Most sites use one or more of these methods, often in combination, to try to balance keeping the system utilized on the one hand but still responsive on the other hand. No method is entirely successful, so it takes dedicated system managers to be constantly monitoring and tuning the methods.

2.3   Utilization Trade-Offs

Managing utilization of the ultra-scale computing platforms requires systems operators to decide among a large number of complex trade-offs. Factors to be considered include:

- Job mix - This includes the categories and size of job described above (for example, large production runs requiring thousands of processors versus smaller development runs to test and validate code). Job mix requires adequate management of memory, internal network bandwidth, and file system concurrently; the risk is that a large capability job may be starved if any single resource is not managed well. This is complicated by the fact that different types of jobs will require memory and CPU resources in differing proportions (for example, large jobs in chemistry versus computational fluid dynamics).
- People priorities - Some users and/or projects might be considered "more equal" than others because they are completing higher priority work. This means that resources must be available to meet the high priority needs – sometimes to the exclusion of other users and other jobs – forcing managers to provide guaranteed access to fewer, key users at the possible cost of lower utilization.

- Learning curves - The optimal target for a platform is usually running on 1/4 to 1/2 of the entire machine. Use of such large fractions of systems, particularly early in existence, is not likely as system operating software is still being developed and applications programmers are still becoming familiar with the scheduling processes and operational algorithms required to make effective use of the ultra-scale platform. One conceivable alternative is to run only small jobs. However, in practice, the only way to ensure that a machine is ready is to subject it to real jobs and real workloads. Therefore, when users are kept off the machine with the goal of fixing all the problems, the net result is serious delays in the development and scaling of applications to make use of the capabilities and features of the system. This in turn leads to further utilization problems.
- Absence of Tools - Because the ultra-scale platforms are first-of-their-kind, tools for measuring efficiency, accounting for use, and for tuning system parameters for higher levels of efficiency are not yet in place. There is an imbalance between the size and diversity of the software needed and the size of the new systems. Initially, accusations of low utilization are often met with anecdotal evidence and little systematic data; time and sponsored efforts are needed to evolve better tools for these platforms.

All of these factors, and the trade-offs that must be made among them, have to be balanced when managing ultra-scale computing platforms. Managers must respond to a highly complex problem with a large number of degrees of freedom. Scheduling efficient use of all of the resources is like a "Tetris" problem; the right job at the right time is needed to consume whatever resources are available. If there is conflict or overlap, utilization efficiency may decrease.

2.4   Utilization Should Not Be the Sole Metric

As these arguments are meant to demonstrate, utilization is not a universally defined term and different organizations use different approaches to define it. The Project participants believe strongly that the true measure of the value of ultra-scale computing systems in the long run should be the scientific output of these systems. Are the systems doing what they were designed and funded to do? How is this measured? The answer is that the overall value of the ultra-scale platform must be assessed to those that have purchased it and taken advantage of its capabilities. This is very effectively achieved by periodic peer review of the facility, as is done with national facilities. In the end, the facilities that operate ultra-scale computing systems should be judged in the same way other national facilities such as accelerators are judged. Typically, periodic peer review is used to assess whether they are meeting their missions and goals. Assessments evaluate and provide guidance in the areas such as: ? Does the facility operate well? Are the systems run well, are they reliable, is the facility meeting user expectations, etc.? ? Is the facility doing the appropriate research and development necessary to keep it at the forefront of its discipline? ? Is the facility doing what it can to ensure, in the aggregate, that the best science is being produced from its resources? Such peer reviews have worked very well to ensure the effectiveness and efficiency of facilities that serve the targeted scientific community. The value of ultra-scale computing facilities and the scientific output of the systems should be evaluated in a similar manner.

There is no single metric for utilization because every platform manager, program, and complex problem to be solved is working towards specific (and somewhat different) objectives. The managers of the programs and the platforms must first define the overall value of the new tool in meeting objectives and then assess how successfully those objectives are being met with respect to the use of this sophisticated

3   A New Conceptual Approach

Although some consideration of utilization is appropriate, a slowdown effect in the system can result when utilization is driven too hard (Figure 4). If the slowdown is significant, the effect of focusing on utilization can be counterproductive on overall system performance and on the ability of the system to be used for the type of applications for which its acquisition was justified. It was found that a "smoothly" running system (for example, ultra-scale computer systems) will find optimum utilization at the "knee" of the curve. One would want to increase utilization from small values until the slowdown becomes too large. Acceptable slowdown values may be different for different operations. For example, the exact slowdown-utilization curve depends on the type of machine, software, and job mix (e.g. Case 1 and Case 2 in the figure). The curves all look the same but have different constants, and hence the knee occurs are different places. Slowdown impacts user behavior which, in turn, affects the amount of load on the system (reduced utilization) and, more importantly, ultimately affects what the user is able to accomplish.

Preliminary examination of the sample data showed that this normally expected "slowdown-utilization" curve does occur although it is not immediately evident from raw trace data. The implication of this hypothesis is that systems operating at the "knee" are operating at the best range for those systems, that is, at the ideal point.

3.1   Trace Data Analysis

As part of the Project, trace data from several sites (see Figure 5) were collected and examined. It should be noted that the data did not cover the same time period or even the same length of time at each site. Furthermore, different machines collected the data, used different schedulers, and had different workloads. Because some of the trace data contained partially complete records, some information was lost as it was converted to a standard format. Despite all these differences across the data sets, a standard pattern was detected. Although acceptable slowdown associated with utilization was found to be near 60%, the data clearly show that there is no absolute acceptable utilization number. For

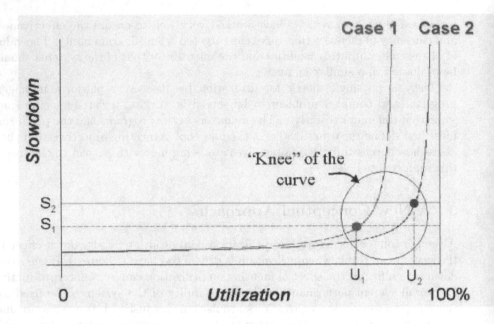

Fig. 4. Slowdown vs. Utilization

the purpose of this section, instantaneous utilization is the percentage of total time that is used by running jobs – not percentage of available time or fraction allocated to jobs.

Before describing the analysis, it is important to highlight a standard queuing theory expectation. It is a well-established fact for service systems that the average response time increases as the "offered load" increases. The response time is flat until the load crosses a threshold, at which point the response time increases exponentially.

Org	Machine	Max CPUs*	Period	#Jobs	#Queues
LANL	SGI Origin	2048	7/24/99 – 8/31/99	30,000	18
LLNL	SP-2	1344	Months	20,000	3
NASA	SGI Origin	256	Months	32,000	2
NPACI	SP-2	128	1/1/99 – 9/27/99	22,000	4
NPACI	T3E	272	5/1/99 – 9/27/99	5,000	40
NPACI	T90	14	1/1/99 – 9/27/99	25,000	45
NCSA	SGI Origin	512	6/30/99 – 7/30/99	10,000	36
NERSC	T3E	644	1/1/99 – 7/1/99	90,000	12

Fig. 5. The data analysis was based on trace logs from these sites. The largest number of CPUs for which trace data were available, not the size of machine are presented.

Since a high performance computer is an example of a service system, such a pattern should occur. In many systems, it is possible to submit jobs to "closed queues" that may not be "opened" for quite some time, for example, the weekend queue. For this and other reasons, the offered load was not used. Instead, the average system utilization during the lifetime of each job was measured. Utilization was taken to be the fraction of the total available CPU hours, during the lifetime of a job, that were being used to execute jobs.

Instead of response time, the related measure of slowdown was computed. Slowdown is defined as the elapsed job time (from submission to completion) divided by the run time. For example, a slowdown of two indicates that a job spent as much time waiting to run as it did actually being run. Some sites have job queues that are active only during certain time periods, such as late night and weekends. A job submitted on Monday, for a weekend queue, would incur at least a five-day waiting time. In this analysis, the submit time was changed to be just before the queue open time. Two other modifications were made to the data: (1) jobs with run times of less than one minute were excluded, and (2) jobs with very high slowdown values (due either to queues that were turned on/off or due to an inability to determine exactly when a queue becomes active) were excluded. Both these job classes obscured the results. Finally, the average instantaneous utilization (considering all the included jobs) is noted on the plots below.

The plots that follow reveal that indeed, at higher utilization levels, the slowdown (for example, response time) does increase. It appears that the facility managers do try to keep the response time reasonable. Two types of anomalous situations were found. The first happens when the response time decreases at higher utilization levels. The other occurs when response time increases at lower utilization levels. Further investigation revealed that one must first separate the jobs into different classes because some systems have batch queues for large jobs, others for interactive daytime jobs, and even queues for very long, highly parallel jobs. The slowdown versus utilization curves all fit the same pattern but each has a different Desired Operation Range (DOR). When the analysis is focused on the important queues, most of the jobs are found to reside in the DOR.

Major conclusions to be drawn from the analysis of trace data are as follows:

- High-end and ultra-scale computer workloads exhibit a pattern of acceptable response time up to a certain instantaneous utilization level, which one refers to as the DOR. When instantaneous utilization is pushed higher than that level, average response time increases precipitously and to levels that negatively impact human productivity.
- For many of the systems studied and for the job classes that matter most, the DOR occurs around 60% instantaneous utilization.
- The location of the DOR can change through improvements in system software (for example, gang scheduling) and scheduler queues that are particularly well matched to the workload characteristics. Thus, more mature systems with more capable system software and a well-characterized workload can achieve desired operation ranges at higher instantaneous utilization lev-

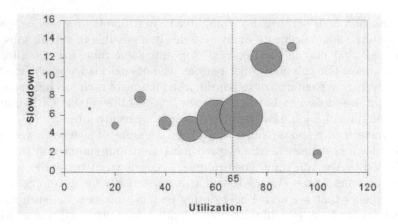

Fig. 6. Site A

els in the later stages of the system life cycle. The figures that follow show average slowdown as a function of system instantaneous utilization for individual sites. This requires some explanation. For each job, the average system instantaneous utilization was computed for the lifetime of that job, and the job was assigned to one of ten utilization buckets (from 10 to 100%). In addition, the slowdown for that job was calculated as the ratio of job lifetime divided by job runtime. Finally, the weight for each instantaneous utilization bucket was computed, expressed as a fraction of the whole weight, and displayed as the size of the bubble. Bubbles with high slowdown values indicate poor system response time. Bubbles with low utilization levels indicate poor system usage. Ideal performance has large bubbles.

A vertical line was drawn indicating the percentage of total node hours for all trace jobs divided by the total number of node hours in the time period. This line is not the average instantaneous utilization of the jobs in the curve, since there may be periods when the system was unusable.

The Site A plot reveals the characteristic rise with most of the big bubbles at the DOR of the curve. At eighty percent, many jobs are seen to suffer from a large slowdown value.

The Site B curve looks very similar to the one before it, except that everything happens at a lower utilization level. At 60% utilization, the response time rises, so the DOR occurs at a lower utilization level.

The Site C curves below show a slightly different pattern. Slowdown values are very low and it is easy to see the increase at higher levels. As one can see, the vertical line appears more to the left than would be evident from the distribution of the bubbles. This is because either a long downtime or a short trace period exists. Site C1 has smaller jobs than Site C2; thus the desired operation ranges are in different places, although both seem to manage their systems very well.

The plot for Site D does not show the typical pattern. Most of the jobs have a low response time (not just most of the jobs, but most of the job weight).

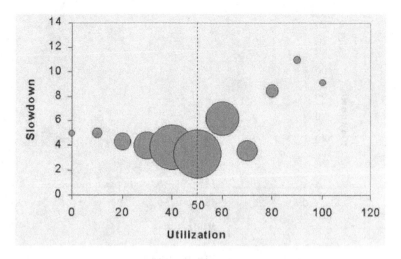

Fig. 7. Site B

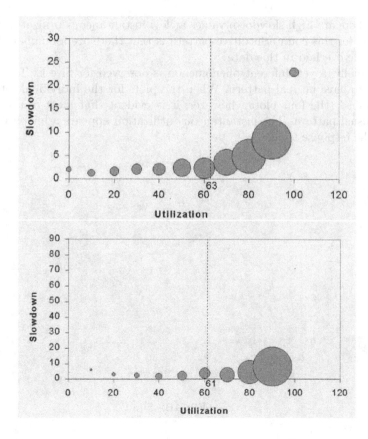

Fig. 8. Site C - C1 is on the top; C2 is on the bottom

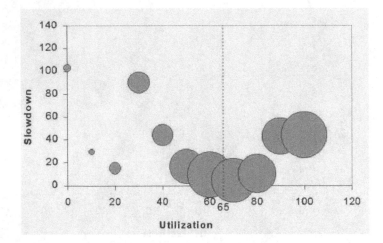

Fig. 9. Site D

But there are high slowdown values at low instantaneous utilization values. The reason for this counterintuitive pattern is that there are a number of job classes that are overlaid in this data.

Finally, a yet different phenomenon is observed for Site E. The bubbles appear to have no real pattern. When the plots for the individual job classes are examined (the four plots), however, it is evident that most of the plots follow the usual pattern. The instantaneous utilization appears a bit on the high side for the response time.

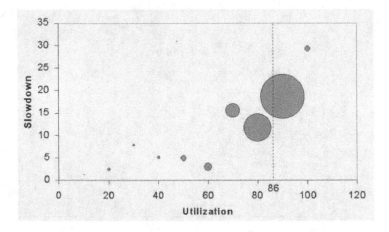

Fig. 10. Site E

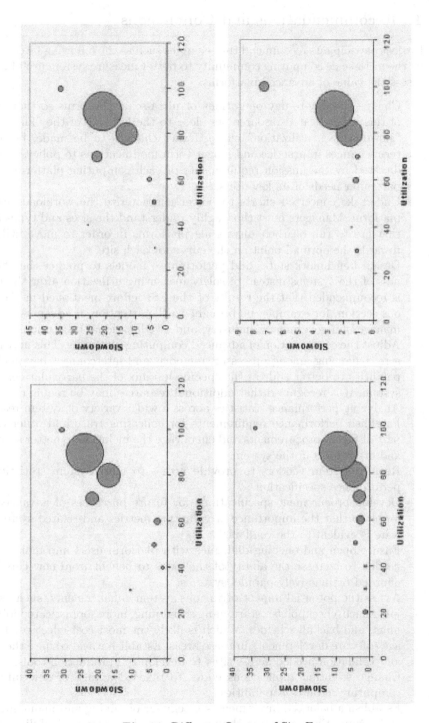

Fig. 11. Different Queues of Site E

4 Recommendations and Conclusions

Project participants recommend that changes such as the following be considered by the ultra-scale computing community to better measure system usefulness and assess the value of advanced platforms:

- Change the day-to-day operations of ultra-scale platforms so that the use of this sophisticated resource lies close to the left side of the "knee" of the "slowdown vs. utilization" curve. Exact changes to be made, both near-term changes in practice and longer-term modifications to policy, should be dictated by the mission requirements of each computing platform and the particular needs of its key users.
- Undertake concerted efforts to better characterize the workloads for each platform. Managers must thoroughly understand the sizes and types of jobs that are to run on their ultra-scale platforms in order to move utilization towards the optimal point on the curve for each site.
- Design benchmark suites and performance models to predict the effectiveness of the systems instead of solely measuring utilization after the fact. It is recommended that the results of the ESP effort mentioned in the previous section, for example, be brought to the attention of advanced platform managers in government, industry, and at educational institutions.
- Adjust the configuration of advanced computing platforms. This may require a re- balancing among processor, memory, and interconnect bandwidth capabilities to better address the specific job mix of the particular computing system. It is recognized that additional resources may be required.
- Analyzing performance statistics across a wider variety of system resources.
- Establish performance requirements for collecting trace and other data as part of future procurements and encourage the inclusion of better schedulers and other tools in the system.
- Require system vendors to provide access to more system statistics as a performance specification.
- Develop procurement specifications for future purchases of advanced platforms so that the importance of valuation metrics and related system software is evident to the vendors.
- Ensure open and ongoing dialogues with platform users and make changes needed to increase the ability of the users to benefit from new capabilities afforded by massively parallel systems.
- Assess the potential impact of various system enhancements, such as faster job launch, checkpoint-restart, gang scheduling, more sophisticated job scheduling, and backfill schemes. Which is likely the most cost-effective? Encourage software developments in these areas. Establish ways to share the testing and validation needed across sites to develop full production tools.
- Change scientific applications codes to take advantage of new ultra-scale computing resource capabilities.
- Establish a balanced investment strategy for obtaining and managing ultra-scale computing platforms that seeks to both improve scheduling and increase the efficiency of individual jobs.

It is important to undertake research in many key areas to accomplish, among other things, at least the following:

- Designing more efficient scheduling algorithms. Determine how to incorporate other job parameters (memory usage, interruptible jobs, and dynamic node size flexibility) into the scheduling software.
- Techniques for increasing the efficiency of applications by employing moldable and malleable jobs. What percentage of user jobs could be configured, with reasonable effort, as interruptible, as adjustable CPUs at job launch time, or as adjustable CPUs during execution? What improvement in system efficiency could be achieved by means of such changes?

The following research questions were identified during the Project:

- Which system software enhancements and operating strategies have the greatest potential for improving system effectiveness?
- How do the job size/run time distributions vary between various HPC centers? How do these distributions vary between different disciplines?
- What percentage of jobs has power-of-two CPU sizes?
- What impact does job size distribution have on system-level efficiency?

The purpose of the Ultra-Scale Computing Valuation Project has been achieved; acceptable ways to evaluate "ultra-scale" computing systems are being defined and a consensus on these approaches is emerging within the ultra-scale computing community. Reaching agreement on understandable and defensible measures is important to the large-scale computing research and applications programs in government and academia, such as the ASCI program at DOE and the PACI program at NSF, as well as others. Presently, generally accepted metrics do not exist for this evaluation. It is evident, however, that the answer is not found by merely assessing node utilization.

The Project Co-Chair's contention given all the system limitations and constraints is that "things are in good shape as far as the running of the advanced computing platforms is concerned," is based on sound peer review of the approaches currently used to manage utilization of advanced computing platforms. Participants agree that a balance of research, development, and implementation considerations is necessary, but argue that the success of high-end computing efforts aimed at enabling new classes of applications should be measured primarily by whether the use does, in fact, result in new knowledge. If so, then the advanced computing tools used were worth the investment.

Participants agreed that the ultra-scale computing community should focus on creating the right-size tools for every scientific and programmatic mission. There is recognition of the responsibility of computing systems managers and the overseeing agencies to determine how best to measure the overall value of each system to its users. In addition, ways must be defined to make needed measurements and compare against recognized benchmarks and to establish operational practices that are optimal for each site and the scientific goals that site is designed to achieve.

System Utilization Benchmark
on the Cray T3E and IBM SP

Adrian Wong, Leonid Oliker, William Kramer, Teresa Kaltz, and David Bailey

National Energy Research Scientific Computing Center, Lawrence Berkeley National
Laboratory, 1 Cyclotron Rd, Berkeley, CA 94720, USA
{atwong, loliker, wtkramer, tlkaltz, dhbailey}@lbl.gov

Abstract. Obtaining maximum utilization of parallel systems continues
to be an active area of research and development. This article outlines
a new benchmark, called the *Effective System Performance* (ESP) test,
designed to provide a utilization metric that is transferable between systems
and illuminate the effects of various scheduling parameters. Results
with discussion are presented for the Cray T3E and IBM SP systems together
with insights obtained from simulation.

1 Introduction

The overall value of a high performance computing system depends not only on
the raw computational speed but also on system management. System characteristics
such as job scheduling efficiency, reboot and recovery times and the level
of process management are important factors in the overall usability and effectiveness
of the system. Common performance metrics such as the LINPACK and
NAS Parallel Benchmarks [1,2] are useful for measuring sustained computational
performance, but give little or no insight into system-level efficiency issues.

In this article, we describe a new benchmark, the *Effective System Performance*
(ESP) benchmark, which measures system utilization [3]. Our primary
motivation in developing this benchmark is to aid the evaluation of high performance
systems. Additionally, it will be used to monitor the impact of configuration
changes and software upgrades in existing systems. We also hope that
this benchmark will provide a focal point for future research and development
activities in the high performance computing community. The emphasis in this
work is on scheduling and resource management and should be viewed as complementary
to performance benchmarks, such as NAS.

The ESP test extends the idea of a throughput benchmark with additional
constraints that encapsulate day-to-day operation. It yields an efficiency measurement
based on the ratio of the actual elapsed time relative to the theoretical
minimum time assuming perfect efficiency. This ratio is independent of the computational
rate and is also relatively independent of the number of processors
used, thus permitting comparisons between platforms.

The test was run on the Cray T3E and the IBM SP at NERSC. The T3E
consists of 512 Alpha EV56 processors at 450 MHz with an aggregate peak of

D.G. Feitelson and L. Rudolph (Eds.): JSSPP 2000, LNCS 1911, pp. 56–67, 2000.
© Springer-Verlag Berlin Heidelberg 2000

614 GFlop/s. The SP consists of 512 Power3 processors at 200 MHz with an aggregate peak of 410 GFlop/s. The SP exhibits higher sustained performance for most applications, however, the T3E has better scalability for tightly-coupled parallel applications. With two systems of the same size but different scheduling characteristics, NERSC is in a unique position to implement and validate the ESP test.

2   Utilization and Scheduling

In this work, we are primarily concerned with parallel applications that require a static number of processors (or partition size). Scheduling several parallel applications concurrently is particularly problematic since time and partition constraints must be satisfied while simultaneously the system utilization should be at a maximum. Utilization, in this sense, is defined as the fraction of busy processors to available processors integrated over time. In day-to-day operation, other constraints and requirements create a situation more complex and subtle. For example, a scheduler may use a *best-fit-first* (BFF) strategy but at a cost of starvation of larger partition jobs. While this may reduce the elapsed time and achieve higher utilization compared to a *first-come-first-serve* (FCFS) strategy it does not address the issues of turnaround, fairness and productivity.

One indirect measurement of utilization is the elapsed time required to process a workload consisting of a number of jobs. If the time for each job is constant, irrespective of whether it is run dedicated or concurrently with other jobs, then the variation in the elapsed time for the workload depends only on the scheduling strategy and system overhead. For a given workload with jobs of varying partition sizes and elapsed times, a utilization efficiency, E, can be defined as,

$$E = \frac{\sum_i p_i t_i}{PT} \tag{1}$$

where p_i and t_i are the partition size and elapsed time, respectively, for the i-th job, T is the observed time for the workload and P is the number of available processors. In the ideal limit of perfect packing with no overhead, the efficiency, E, approaches unity. Here the numerator and denominator are in units of CPU-hours (or CPU-seconds), a unit of that is useful for discussing parallel resources. Note, there is a distinction between perfect packing and optimal scheduling. Some of the possible parameters include; preemption, backfilling, variable deadlines, multiple resource requirements, scheduling dependencies and job priorities. Not surprisingly this problem is NP-hard and many heuristic techniques have been developed to approximate a good solution. Examples of recent work for non-preemptive, preemptive and multiple resource schemes include [4,6,5,7].

Particular scheduling strategies depend on the availability of certain key system functionality. As shown in Table 1, the systems examined in this work differ considerably in available functionality. *Checkpoint/restart* is the ability to save to disk and subsequently restore a running job. System-initiated checkpointing of long-running jobs affords flexibility in scheduling and maintenance. Without checkpointing, one is faced with the undesirable choice between waiting to idle the machine or the premature termination of jobs. *Swapping* and *gang-scheduling* is the parallel analog of time-slicing on single processor machines but usually with a course granularity. This allows oversubscription (multiple processes per processor), increasing the apparent number of processors available and allowing greater flexibility in scheduling. *Job migration/compaction* refers to the capability to move a running job to a different set of processors. This aids in defragmentation and scheduling large partitions. *Priority preemption* is the ability to launch a higher priority job with the resulting effect of swapping out lower priority jobs. This is useful to improve turnaround and prevent starvation of large partition jobs. *Backfill* is the insertion of smaller, shorter jobs ahead of earlier jobs in the queue to fill empty slots. More sophisticated backfill algorithms exploit *a priori* run time information such that jobs have a guaranteed launch time but may be promoted ahead to fill empty slots. Systems with *disjoint partitions* do not require contiguous (in a topological sense) parallel partitions on the interconnect and, therefore, fragmentation is not an issue.

Table 1. System Functionality on T3E and SP

Function	T3E	SP
Checkpoint/restart	X	
Swapping/Gang-scheduling	X	
Job migration/compaction	X	
Priority preemption	X	
Backfill	X	X
Disjoint partitions		X

The first four functions mentioned, namely, checkpoint/restart, swapping, migration and preemption, all depend on the fundamental kernel operation of preemptively changing process images between run and idle states and moving them to memory and disk. Unfortunately, this is either not implemented in stock operating systems or is not exposed to the global scheduling/queuing software.

The Cray T3E at NERSC has demonstrated high utilization due to system management and the availability of checkpoint/restart and priority preemption [9,8].Scheduling on the T3E comprises two interacting subsystems; a batch queue (NQS) and the *global resource manager* (GRM). NQS schedules at a coarse grain and launches jobs from queues based on site policies. Multiple NQS queues for different partition sizes are used. The number of released jobs for each queue may be limited by the NQS configuration. Therefore, the profile of jobs launched may be adjusted according to the time of the day. For example, at night, larger partition jobs are preferentially launched by limiting small partition jobs. Dynamic management of currently launched jobs is implemented by GRM using swapping, priority preemption and compaction. Two priority rankings are recognized by GRM; normal and prime. The prime rank is used to preemptively insert jobs to run immediately with the effect of swapping out running jobs. Within each priority rank, there maybe more processors subscribed than physically available, in which case, GRM can either gang-schedule between jobs or hold jobs pending a suitable partition. GRM uses a BFF strategy to launch held jobs. To prevent starvation of larger jobs, NQS must be appropriately configured and prime rankings judiciously assigned to larger jobs.

Loadleveller is used on the SP for scheduling batch jobs. In general, each job is assigned dedicated processors and runs to completion without swapping. Different job *classes* with varying requirements and priorities may be defined within Loadleveller. Loadleveller uses an overall FCFS strategy with backfill to launch jobs from the queue. The ordering of jobs considered for launch maybe adjusted using system and/or user assigned priorities. Efficient backfill requires *a priori* estimated run times.

3   Benchmark Design

A throughput benchmark was the initial starting point for the design of the ESP test. It consists of a set of jobs of varying partition sizes and times with the objective of obtaining the shortest elapsed run time. By reporting the utilization efficiency, E, instead of the absolute time, the ESP test is independent of the computational rate. A theoretical minimum elapsed time of 4 hours (or 4×512 CPU-hours) on the T3E was chosen for the benchmark. This choice was a compromise between a longer simulation more representative of actual production and a shorter time more amenable to benchmarking.

The turnaround of larger partition jobs has always been a concern. In order to encapsulate this problem, the test includes two jobs with partition sizes equal to the number of available processors (*full configuration* jobs). The test stipulates that upon submission, the full configuration jobs must be run before any further jobs are launched. The first full configuration job can only be submitted after 10% of the theoretical minimum time has elapsed such that it is non-trivial to schedule. Similarly, the second full configuration job must complete within 90% of the test and is not simply the last job to be launched. The requirement to run these two full configuration jobs is a difficult test for a scheduler but it is, nonetheless, a common scenario in production environments.

Outages, both scheduled and unscheduled, are common in these systems and the time to shutdown and reboot has a significant impact on utilization over the lifetime of a system. The ESP test includes a shutdown with reboot which is required to start immediately after the completion of the first full configuration job. In practice, the shutdown and reboot cycle is difficult to implement without manual intervention during the test. If the shutdown/reboot time, S, is known in advance then the operation need not be performed. The denominator in Equation 1 is now simply, $P(T + S)$. Figure 1 is a schematic of the ESP test which shows the relative locations of the full configuration and shutdown/reboot sections.

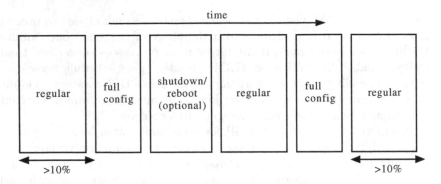

Fig. 1. ESP Schematic

There are several issues with the submission of jobs. Ideally, the rate of submission and profile of sizes should reflect the actual workload. However, a complex scheme of submission of individual jobs at pseudo-random intervals may be error prone and produce irreproducible results. Furthermore, it is possible to inadvertently reduce utilization due to insufficient queued work. Alternatively, all jobs might be submitted simultaneously at the beginning. This has the advantages of simplicity and allowing the scheduler maximum flexibility. The disadvantage is that *a priori* knowledge of the complete workload submission may allow artificial configurations specific to the test. For the ESP test, a compromise was chosen between the two extremes. The order of submission is determined from a reproducible pseudo-random sequence and this list divided into three blocks. The total number of CPUs requested in the first block is at least twice the available processors and the number of CPUs in the second block at least equal to the available processors. The remaining jobs constitute the third block. The first block is submitted at the start with the second and third blocks submitted 10 and 20 minutes thereafter, respectively. This structure was designed to forestall artificially configured queues specific to this test and, at the same time, provide sufficient queued work to allow flexibility in scheduling. No manual intervention is allowed once the test is initiated.

We consider it important that the job mix be representative of the user workload. Accounting records for three months from the T3E were distilled into a workload profile. User jobs were sorted into classes defined by run time and partition size. Table 2 shows the workload profile expressed as a percentage of the available CPU-hours. Using the 4 hour elapsed time (2048 CPU-hours) for the test, Table 2 allows one to calculate the amount of CPU-hours for each class. For example, the class of jobs with a partition size of 64 and taking 1000-3600 seconds, represents 209 CPU-hours (= 209/64 hours). It is important to note that while the profile reflects the application and problem-size constraints of users (for example, a minimum of aggregate memory), there is also a secondary effect of the scheduling policy enforced on the system. That is, the users will naturally adapt their pattern of usage to maximize their productivity for a given queue structure.

Table 2. Workload Profile on the T3E at NERSC (%)

Size (procs)	8	16	32	64	128	256
Time(s)						
300- 900	0.5	0.7	1.9	4.5	0.5	1.3
1000-3600	0.5	1.4	3.4	10.2	2.8	4.0
3700-9600	2.0	4.2	7.6	35.1	17.3	2.4

The applications in the job mix originate from our user community and are used in production computing. Furthermore, the job mix profile was designed to span the diverse scientific areas of research amongst our users. Attention was also paid to diversify computational characteristics such as the amount of disk I/O and memory usage. For each class, an application and problem set was selected to satisfy the time and partition size constraints. The number of instances (Count) of each application/problem was adjusted such that aggregate CPU-hours reflected the workload profile. Table 3 lists the final job mix for the ESP benchmark with the elapsed times for each job on the T3E and SP.

4   Results and Discussion

Two test runs were completed on the T3E. In both cases, a separate queue was created for full configuration jobs and was marked to preempt running jobs. The full configuration jobs can thus be launched immediately on submission independent of the queue of general jobs. Process migration/compaction was also enabled for both runs. In the first run, labeled *Swap*, the system was oversubscribed by two and gang-scheduled with a time-slice of 20 minutes. A single NQS queue was used for the general job mix. In the second run, labeled *NoSwap*, the system was not oversubscribed. Each job ran uninterrupted until completion. Six queues for different maximum partition sizes; 256, 128, 64, 32, 16, with decreasing priority were used.

On the SP, two classes (queues) were created in Loadleveller; a general class for all jobs and a special high priority class for the full configuration jobs. It is not possible to *selectively* backfill with Loadleveller. Our preliminary runs showed that backfill would defer launching of the full configuration job until the end of the test. This would clearly violate the intent of the test. Backfill was implicitly disabled by assigning large wallclock times (several times greater than the complete test) to all jobs. Thus Loadleveller was reduced to a strictly FCFS strategy.

The results of the ESP test for the T3E and the SP are summarized in Table 4. Two efficiency measurements, with and without the shutdown/reboot time factored in, are reported. Figures 2, 3 and 4 show the details of the three runs where the instantaneous utilization is plotted against time and the time axis has been rescaled by the theoretical minimum time. Additionally, the start

Table 3. ESP Application Job Mix

Application	Discipline	Size	Count	Time(s)	
				T3E	SP
gfft	Large FFT	512	2	30.5	255.6
md	Biology	8	4	1208.0	1144.9
md		24	3	602.7	583.3
nqclarge	Chemistry	8	2	8788.0	5274.9
nqclarge		16	5	5879.6	2870.8
paratec	Material Science	256	1	746.9	1371.0
qcdsmall	Nuclear Physics	128	1	1155.0	503.3
qcdsmall		256	1	591.0	342.4
scf	Chemistry	32	7	3461.1	1136.2
scf		64	10	1751.9	646.4
scfdirect	Chemistry	64	7	5768.9	1811.7
scfdirect		81	2	4578.0	1589.1
superlu	Linear Algebra	8	15	288.3	361.2
tlbebig	Fusion	16	2	2684.5	2058.8
tlbebig		32	6	1358.3	1027.0
tlbebig		49	5	912.9	729.4
tlbebig		64	8	685.8	568.7
tlbebig		128	1	350.0	350.7

Table 4. ESP Results

	T3E		SP
	Swap	*NoSwap*	
Available processors	512	512	512
Jobmix work (CPU-seconds)	7437860	7437860	3715861
Elapsed Time (seconds)	20736	17327	14999
Shutdown/reboot (seconds)	2100	2100	5400
Efficiency	0.64	0.75	0.36
Efficiency (w/o reboot)	0.70	0.84	0.48

time for each job is indicated by an impulse where the height equals the partition size.

The obvious point is the significantly higher utilization efficiency of the T3E compared to the SP. This is due to the lack of a suitable mechanism to immediately launch full configuration jobs on the SP. On submission of the full configuration jobs, a considerable amount of time was spent waiting for running jobs to complete. This is evident in Figure 4 which shows two large regions where the instantaneous utilization drops very low. Without this drawback, it is likely

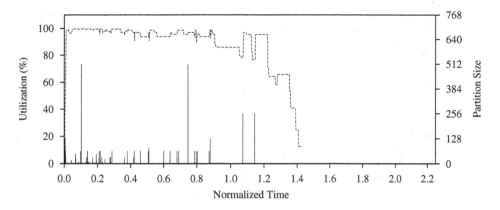

Fig. 2. T3E Swap : Utilization Chronology

the utilization on the SP would be comparable to the T3E. The time lag to run preferential jobs is indicative of the difficulty in changing modes of operation on the SP. This is important for sites that routinely change system characteristics, for example, between interactive and batch or between small and large partitions. The most desirable remedy would be to either checkpoint or dynamically swap out running jobs. It is noteworthy that the SP completed the test in less time due to its higher computational rate.

As seen in Figure 2, the BFF mechanism on the T3E deferred large partition jobs ($\geq$ 128) until the end. Consequently, at the end of the test there were large gaps that could not be filled by small jobs. On the SP, a FCFS strategy was indirectly enforced which can be seen illustrated in Figure 4 where the distribution of job start times is unrelated to partition size. It is evident from Figures 2 and 3 that a significant loss of efficiency on the T3E is incurred at the tail end of the test. In an operational setting, however, there are usually more jobs to launch. That is, the fact the ESP test is finite poses a problem since we are interested in a continual utilization given a hypothetical infinite number of queued jobs. Suggested solutions to this dilemma have proven to be awkward and require manual intervention. How the test should be terminated and post-analyzed will be reexamined in the next design of the ESP test.

The distribution of start times is qualitatively similar between the Swap and NoSwap runs on the T3E although the queue set up was different. In the second run, we deliberately assigned increasingly higher priorities to larger partition queues in an attempt to mitigate starvation. However, shortly after the start, it is unlikely that a large pool of idle processors would become coincidently available. In this scenario, the pattern of job submission reverts back to BFF and the queue set up has little impact. On the other hand, there is considerable difference in efficiency between the two T3E runs. This is attributed to the overhead of swapping which is significant when the oversubscribed processes cannot simultaneously fit in memory and process images must be written to disk.

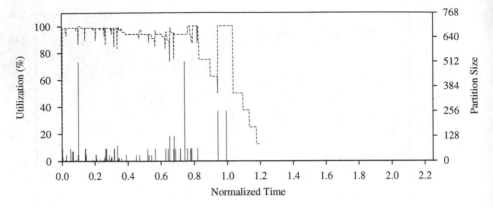

Fig. 3. T3E NoSwap : Utilization Chronology

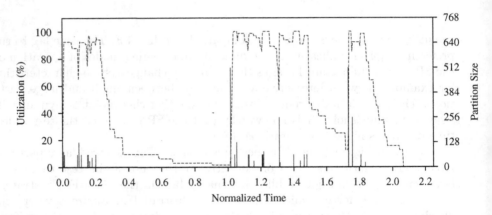

Fig. 4. SP : Utilization Chronology

It is recognized that backfill is the standard strategy used on the SP. To illustrate the effect of backfill on the utilization, Figure 5 shows the plot of the test run with backfill enabled. In this case, Loadleveller was provided *a priori* runtime estimates. Clearly backfill significantly improves the instantenous utilization especially at the beginning of the test. However, since the two full configuration jobs were deferred until the end and violated the intent of the test it was considered an invalid run. Note that large partition jobs ran near the end of the test. While this may appear to be starvation this is due to the granularity of job run times relative to the overall test. In other words, upon submission, the large jobs were reserved run times in the future, however, due to some lengthy running jobs, the reservation time is near the end of the test. To fully demonstrate the effect of backfill, the run times for individual jobs have to be at a finer granularity with respect to the overall time for the test.

To aid the evaluation of the performance and sensitivity of the ESP test, a simulator was developed to predict the runtime of this workload using various

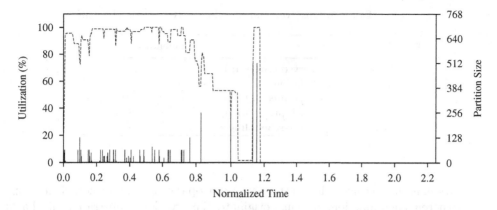

Fig. 5. SP with Backfill: Utilization Chronology

scheduling schemes. Several simple scheduling algorithms, such as FCFS and BFF were implemented together with the option of using backfill schemes and priority preemption. The simulator was used in the definition of the ESP test in order to ensure that the test did not exhibit pathological behavior. We have also used the simulator to estimate results of the ESP test on various system configurations and compared them to observed results.

Table 5 compares observed efficiency against various simulator efficiencies without shutdown/reboot. The simulated efficiencies are somewhat optimistic since they do not account for system overhead such as I/O contention, swapping and processor fragmentation. A gang-scheduled simulation of the ESP test with a 1000 second time-slice and oversubscription of two achieved a utilization efficiency of 0.86. However, this is overly optimistic as the observed efficiency of 0.70 from the Swap run indicate that there is a significant overhead incurred with gang-scheduling. Furthermore, this is only a slight increase compared to the preemption simulation with an efficiency of 0.84 without the use of gang-scheduling. The most noticeable result obtained from the simulations has been the assessment of the preemption functionality. The simulated efficiency of the ESP test using a BFF algorithm increased from 0.49 to 0.84 when preemption was employed. These results indicate that preemption can have a very significant impact on system utilization in a real operational setting which agrees with the conclusion from the SP run.

5 Conclusion

In this work we described a new utilization benchmark that we successfully ran on two parallel computer systems. It has provided quantitative data on utilization and scheduling efficacy of these resources and useful insights on how to manage these systems. The most important conclusion is that certain system functionality; including checkpoint/restart, swapping and migration, are critical for efficient scheduling strategies. Unfortunately, the scheduling of parallel

Table 5. Observed and Simulation Results on the T3E

	Efficiency
Observed (NoSwap)	0.84
Simulation	
+ w/o preemption	0.49
+ with preemption	0.84
+ gang-scheduling	0.86

systems has received little attention from operating system kernel developers wherein such functionality must originate. This work demonstrated that backfill has the potential to significantly enhance utilization while simultaneously preserving fairness. The only detraction is that it is not possible to forcibly insert a higher priority job to run immediately.

Future work will also include testing other parallel platforms with different scheduling and system functionality. We are interested in quantifying the effects of different schedulers with Loadleveller and particularly interested in using backfill in a valid run. The scalability of the test at larger number of processors and the difficulty with the tail end of the test will have to addressed. Finally we intend to conduct a theoretical analysis of the ESP test in the context of multiple resource requirements. At some point, we hope to make the test freely available. We hope that this test will be of use to other sites and spur both industry and research to improve system utilization.

Acknowledgments

This work was supported by the Office of Computational and Technology Research, Division of Mathematical, Information and Computational Sciences of the U.S. Department of Energy, under contract DE-AC03-76SF00098. The authors would like to acknowledge the assistance of the system administrators on the T3E and SP; Tina Butler, Nicholas Cardo and Jacqueline Scoggins, in setting up the ESP test. We would like to thank the developers of the applications for allowing their software to be included in this test, including; Environmental Molecular Science Laboratory (NWChem), George Vahala (tlbe), Gregory Kilcup (qcd), Xiaoye Li (SuperLU) and Andrew Canning (paratec).

References

1. Dongara J: Performance of Various Computers Using Standard Linear Algebra Software in a Fortran Environment, Available at:
   http://www.netlib.org/benchmarks/performance.ps.
2. Bailey D. H: The NAS Parallel Benchmarks. Int. J. Supercomputer Applications **5** (1991) 66

3. Wong A., Oliker L., Kramer W. T., Kaltz T. and Bailey D.H.:, Evaluating System Effectiveness in High Performance Computing Systems, Available at http://www.nersc.gov/ďhbailey
4. Talby D., Feitelson D. G.: Supporting priorities and improving utilization of the IBM SP2 scheduler using slack-based backfilling, 13th International Parallel Processing Symposium (1999) 513
5. Feitelson D.G., Jette M.A.: Improved Utilization and Responsiveness with Gang Scheduling In: Feitelson D.G., Rudolph L. (eds): Workshop in Job Scheduling Strategies for Parallel Processing. Lecture Notes in Computer Science, Vol 1291, Springer-Verlag (1997) 238–261
6. Feitelson D.G., Rudolph L., Schwiegelshohn U., Sevcik K.C., Wong P.: Theory and Practice in Parallel Job Scheduling In: Feitelson D.G., Rudolph L. (eds): Workshop in Job Scheduling Strategies for Parallel Processing. Lecture Notes in Computer Science, Vol 1291, Springer-Verlag (1997) 1–34
7. Leinberg W., Karypis G., Kumar V.: Job Scheduling in the presence of Mulitple Resource Requirements Computer Science Department, University of Minnesota **TR 99-025** (1999)
8. Blakeborough J., Welcome M.: T3E Scheduling Update, 41st Cray User Group Conference Proceedings (1999)
9. Simon H., Kramer W., Lucas R.: Building the Teraflops/Petabytes Production Supercomputing Center, Fifth International Euro-Par Conference Proceeding (1999) 61

A Critique of ESP

Dror G. Feitelson

School of Computer Science and Engineering,
The Hebrew University, 91904 Jerusalem, Israel,
feit@cs.huji.ac.il,
http://www.cs.huji.ac.il/~feit

Abstract. This note is an elaboratin of a panel presentation, and is
meant as a constructive critique of ESP. It should be remembered that
the bottom line is that ESP is a big step in an important direction —
otherwise we wouldn't bother with this discussion...

1 Introduction

The evaluation of parallel systems is very important, mainly for costly acquisition decisions, and has therefore been practiced for a long time. However, such evaluations typically focus on the computational aspects of the system. They typically use a small set of benchmark applications, and measure the performance of these applications in isolation [2,3,7,1]. The results reflect the performance of the processor, the memory hierarchy, the interconnection network, and the relationship between these factors.

ESP is different — it targets the *system-level* performance rather than the hardware [8]. Issues include the efficiency of the scheduling, its flexibility, and mundane details such as booting time. While this is a very welcome shift in focus, there are some potential problems that have to be addressed. The purpose of this note is to point them out.

2 Good Points

The most important point in ESP is the objective of including the system in the evaluation. This should not be underestimated. Many large-scale parallel systems, costing tens of millions of dollars, suffer from very low utilization (e.g. [6]). This is at least partly due to the fact that vendors emphasize single-job performance, and that is where they invest most of their development effort. It is high time that system performance receive similar treatment.

The way to measure system performance is to measure how the system performs under a representative workload. The choice of workload is crucial, as different workloads can lead to very different performance results. It seems that ESP has made a very reasonable choice in this respect. The proposed workload conforms to various features of workloads observed in production installations [4], including

D.G. Feitelson and L. Rudolph (Eds.): JSSPP 2000, LNCS 1911, pp. 68–73, 2000.

- The distribution of job sizes, which is mostly powers of two, but not only
- The existence of a large variance in the distribution of runtimes
- The repetition of certain jobs

The size of the test — 82 jobs — is also a reasonable compromise between the desire to have enough jobs to exercise the system scheduler, and the need to complete the test in a reasonable time (a few hours).

3 Debatable Points

While ESP is in general a very promising system-level benchmark, the details of its definition contain some potential problems. Some of these originate from the attempt to bundle everything into a result that is expressed as a single number.

3.1 The Arrival Pattern

The ESP benchmark is composed of a set of 82 jobs. 80 of these jobs arrive in three batches 10 minutes apart. While the set of jobs is fixed, their division into these three batches is randomized. The other two jobs are so-called "full configuration jobs" that require all the processors in the system, and arrive later.

There are two problems with this arrival pattern. One is that essentially all the jobs arrive at the beginning, within 20 minutes of a test that takes several hours. In particular, there is a distinct possibility that towards the end of the test the system will start to drain and utilization will drop. In a real setting, where jobs continue to arrive, this would not happen.

The second problem is that the user feedback cycle is missing. In real systems, users often do not submit additional work until their previous work is done. This tends to automatically spread out the load, and reduces the risk that the system will saturate; it is part of the on-line nature of real scheduling work. EPS, on the other hand, is closer to off-line scheduling, with all jobs available (nearly) at the outset.

While these problems are very disturbing, there is no obvious way to solve them. Changing the arrival pattern so as to spread the jobs out throughout the test risks all sorts of interactions with the load, especially considering that the jobs have different runtimes on different platforms. A partial solution might be to ignore idle time at the end of the test, and not include it in the utilization measure. This at least reduces the effect of the system drainage towards the end. This idea is elaborated upon in Section 3.4.

3.2 Including Booting the System

The ESP metric of efficiency calculates the useful computation time as a fraction of the total runtime including a system boot. This implies an expectation that the system will be booted every 82 jobs, which is unreasonable and puts too much emphasis on booting. It also gives vendors an oppportunity to improve their score significantly by reducing boot time, without any modifications to the scheduler, which is more important for normal use.

The correct way to incorporate booting time would be to estimate the MTTB — the mean time to boot. Systems with a high MTTB would add less of the boot time to the denominator of the metric formula. However, there is no easy way to estimate the MTTB of a system. It may therefore be preferable to leave booting time as a separate metric, rather than trying to incorporate it into the efficiency metric.

3.3   Features and Restrictions

The definition of ESP makes special provisions for the full-configuration jobs: they are given higher priority, and must be run as soon as possible after being submitted. This favors computers with the capability to checkpoint current jobs, because they can then make room for the full configuration jobs immediately. Computers lacking this capability are forced to idle their nodes as they collect them when the current jobs terminate. Backfilling is deemed undesirable, as it may actually delay the high-priority full-configuration jobs (even if the conservative version is used). As a side issue, even if backfilling is used, it is not clear what runtime estimates should be given, as accurate estimates are not necessarily the best, but normal user estimates are worse [5].

While favoring machines with checkpoint and restart is reasonable for a system-level metric, the effect in this case may be too extreme. A more balanced approach would be to first run the workload with no special requirements, and allowing all the features that exist in the scheduler. Then a second test would be administered to see how well the system handles special requirements, such as the need to run certain jobs immediately. This would then be able to use specialized metrics, such as the waiting time of the high-priority jobs. With the current efficiency metric, the advantage of checkpointing jobs in order to run the full configuration jobs immediately only has a secondary effect on the score, and might have practically no effect if backfilling is used. A system without checkpointing or preemption that causes a high-priority job to wait should be penalized by more than some added idle time.

Finally, submitting the first full configuration job after all the others, and requiring the second to terminate within 90% of the test duration, are artificial mechanisms to ensure that the full configuration jobs are not placed at the ends. The cause of this problem is that the test length, only 82 jobs, may be too short. Alternative solutions are therefore to either enlarge the test, or use only a single full configuration job.

3.4   Calculating the Score

The ESP efficiency metric is supposed to lie in the range [0, 1], with a value of 1 representing the perfect score. However, due to the impossibility of a perfect packing, a score of 1 is unattainable (even if the booting time is not included).

In fact, the top possible score is unknown, partly because this also depends on the runtimes of the jobs on the measured system and on the randomized order in which they are submitted.

One way to ensure that a top score of 1 is attainable is to ignore idle time at the end of a schedule. Thus the denominator of the efficiency metric will not be $P \cdot T$, but rather $\sum_{i=1}^{P} T_{p_i}$, where T_{p_i} is is the time from the start of the test to the last instant in which processor p_i is used. With this definition, a largest-job-first algorithm that does not reuse any processor once it is idled can create a perfect packing, with all the idle time at the end. The problem is that this is a very wasteful schedule, and is based on avoiding any attempts for dense packing — exactly the opposite of what we want!

To prevent such situations, it is possible to use a predefined scheduling algorithm as the comparison point. For example, we can choose "most work first" (MWF), which sorts the jobs according to the product of their runtime and number of processors. Using this reference algorithm, we calculate the IAE (idle at end) time as follows:

$$IAE^{MWF} = \sum_{i=1}^{P} T^{MWF} - T_{p_i}^{MWF}$$

where T^{MWF} is the total time for the schedule generated by MWF, and $T_{p_i}^{MWF}$ is the last instant processor p_i is used under MWF. The efficiency metric of ESP is then calculated as

$$\frac{\sum_{j=1}^{82} p_j \cdot t_j}{P \cdot T - IAE^{MWF}}$$

i.e. the IAE time calculated for the reference algorithm is deducted from the denominator. This avoids the unfair penalty due to drainage at the end to some degree. while it may happen that a superb scheduling algorithm would create a dense packing leading to a metric larger than 1, this is not very probable, and even if it happens there is a good interpretation: the algorithm is better than MWF.

3.5   Using Real Applications

The question of using real vs. synthetic applications is perhaps the hardest to settle. Real applications have the advantage of being good for comprehensive system valuation, including the processor, the communications infrastructure, the memory hierarchy, and so on. They really evaluate how all the system components work together, and foster a very wide interpretation for the word "system".

However, due to the way in which they interact with the hardware, real applications are problematic if you want to evaluate the "system" in a more narrow interpretation, namely the operating system components such as the scheduler. For example, the runtimes of different jobs may be totally different on different platforms, and even the relations between the jobs (which is longer than the other) may change. Therefore schedulers on different platforms are actually faced with a different workload when scheduling the same real applications! If you want to compare *only the schedulers*, this will not do.

It seems that in the case of ESP the choice of using real applications is the correct one. This is so for two reasons:

- ESP is designed to evaluate full system performance. This indeed *includes* the scheduler, but is not *limited* to the scheduler. Thus if the scheduler on a certain platform benefits from the fact that certain jobs run faster on that platform, so be it — the platform is indeed better.
- Using synthetic applications requires the benchmark designer to give answers to many hard questions, that are implicitly hidden by the choice of job mix. These include
  1. What should the memory requirements of the jobs be?
  2. What degree of locality should they display?
  3. What should be the granularity of communications?
  4. What should be the patterns of communications?
  5. How much I/O should the applications perform?
  6. What should be the correlations among the above parameters?

  These questions should be answered based on a detailed workload analysis, which is extremely hard to do. No real data about these issues exists to date.

However, different installations may opt to use different sets of applications that are more representative of their local workload. If this happens, ESP will become more of a framework than a well-defined metric.

4   Conclusions

It seems that there are a number of points in the current ESP definition that should be addressed. However, this critique should not be understood as saying that ESP is bad. On the contrary, it is a very significant first step in a very important direction. It is just that the problem of how to evaluate a complete systems is a hard one, and cannot be expected to be solved in one step.

References

1. D. H. Bailey, E. Barszcz, L. Dagum, and H. D. Simon, *"NAS parallel benchmark results"*. *IEEE Trans. Parallel & Distributed Syst.* **1(1)**, pp. 43–51, Feb 1993.
2. G. Cybenko, L. Kipp, L. Pointer, and D. Kuck, *"Supercomputer performance evaluation and the Perfect Benchmarks"*. In *Intl. Conf. Supercomputing*, pp. 254–266, Jun 1990.
3. J. J. Dongarra, *"Performance of various computers using standard linear equations software"*. *Comput. Arch. News* **18(1)**, pp. 17–31, Mar 1990.
4. A. B. Downey and D. G. Feitelson, *"The elusive goal of workload characterization"*. *Perf. Eval. Rev.* **26(4)**, pp. 14–29, Mar 1999.
5. D. G. Feitelson and A. Mu'alem Weil, *"Utilization and predictability in scheduling the IBM SP2 with backfilling"*. In 12th *Intl. Parallel Processing Symp.*, pp. 542–546, Apr 1998.

6. J. P. Jones and B. Nitzberg, *"Scheduling for parallel supercomputing: a historical perspective of achievable utilization"*. In *Job Scheduling Strategies for Parallel Processing*, D. G. Feitelson and L. Rudolph (eds.), pp. 1–16, Springer-Verlag, 1999. Lect. Notes Comput. Sci. vol. 1659.
7. J. P. Singh, W-D. Weber, and A. Gupta, *"SPLASH: Stanford parallel applications for shared-memory"*. *Comput. Arch. News* **20(1)**, pp. 5–44, Mar 1992.
8. A. Wong, L. Oliker, W. Kramer, T. Kaltz, and D. Bailey, *"System utilization benchmark on the Cray T3E and IBM SP2"*. In *Job Scheduling Strategies for Parallel Processing*, D. G. Feitelson and L. Rudolph (eds.), p. 58–70, Springer Verlag, 2000. Lect. Notes Comput. Sci. vol. 1911.

Resource Allocation Schemes
for Gang Scheduling

Bing Bing Zhou[1], David Walsh[2], and Richard P. Brent[3]

[1] School of Computing and Mathematics, Deakin University,
Geelong, VIC 3217, Australia
[2] Department of Computer Science, Australian National University,
Canberra, ACT 0200, Australia
[3] Oxford University Computing Laboratory, Wolfson Building, Parks Road,
Oxford OX1 3QD, UK

Abstract. Gang scheduling is currently the most popular scheduling scheme for parallel processing in a time shared environment. In this paper we first describe the ideas of job re-packing and workload tree for efficiently allocating resources to enhance the performance of gang scheduling. We then present some experimental results obtained by implementing four different resource allocation schemes. These results show how the ideas, such as re-packing jobs, running jobs in multiple slots and minimising the average number of time slots in the system, affect system and job performance when incorporated into the buddy based allocation scheme for gang scheduling.

1 Introduction

Many job scheduling strategies have been introduced for parallel computing systems. (See a good survey in [4].) These scheduling strategies can be classified into either *space sharing*, or *time sharing*. Because a time shared environment is more difficult to establish for parallel processing in a multiple processor system, currently most commercial parallel systems only adopt space sharing such as the LoadLeveler scheduler from IBM for the SP2 [9]. However, one major drawback of space sharing is the blockade situation, that is, small jobs can easily be blocked for a long time by large ones. For parallel machines to be truly utilised as general-purpose high-performance computing servers for various kinds of applications, time sharing has to be seriously considered.

It is known that coordinated scheduling of parallel jobs across the processors is a critical factor to achieve efficient parallel execution in a time-shared environment. Currently the most popular strategy for coordinated scheduling is *explicit coscheduling* [7], or *gang scheduling* [5]. With gang scheduling processes of the same job will run simultaneously for a certain amount of time which is called, *scheduling slot*, or *time slot*. When a time slot is ended, the processors will context-switch at the same time to give the service to processes of another job. All parallel jobs in the system take turns to receive the service in a coordinated manner. If space permits, a number of jobs may be allocated in the

D.G. Feitelson and L. Rudolph (Eds.): JSSPP 2000, LNCS 1911, pp. 74–86, 2000.

same time slot and run simultaneously on different subsets of processors. Thus gang scheduling can be considered as a scheduling strategy which combines both space sharing and time sharing together.

Currently most allocation strategies for gang scheduling only consider processor allocation within the same time slot and the allocation in one time slot is independent of the allocation in other time slots. One major disadvantage in this kind of resource allocation is the problem of fragmentation. Because resource allocation is considered independently in different time slots, some freed resources due to job termination may remain idle for a long time even though they are able to be re-allocated to existing jobs running in other time slots. One way to alleviate the problem is to allow jobs to run in multiple time slots whenever possible [2,10]. When jobs are allowed to run in multiple time slots, the buddy based allocation scheme will perform much better than many other existing allocation schemes in terms of average job turnaround time [2].

The buddy based scheme was originally developed for memory allocation [8]. To allocate resources to a job of size p using the buddy based scheme, the processors in the system are first divided into subsets of size n for $n/2 < p \leq n$. The job is then assigned to one such subset if there is a time slot in which all processors in the subset are idle. Although the buddy scheme causes the problem of internal fragmentation, jobs with about the same size tend to be head-to-head aligned in different time slots. If one job is completed, the freed resources can easily be reallocated to other jobs running on the same subset of processors. Therefore, jobs have a better chance to run in multiple time slots.

To alleviate the problem of fragmentation we proposed another scheme, namely job re-packing [11]. In this scheme we try to rearrange the order of job execution on the originally allocated processors so that small fragments of idle resources from different time slots can be combined together to form a larger and more useful one in a single time slot. When this scheme is incorporated into the buddy based system, we can set up a *workload tree* to record the workload conditions of each subset of processors. With this workload tree we are able to simplify the search procedure for resource allocation and also to balance the workload across the processors.

In this paper we shall present some simulation results to show how the ideas, such as re-packing jobs, running jobs in multiple slots and minimising the number of time slots in the system, affect system and job performance when incorporated into the buddy scheduling system. In Section 2 we briefly discuss job re-packing. The construction of the binary workload tree for the buddy based system is described in Section 3. Section 4 first discusses four different allocation schemes to be compared and the workload model used in our experiments and then presents some simulation results. Finally the conclusions are given in Section 5.

2   Job Re-packing

One way to alleviate the problem of fragmentation is to allow jobs to run in multiple time slots whenever possible. A simple example is depicted in Fig. 1.

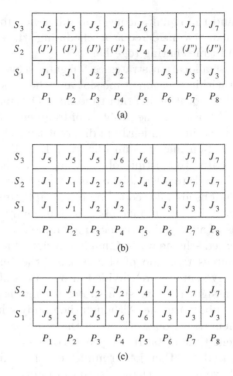

Fig. 1. An example of alleviating the fragmentation problem by (b) running jobs in multiple time slots and (c) re-packing job to reduce the total number of time slot.

In this example the system has eight processors and originally three slots are created to handle the execution of nine jobs. Now assume that two jobs J' and J'' in slot S_2 are terminated. If jobs are allowed to run in multiple time slots, jobs J_1 and J_2 in slot S_1 and job J_7 on S_3 can occupy the freed resources in S_2, as shown in Fig. 1(b). Therefore, most processors can be kept busy all the time. However, this kind of resource reallocation may not be optimal when job performance is considered. Assume now there arrives a new job which requires more than one processor. Because the freed resources have been reallocated to the running jobs, the fourth time slot has to be created and then the performance of the existing jobs which run in a single time slot will be degraded.

Now consider job re-packing. We first shift jobs J_1 and J_2 from slot S_1 to slot S_2 and then move jobs J_5 and J_6 down to slot S_1 and job J_7 to slot S_2. After this rearrangement or re-packing of jobs, time slot S_3 becomes completely empty. We can then eliminate this empty slot, as shown in Fig. 1(c). It is obvious that this type of job re-packing can greatly improve the overall system performance. Note that during the re-packing jobs are only shifted between rows from one time slot to another. We actually only rearrange the order of job execution on their originally allocated processors in a scheduling round and there is no process migration between processors involved. This kind of job rearrangement is particularly suitable for distributed memory machines in which process migration is expensive.

Since processes of the same job need coordination and they must be placed in the same time slots all the time during the computation, therefore, we cannot re-pack jobs in an arbitrary way. A shift is said to be legal if all processes of the same job are shifted to the same slot at the same time. In job re-packing we always utilise this kind of legal shift to rearrange jobs between time slots so that small fragments of available processors in different time slots can be combined into a larger and more useful one. This kind of job re-packing can effectively be done based on the following two simple properties [11].

Property 1. Assume that processors are logically organised as a one-dimensional linear array. Any two adjacent fragments of available processors can be grouped together in a single time slot.

Property 2. Assume that processors are logically organised as a one-dimensional linear array. If every processor has an idle fragment, jobs in the system can be re-packed such that all the idle fragments will be combined together in a single time slot which can then be eliminated.

Note that adopting job re-packing may increase the scheduling overhead in a clustered computing system because messages notifying the changes in the global scheduling matrix have to be broadcast to processors so that the local scheduling tables on each processor can be modified accordingly. However, there is no need to frequently re-pack jobs between time slots. The re-packing is applied only when the working condition is changed, e.g., when a job is terminated, or when a new job arrives. Thus the extra system cost introduced by the re-packing may not be high. In the next section we shall see that, when job re-packing is incorporated in the buddy based system, we can set up a workload tree. With this workload tree the procedure for searching available resources can be simplified and then the overall system overhead for resource allocation is actually reduced.

3   Workload Tree

Based on job re-packing we can set up a *workload tree* (WLT) for the buddy scheduling system, as depicted in Fig. 2, to balance the workload across the processors and also to simplify the search procedure for resource allocation.

The workload tree has $logN + 1$ levels where N is the number of processors in the system. Each node in the tree is associated with a particular subset of processors. The node at the top level is associated with all N processors. The N processors are divided into two subsets of equal size and each subset is then associated with a child node of the root. The division and association continues until the bottom level is reached. Each node in the tree is assigned an integer value. At the bottom level the value assigned to each leaf node is equal to the number of idle time slots on the associated processor. For example, the node

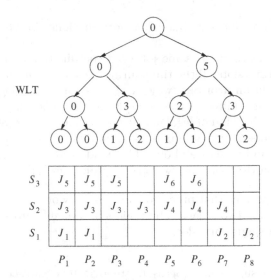

Fig. 2. The binary workload tree (WLT) for the buddy based allocation system.

corresponding to processor P_1 is given a value 0 because there is no idle slot on that processor, while the value assigned to the last node is equal to 2 denoting there are currently two idle slots on processor P_8. For a non-leaf node the value will be equal to the sum of the values of its two children when both values are nonzero. Otherwise, it is set to zero denoting the associated subset of processors will not be available for new arrivals.

For the conventional allocation method, adding this workload tree may not be able to assist the decision making for resource allocation. This is because the information contained in the tree does not tell which slot is idle on a processor, but processes of the same job have to be allocated in the same time slot. With job re-packing, however, we know that on a one-dimensional linear array any two adjacent fragments of available processors can be grouped together to form a larger one in a single time slot according to Property 1 presented in the previous section. To search for a suitable subset of available processors, therefore, we only need to check the values at a proper level. Consider the situation depicted in Fig. 2 and assume that a new job of size 4 arrives. In this case we need only to check the two nodes at the second level. Since the value of the second node at that level is nonzero (equal to 5), the new job can then be placed on the associated subset of processors, that is, the last four processors. To allocate resources we may first re-pack job J_6 into time slot S_1 and then place the new job in time slot S_3. Since the workload conditions on these processors are changed after the allocation, the values of the associated nodes need to be updated accordingly.

There are many other advantages in using this workload tree. To ensure a high system and job performance it is very important to balance workloads across the processors. Using the workload tree it will become much easier for us to handle the problem of load balancing. Because the value of each node reflects the information about the current workload condition on the associated processor subset, the system can easily choose a subset of less active processors for an incoming job by comparing the node values at a proper level.

To enhance the efficiency of resource utilisation jobs should be allowed to run in multiple time slots if there are free resources available. Although the idea of running jobs in multiple time slots was originally proposed in [2,10], there were no methods given on how to effectively determine whether an existing job on a subset of processors can run in multiple time slots. Using the workload tree this procedure becomes simple. In Fig. 2, for example, the rightmost node at the third level of the workload tree is nonzero and job J_2 is currently running within the associated subset of processors. It can then be allocated an additional time slot (S_3 in this case) and run in multiple time slots.

To enhance the system and job performance it is also important to minimise the number of time slots in the system. (See our experimental results presented in the next section.) Since the root of the workload tree is associated with all the processors, we are able to know quickly when a time slot can be deleted by simply checking the node value. If it is nonzero, we immediately know that there is at least one idle slot on each processor. According to Property 2 presented in the previous section these idle fragments can be combined together in a single time slot which can then be eliminated. Assume that job J_1 in Fig. 2 is terminated. The values of the leaf nodes associated with processors P_1 and P_2 become nonzero. This will cause the value of their parent node to become nonzero. The information about the change of workload condition is continuously propagated upward and then the root value will become nonzero. It is easy to see in this particular example that, after job J_2 is legally shifted to time slot S_3, time slot S_1 will become completely empty and can then be deleted.

4   Experiments

In this section we present some experimental results to show how the techniques of re-packing jobs, running jobs in multiple slots and minimising the average number of time slots in the system, affect system and job performance when incorporated into the buddy based allocation system for gang scheduling.

4.1   Allocation Schemes

Four different resource allocation schemes are evaluated in the experiment. The first one is just the conventional buddy (BC) system in which the workload balancing is not seriously considered and each job only runs in a single time slot. The second scheme (BR) utilises the workload tree to balance the workload across the processors and re-packs jobs when necessary to reduce the average number of time slots in the system, but it does not consider to run jobs in multiple time slots. The third allocation scheme (BRMS) is a modified version of the second one, in which jobs are allowed to run in multiple time slots whenever possible. When a job is given an extra time slot in this scheduling scheme, it will keep running in multiple time slots to completion and never relinquish the extra resources gained during the computation. The fourth allocation scheme (BRMMS) is designed to consider the minimisation of the average number of time slots in the system while allowing jobs to run in multiple slots. In this scheme jobs running in multiple time slots may have to relinquish the additional resources gained during the computation if a new arrival cannot fit into the existing time slots, or if a time slot in the system can be deleted. Therefore, we can expect that the average number of time slots in the system will never be greater than the number created by using the second scheduling scheme BR.

4.2   The Workload Model

Experimental results show that the choice of workload alone does not significantly affect the relative performance of different resource management algorithms [6]. To compare the performance of the above four different resource allocation schemes, we adopted one workload model proposed in [1]. Both job runtimes and sizes (the number of processors required) in this model are distributed uniformly in log space (or uniform-log distributed), while the interarrival times are exponentially distributed. This model was constructed based on observations from the Intel Paragon at the San Diego Supercomputer Center and the IBM SP2 at the Cornell Theory Center and has been used by many researchers to evaluate their parallel job scheduling algorithms.

Since the model was originally built to evaluate batch scheduling policies, we made a few minor modifications in our simulation for gang scheduling. In many real systems jobs are classified into two classes, that is, interactive and batch jobs. A batch job is one which tends to run much longer and often requires a larger number of processors than interactive ones. Usually batch queues are enabled for execution only during the night. In our experiments we only consider interactive jobs. Job runtimes will have a reasonably wide distribution, with many short jobs but a few relatively large ones and they are rounded to the number of time slots within a range between 1 and 120. Assuming the length of a time slot is five second, the longest job will then be 10 minutes and the average job length is about two minutes.

4.3   Results

We assume that there are 128 processors in the system. During the simulation we collect the following statistics:

- average processor active ratio r_a: the average number of time slots in which a processor is active divided by the overall system computational time in time slots. If the resource allocation scheme is efficient, the obtained result should be close to the estimated average system workload ρ which is defined as $\rho = \lambda \bar{p} \bar{t} / P$ where λ is job arrival rate, $\bar{t}$ and $\bar{p}$ are the average job length and size and P is the total number of processors in the system.

Table 1. Some experimental results obtained in the first experiment.

scheme	ρ	r_a	n_l	n_a	t_{ta}	t_{sa}	t_{ma}	t_{la}
BC	0.20	0.19	3	1.16	31.10	5.67	40.52	112.45
BR		0.19	3	0.45	30.01	5.52	39.29	108.18
BRMS		0.19	4	0.57	29.25	5.37	37.86	106.56
BRMMS		0.19	3	0.44	28.66	5.24	37.09	104.68
BC	0.50	0.46	6	2.84	70.00	14.04	89.27	246.08
BR		0.46	5	2.27	58.65	11.68	75.23	206.45
BRMS		0.45	15	6.11	57.28	15.99	73.83	184.98
BRMMS		0.47	5	2.06	44.05	8.77	55.82	159.75
BC	0.70	0.55	10	5.23	129.65	25.03	166.21	456.72
BR		0.58	8	4.09	102.21	20.27	130.17	359.00
BRMS		0.53	30	14.39	96.95	35.78	128.23	271.12
BRMMS		0.61	7	3.58	66.23	13.96	83.19	234.05
BC	0.90	0.58	14	7.62	189.60	35.91	246.73	670.42
BR		0.65	11	6.00	150.18	29.50	195.49	526.64
BRMS		0.56	43	20.17	120.53	51.84	170.61	356.94
BRMMS		0.68	10	5.51	98.51	20.80	124.69	345.48

- average number of time slots n_a: If t_i is the total time when there are i time slots in the system, the average number of time slots in the system during the operation can be defined as $n_a = \sum_{i=0}^{n_l} it_i / \sum_{i=0}^{n_l} t_i$ where n_l is the largest number of time slots encountered in the system during the computation.
- average turnaround time t_a: The turnaround time is the time between the arrival and completion of a job. In the experiment we measured the average turnaround time t_{ta} for all 200 jobs. We also divided the jobs into three classes, that is, small (between 1 and 12 time slots), medium (between 13 and 60) and large (greater than 60) and measured the average turnaround time for these classes, t_{sa}, t_{ma} and t_{la}, respectively.

We conducted two experiments. In our first experiment we measured transient behaviors of each system. Each time only a small set of 200 jobs were used to evaluate the performance of each scheduling scheme. For each estimated system workload, however, 20 different sets of jobs were generated using the workload model and the final results are the average of the 20 runs for each scheduling scheme.

Some experimental results are given in Table 1. First consider that jobs only run in a single time slot. When job re-packing is applied to reduce the number of time slots in the system and the workload tree is used to balance the workload across the processors, we expect that both job performance and system resource utilisation should be improved. Our experimental results confirm this prediction.

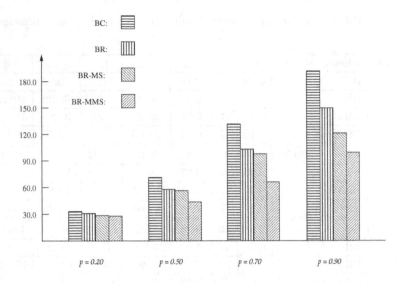

Fig. 3. Average turnaround time for all jobs t_{ta}.

It can be seen from the table that scheme BR consistently outperforms BC under all categories although the improvement is not significant for the estimated system workload $\rho = 0.20$.

When jobs are allowed to run in multiple time slots, situations become a bit more complicated. We can see that both n_l and n_a are dramatically increased when the third scheduling scheme BRMS is adopted. In order to give a better view for the comparison we show three pictures for average turnaround time for all jobs t_{ta}, average turnaround time for short jobs t_{sa} and average processor active ratio r_a, respectively.

The average turnaround time for all jobs is depicted in Fig. 3. It is seen that schemes BRMS and BRMMS which allow jobs to run in multiple slots can reduce t_{ta}. This is understandable since a job running in multiple slots may have a shorter turnaround time. An interesting point, however, is that applying BRMS will result in a much longer average turnaround time for short jobs as shown in Fig. 4. From the user's perspective it is short jobs that need to be completed more quickly. The main reason why BRMS can cause a longer average turnaround time for short jobs may be as follows: If jobs are allowed to run in multiple slots and do not relinquish additional slots gained during the computation, the number of time slots in the system may become very large most of the time. Note that long jobs will stay in the system longer and then have a better chance to run in multiple time slots. However, the system resources are limited. When a short job arrives, it can only obtain a very small portion of CPU utilisation if allocated only in a single time slot.

It seems that we can increase the average processor active ratio if jobs are allowed to run in multiple time slots. However, another interesting point is that using the allocation scheme BRMS will eventually decrease the efficiency in

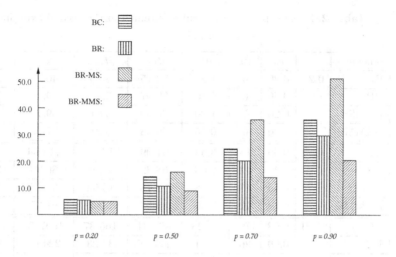

Fig. 4. Average turnaround time for small jobs t_{sa}.

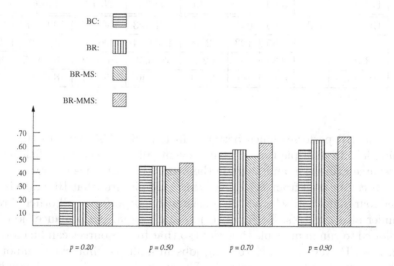

Fig. 5. Average processor active ratio r_a.

resource utilisation. As shown in Fig. 5 the average processor active ratio can even be lower than that obtained by using the conventional buddy scheduling scheme BC. The main reason may be that, when a job running in multiple slots finishes, the processors on which it was running will be idle in those time slots until a change in workload condition occurs such as a new job arriving to fill the freed resources, or some slots becoming totally empty which can be eliminated.

In our second experiment we measured the steady state performance of each system by increasing the number of jobs in each job set to 20,000. Some experimental results are depicted in Table 2. The results are obtained by taking the average of 5 runs using different job sets. It can be seen that the allocation

Table 2. Some experimental results obtained in the second experiment.

scheme	ρ	r_a	n_l	n_a	t_{ta}	t_{sa}	t_{ma}	t_{la}
BC	0.20	0.20	6	1.21	32.15	5.70	40.62	114.25
BR		0.20	6	0.46	30.97	5.52	39.16	109.77
BRMS		0.20	7	1.20	30.99	5.51	39.11	110.15
BRMMS		0.20	6	0.45	29.58	5.21	37.20	105.60
BC	0.50	0.49	18	3.64	91.09	17.33	115.54	317.90
BR		0.49	13	2.60	68.32	12.95	86.93	237.94
BRMS		0.49	17	3.78	78.78	15.64	99.75	272.78
BRMMS		0.49	12	2.30	48.93	9.47	61.25	172.04
BC	0.70	0.68	79	35.28	874.81	166.87	1097.78	3077.22
BR		0.69	26	7.21	177.75	34.23	224.62	620.55
BRMS		0.69	64	23.37	441.42	91.33	551.02	1531.94
BRMMS		0.69	23	5.39	94.78	20.10	118.61	326.51
BC	0.90	0.69	645	346.33	8713.93	1603.65	10955.74	30834.47
BR		0.85	123	62.48	1151.24	296.40	1952.93	5438.99
BRMS		0.82	357	202.71	3836.59	800.92	4830.35	13191.87
BRMMS		0.86	90	39.94	716.46	151.14	887.45	2490.94

scheme BR performs much better than BRMS. This conforms that simply running jobs in multiple time slots can eventually decrease the efficiency of system resource utilisation and degrade the overall performance of jobs.

It can be seen from the above tables and pictures that BRMMS is the best of the four allocation schemes. It consistently outperforms all other three schemes under all categories. To improve job and system performance, jobs should be allowed to run in multiple time slots so that free resources can be more efficiently utilised. However, simply running jobs in multiple time slots cannot guarantee the improvement of performance. The minimisation of average number of time slots in the system has to be seriously considered.

5   Conclusions

One major drawback of using gang scheduling for parallel processing is the problem of fragmentation. A conventional way to alleviate this problem was to allow jobs to run in multiple time slots. However, simply adopting this idea alone may cause several problems. The first obvious one is the increased system scheduling overhead. This is because simply running jobs in multiple time slots can greatly increase the average number of time slots in the system and then the system time will be increased to manage a large number of time slots. The second problem is the unfair treatment to small jobs. Long jobs will stay in the system for relatively a long time and then have a better chance to run in multiple time slots. However, the system resources are limited and in consequence a newly arrived short job may only obtain relatively a very small portion of CPU utilisation. Another very interesting point obtained from our experiment is that simply running jobs in multiple time slots may not solve the problem of fragmentation, but on the contrary it may eventually degrade the efficiency of system resource utilisation.

With job re-packing we try to rearrange the order of job execution on their originally allocated processors to combine small fragments of available processors into a larger and more useful one. Based on job re-packing we can set up a workload tree to greatly improve the performance for the buddy scheduling system. With the workload tree we are able to simplify the search procedure for resource allocation, to balance the workload across the processors and to quickly detect when a job can run in multiple time slots and when the number of time slots in the system can be reduced. More importantly we are able to properly combine the ideas of job re-packing, running jobs in multiple time slots and minimising the average number of time slots in the system together to reduce job turnaround times and to enhance the efficiency of system resource utilisation. Our experimental results show that this combined allocation scheme, i.e., our fourth allocation scheme BRMMS can indeed improve the system and job performance significantly. Because there is no process migration involved, this scheme is particularly suitable for clustered parallel computing systems.

It should be noted that in our experiment we assumed that the memory space is unlimited and characteristics of jobs are totally unknown. In practice, however, the size of memory in each processor is limited. Thus jobs may have to come to a waiting queue before being executed and large running jobs may have to be swapped when the system becomes busy. Along with the rapid development of high-performance computing libraries characteristics of jobs may no longer be considered completely unknown before being executed. These conditions will be considered in our future research.

References

1. A. B. Downey, A parallel workload model and its implications for processor allocation, *Proceedings of 6th International Symposium on High Performance Distributed Computing*, Aug 1997.
2. D. G. Feitelson, Packing schemes for gang scheduling, In *Job Scheduling Strategies for Parallel Processing*, D. G. Feitelson and L. Rudolph (eds.), Lecture Notes Computer Science, Vol. 1162, Springer-Verlag, 1996, pp.89-110.
3. D. G. Feitelson and L. Rudolph, Distributed hierarchical control for parallel processing, *Computer*, 23(5), May 1990, pp.65-77.
4. D. G. Feitelson and L. Rudolph, Job scheduling for parallel supercomputers, in Encyclopedia of Computer Science and Technology, Vol. 38, Marcel Dekker, Inc, New York, 1998.
5. D. G. Feitelson and L. Rudolph, Gang scheduling performance benefits for fine-grained synchronisation, *Journal of Parallel and Distributed Computing*, 16(4), Dec. 1992, pp.306-318.

6. V. Lo, J. Mache and K. Windisch, A comparative study of real workload traces and synthetic workload models for parallel job scheduling, In *Job Scheduling Strategies for Parallel Processing*, D. G. Feitelson and L. Rudolph (Eds.), Lecture Notes Computer Science, Vol. 1459, Springer-Verlag, 1998, pp.25-46.
7. J. K. Ousterhout, Scheduling techniques for concurrent systems, *Proceedings of Third International Conference on Distributed Computing Systems*, May 1982, pp.20-30.
8. J. L. Peterson and T. A. Norman, Buddy systems, *Comm. ACM*, 20(6), June 1977, pp.421-431.
9. J. Skovira, W. Chan, H. Zhou and D. Lifka, The EASY - LoadLeveler API project, In *Job Scheduling Strategies for Parallel Processing*, D. G. Feitelson and L. Rudolph (Eds.), Lecture Notes Computer Science, Vol. 1162, Springer-Verlag, 1996.
10. K. Suzaki, H. Tanuma, S. Hirano, Y. Ichisugi and M. Tukamoto, Time sharing systems that use a partitioning algorithm on mesh-connected parallel computers, *Proceedings of the Ninth International Conference on Distributed Computing Systems*, 1996, pp.268-275.
11. B. B. Zhou, R. P. Brent, C. W. Johnson and D. Walsh, Job re-packing for enhancing the performance of gang scheduling, *Proceedings of 5th Workshop on Job Scheduling Strategies for Parallel Processing*, San Juan, April 1999, pp.129-143.

A Tool to Schedule Parallel Applications on Multiprocessors: The NANOS CPU MANAGER

Xavier Martorell[1], Julita Corbalán[1], Dimitrios S. Nikolopoulos[2],
Nacho Navarro[1], Eleftherios D. Polychronopoulos[2],
Theodore S. Papatheodorou[2], and Jesús Labarta[1]

[1] European Center for Parallelism of Barcelona
Departament d'Arquitectura de Computadors
Universitat Politècnica de Catalunya, Spain
{xavim,juli,nacho,jesus}@ac.upc.es
[2] High Performance Information Systems Laboratory
Department of Computer Engineering And Informatics
University of Patras, Greece
{dsn,edp,tsp}@hpclab.ceid.upatras.gr

Abstract. Scheduling parallel applications on shared–memory multi-processors is a difficult task that requires a lot of tuning from application programmers, as well as operating system developers and system managers.

In this paper, we present the characteristics related to kernel–level scheduling of the NANOS environment and the results we are achieving. The NANOS environment is designed and tuned specifically to achieve high performance in current shared–memory multiprocessors.

Taking advantage of the wide and efficient dialog established between applications and the NANOS environment, we are designing powerful scheduling policies. The information exchanged ranges from simply communicating the number of requested processors to providing information of the current speedup achieved by the applications. We have devised several scheduling policies that use this interface, such as Equipartition, Variable Time Quantum DSS and Dynamic Performance Analysis.

The results we have obtained with these policies indicate that there is a lot of work to do in the search for a "good" scheduling policy, which can include characteristics like sustainable execution times, fairness and throughput. For instance, we show through several experiments that benefits in execution time range from 15% to 100%, depending on the policy used and the characteristics of the workload.

1 Introduction

Current multiprocessor machines are used by multiple users to execute several parallel applications at a time, which may share the available resources. Processor scheduling strategies on contemporary shared–memory multiprocessors range between the two extremes of time–sharing and space–sharing. Under time–sharing, applications share processors in time slices. The partitioning is highly

D.G. Feitelson and L. Rudolph (Eds.): JSSPP 2000, LNCS 1911, pp. 87–112, 2000.
© Springer-Verlag Berlin Heidelberg 2000

dynamic and processors are allowed to freely flow among applications. On the other hand, under space–sharing, partitions of the machine are established at the starting of the execution and maintained for a long–term period.

Time–sharing usually causes lots of synchronization inefficiencies to applications due to the uncontrolled movements of processors. On the other side, space–sharing looses processor power when applications do not use the same number of processors along their execution (e.g. an application that has significant sequential portions). As a result, the scheduling of parallel applications should take the good characteristics of both environments to achieve good performance from applications and processors.

Current machines, from low–end workstations to big mainframes, provide execution environments that fit between the previous two extremes. Small shared–memory multiprocessor machines are available from a great number of computer builders: Silicon Graphics, SUN Microsystems, Compaq/DEC, Hewlett Packard, Intel, Sequent, Data General, etc. Some of them also build big mainframes. Examples of current shared–memory multiprocessor mainframes are the Origin2000 [17] from Silicon Graphics, the SUN Enterprise 10000 [6], the Digital AlphaServer [11], etc. Small–scale SMP systems rely usually on variants of time–sharing to support multidisciplinary workloads, while large–scale servers provide both time–sharing and space–sharing capabilities, usually realized through batch queueing systems.

Experience on real systems shows that with contemporary kernel schedulers, parallel applications suffer from performance degradation when executed in an open multiprogrammed environment. As a consequence, intervention from the system administrator is usually required, in order to guarantee a minimum quality of service with respect to the resources allocated to each parallel application (CPU time, memory etc.). Although the use of sophisticated queuing systems and system administration policies may improve the execution conditions for parallel applications, the use of hard limits for the execution of parallel jobs with queuing systems may jeopardize global system performance in terms of utilization and fairness.

Even with convenient queueing systems and system administrator's policies, application and system performance may still suffer because users are only able to provide very coarse descriptions of the resource requirements of their jobs (number of processors, CPU time, etc.). Fine–grain events that happen at execution time (spawning parallelism, sequential code, synchronizations, etc.), which are very important for performance, can only be handled at the level of the run-time system, through an efficient communication interface with the operating system.

In this paper, we present the work related to the previous issues that we are doing in the context of the NANOS Esprit Project. NANOS tackles medium to short–term scheduling and pursues global utilization of the system at any time. The NANOS execution environment consists of three main levels of operation, namely application, user–level execution environment and operating system. In the paper, we will focus at the operating system level to provide high performance to parallel applications.

Kernel–level scheduling solves the problem of having a limited number of physical resources where to execute the applications. Each application maps user–level threads (nano–threads in our model) to the virtual processors offered by the operating system. The operating system maps the virtual processors to physical processors, allowing that all applications execute in a shared environment.

Usually, each application assumes that the operating system assigns a physical processor to each one of its virtual processors. This is not always possible because the demand for virtual processors in the system can exceed the number of physical processors. The total current demand for virtual processors is known as the load of the system.

The role of the operating system dealing with processor scheduling becomes important when the load of the machine is high, when physical processors must be shared by a larger number of virtual processors. This work concentrates in providing new techniques and mechanisms for supporting well–known and new scheduling policies.

Evaluating scheduling policies at kernel–level on real systems usually requires kernel modifications and root privileges, which is very restrictive and limits the ability of the kernel developers to experiment extensively and tune their policies. We have developed a framework for developing and analyzing scheduling policies entirely at user–level, based on a user–level process, the CPU MANAGER, which interacts with the applications running under its control.

This framework not only serves as a tool for comparing scheduling policies, but also as a tool for improving throughput on an actual production system, since the performance of some of the scheduling policies developed in the CPU MANAGER is comparable or better to the performance of native kernel schedulers such as that of IRIX.

The paper is organized as follows: Section 2 presents an overview of the NANOS execution environment, and Section 3 is centered on the kernel–level scheduling issues and compares NANOS with related work. Section 4 presents the characteristics of some of the policies implemented inside the CPU MANAGER. Section 5 sketches the implementation of the CPU MANAGER and Section 6 presents the evaluation of the scheduling policies to demonstrate the usefulness of the tool. Finally, Section 7 presents the conclusions of this paper and the work we have planned for the future.

2   Execution Environment

In the NANOS environment, OpenMP [26] applications compete for the resources of the parallel machine. Applications are parallelized through the NANOS-COMPILER [4,2,3] and the parallel code is executed on top of the NTHLIB [21,20] threads library.

2.1 The Nano-threads Library (NTHLIB)

The Nano-threads Library, NTHLIB is a user–level threads package specially designed for supporting parallel applications. The role of NTHLIB is two–fold. On one hand, NTHLIB provides the user–level execution environment in which applications execute. On the other hand, NTHLIB cooperates with the operating system level. NTHLIB and the operating system cooperate by interchanging significant fine–grain information on accurate machine state and resource utilization, throughout the execution of the parallel application.

When the load of the system is high, each application should run as if executing in a smaller (dedicated) machine. In this case, resource sharing is unavoidable and usually prevents achieving a performance comparable to the individual applications execution, due to conflicts in processors, memory, etc.

Supplying accurate information to the operating system about resource needs is a key aspect for getting a good compromise between time– and space–sharing. When the application shrinks its parallelism, processors could become quickly available for other applications running in the system, reducing idle time. On the other hand, when an application needs more processors, it is guaranteed that the request will be taken into account in a short enough amount of time. Applications generated by the NANOSCOMPILER are malleable [14] and adapt their structure of parallelism to the available resources.

2.2 Application Adaptability to the Available Resources

The execution of a nano–threaded application is able to adapt to changes in the number of processors assigned to it. The adaptation is dynamic, at run–time, and includes three important aspects: first, the amount of parallelism that the application generates at any time is limited someway by both the number of processors assigned to the application and the current amount of work already pending to be executed. Second, the application is able to request and release processors at any time. And third, the application should be able to adapt to processor preemptions and allocations resulting from the operating-system allocation decisions.

With respect to the first aspect, the nano-thread starting the execution of a parallel region takes the decision about how many processors to use for spawning the parallelism. The operating system has to provide some interface to allow the application to check which is the number of processors available for spawning parallelism. By checking the number just before spawning parallelism, the application ensures that it is going to use the processors currently allocated to it.

The second aspect, enabling the request for processors, requires from the operating system interface to set the number of processors each application wants to run on. The operating system should guarantee that the number of requested processors from each application is considered as soon as it distributes processors among applications.

The third aspect, applications being able to adapt to processor preemptions, requires also some help from the operating system. The operating system moves processors from one application to another following some scheduling policy (e.g., time–sharing). The requirement from the application point of view is that preemptions must not occur. As this is usually not possible, the run-time execution environment may help to provide such a feeling, by recovering preemptions. A good solution from the operating system point of view is, on one hand, to provide some mechanism to reduce preemptions at a minimum. And on the other hand, to provide a complete interface for preemption recovery.

2.3 Operating System Scheduling Policies

Kernel–level scheduling consists of a set of policies to distribute processors to applications. Several kernel–level scheduling policies are already developed in order to achieve good performance results in the NANOS environment.

At any time, there is a current active scheduling policy, applied to all applications running in the system. The active policy can be dynamically changed without incurring any overhead to the running applications. Applications notice only the performance differences obtained from the processor allocation decisions taken by the policy newly established. Different application workloads can benefit from different policies [10,18].

The active scheduling policy is in charge of looking at the requirements of all running applications and decide which resources to allocate to each one. Each parallel application is considered as a whole. This is the way space-sharing is established in the NANOS environment. As long as the policy decides to allocate a number of processors to each application, a portion of the machine is effectively given to that application and the application decides what to do with the processors. The mechanism in charge of determining the exact processors to be assigned to each application ensures that the processors assigned to the application are going to be the ones that more recently have been running on it, if any, thus enforcing data locality. Specific architectural characteristics, such as a NUMA memory subsystem can also be taken into account at that point.

The benefit of looking at applications as a whole is that in short term scheduling decisions, processors know where to look first for work (the application where they are assigned to). In case the application has no work to perform, its cooperation with the operating system makes it to release some processors, which will search for work in other applications. The scheduling policies implemented and evaluated in this work are presented in Section 4.

3 Kernel–Level Scheduling in NANOS

In this section, we present the main characteristics of the kernel–level scheduling in the NANOS environment, and compare them with the related work.

3.1   Sharing Information with the Upper Levels

Each application executing on the NANOS parallel execution environment shares information with the operating system. The information dynamically flows from the application to the operating system and vice–versa.

The information includes, but is not limited to, the number of processors on which the application wants to run at any moment and the number of processors currently allocated by the operating system to the application. From the number of requested processors, the operating system decides, in a first step, how many processors to allocate to each application. Processors are moved, in a second step, from one application to another. Each moved processor leaves a virtual processor preempted in the source application. It is possible that between the two steps, some time passes to allow the application to voluntarily release the processors to be moved. This functionality is designed to avoid as much as possible the preemption of running processes by the operating system.

Along with the number of requested and allocated processors, information about each one of the virtual processors can be checked by the user–level execution environment during synchronizations, and help the application progress when the operating system decides to reallocate processors to another application.

The amount and quality of the information shared between an application and the operating system is a significant difference with other related work. Process Control [38] already proposed to share a counter of running processes, but the amount of parallelism was not set by the application, but deduced by the operating system (knowing the number of processes created by the application).

Process Control, Scheduler Activations [1] and First–Class Threads [19] use signals or upcalls to inform the user–level about preemptions. The best mechanism for this is shared memory, which is asynchronous and does not disturb further the execution of the application. The application does not need to know about preemptions till it reaches a synchronization point, where it can check the shared memory.

Our approach is similar to the kernel–level NanoThreads [9], which provides a per-application shared memory area containing register save areas (RSA's) to save/restore the user–level threads state at blocking and preemption points.

The SGI–MP LIBRARY shipped with IRIX 6.4/6.5 incorporates a user–level mechanism [34] for detecting situations in which the load of the system is high and the application performs bad and tries to correct this situation by reducing the number of active processes. This solution has the problem that the view of the status of the system obtained by each application can be different and nothing ensures that the response given by the individual applications can help to solve the global problem of the system. A similar mechanism was also proposed in [32].

3.2   Synchronization and Processor Preemptions

Each time an application needs to do some operation which depends on the number of running processors, it uses the number of processors allocated provided by the NANOS kernel interface [29]. This ensures that, at least during a short amount of time, such processors are available (in average, during half a scheduling period or quantum). This means that most of the times, threads are not going to lose a synchronization point, so they are not going to delay the whole application execution.

In these situations, the behavior of the application depends, during a certain amount of time, on the number of processors allocated. Typically, this happens when the application spawns parallelism, checking the number of processors allocated to know how many processors are going to participate in the parallelism. From that point to the next synchronization point, in a barrier, or while joining the parallelism, the processors should remain assigned to the application, avoiding that a delay in the synchronization slows down the execution of the application. If the operating system decides to reallocate some processors during the execution of the parallelism, some of the virtual processors will be preempted. This can occur, and the NANOS user–level execution environment will be always informed, thus detecting the preemptions when reaching the next synchronization point. No time will be lost waiting for a synchronization with a preempted processor.

Also, when a preemption is detected, any processor of the application (usually the one that detects the preemption) can be directly transferred to execute the preempted work, recovering the application progress.

3.3   The Application as the Scheduling Target

The NANOS operating system environment distributes processors among the running applications, having into account the applications as a whole and their exact requests. Looking at the requests of all the running applications, along with their priorities, the operating system can figure out which is the load of the machine, which applications have more priority to be executed and it can distribute processors accordingly.

To minimize movements of processors between applications, a processor allocated to an application searches for work in that application first. In case there is no ready virtual processor to run in its application, the processor is allowed to automatically assign itself to another application and get work from it. Usually, the scheduling policy applied at each quantum prepares a list of applications which have been given less processors than requested. Those applications are the candidates to receive the processors that become free due to some application termination.

The scheduling policies implemented on the NANOS environment range from the well–known equipartition, batch or round–robin policies to other kind of policies that can make more use of the information provided by the applications. They are described in section 4.

Sometimes, operating systems offer Gang Scheduling [27], combined with two–level synchronization methods at user–level [15,39,14]. This solution is not general enough to perform well in all situations. For instance, in current versions of IRIX, it is not recommended to run applications using Gang Scheduling. We have observed that even with Gang Scheduling is very hard that processes remain assigned as a whole to an application. A process doing I/O or taking a page fault may motivate a context switch in its physical processor, which can take off all the processors of the application, causing cascades of movements across the system and degrading performance.

Another drawback of gang scheduling is that it often compromises the memory performance of parallel applications. When multiple programs are gang-scheduled on the same processors, their working sets interfere in the caches, thus incurring the cost of cache reloads. Parallel applications running on multiprogrammed shared-memory multiprocessors and particularly on NUMA systems, are extremely sensitive to this form of interferences [15].

3.4   Processor Affinity

Processor affinity is an important issue to consider in kernel–level scheduling because of the different access latencies to cached, local and remote memory locations. Cache memory is always of importance, both in SMP and CC-NUMA machines [37,24,36]. When a processor runs inside an application, the processor caches are filled with data which is usually accessed several times. Moving processors from one application to another causes a total or partial cache corruption. Processor affinity is useful to take advantage of the data remaining in the cache when the processor is allocated again to the same application.

In CC-NUMA machines, local and remote memory accesses are also important to consider due to the different access times, which can range from 0.3 to 2 microseconds. Usually, in NUMA machines, the operating system places data near the processor that has accessed it for the very first time. This means that other application threads accessing the same data can benefit of being scheduled on the same processor. The benefits in this case will be greater, if the data already is in the cache of the processor. Otherwise, at least the cost accessing local memory will be lower than accessing remote memory.

Scheduling at the operating system level in the NANOS execution environment uses two levels of affinity. In a first step, a processor is assigned to an application on which it has run before. In a second step, inside an application, a processor is assigned to a virtual processor on which it run before, if any.

4   Kernel–Level Scheduling Policies

In this paper, we are using the environment presented to test several policies and compare them with existing operating system scheduling policies. The policies proposed have been already explained in more detail in [29,30,7]. We summarize here their characteristics.

4.1   Equipartition (Equip)

Equipartition [23,14,22] is the simplest policy included in the NANOS environment. This policy divides the number of physical processors by the number of running applications, and assigns the resulting number of processors to each application. When an application requests less processors than the result of the division, the processors exceeding that number are not assigned to any application. In case there are more applications than processors, only the first P applications are executed, assuming there are P processors.

Some processors can remain unallocated when using this policy, depending on the amount of applications and the requests of each application. Equipartition is implemented to obtain a reference, given by such a simple policy, to which the behavior of the other policies could be compared.

applications not receiving all the requested processors will receive some of them when processors are voluntarily released by other applications. that those applications not receiving all the requested processors will receive some of them when processors are voluntarily released by other applications.

4.2   Processor Clustering (Cluster)

The Processor Clustering policy allocates processors in clusters of four processors. The reasons for selecting this number are to achieve good locality in systems with physically distributed shared–memory. Allocating four processors at a time allows the CPU Manager to better select four neightbour processors, which will improve performance due to smaller memory latencies, assuming first–touch placement. In addition, our experience indicates that applications usually request a number of processors which is a multiple of four. Also, applications usually get better performance when running on an even number of processors.

In a first step, this policy allocates a cluster of four processors to all running applications. If some applications are not receiving processors because there is a large number of applications in the system, they are candidates to receive any processor released from the applications selected to run during the next quantum. In case a number of processors remain unallocated, this policy starts a second step, allocating again in clusters of four. And so on, till all the processors have been allocated or all the requests have been satisfied. When less than four processors remain to be allocated, some applications can receive two or even one processor to maintain working all processors available in the machine.

4.3   Dynamic Space Sharing (DSS)

Dynamic Space Sharing (DSS) [30,29] is a two–level scheduling policy. The high level space–shares the machine resources among the applications running in the system. The low level improves the memory performance of each program by enforcing the affinity of kernel threads to specific physical processors.

DSS distributes processors as evenly as possible among applications taking into account the full workload of the system and the number of processors requested by each application. Each application receives a number of processors which is proportional to its request and inversely proportional to the total workload of the system, expressed as the sum of processor requests of all jobs in the system.

Time–sharing is then applied to DSS to obtain several derived policies, which are explained in the following subsections.

Sliding Window DSS (SW–DSS) Sliding Window DSS partitions all applications on execution in groups of applications called *gangs*. A gang is defined as a group of applications requesting a number of processors which is not more than kP, where P is the number of processors and k is a tunable parameter of the policy.

Each gang is submitted for execution during a constant time quantum (usually of 100 ms.) After the expiration of the quantum, the next neighbouring gang of applications is scheduled and so on. The view of these gangs passing through execution is as a moving window sliding across the workload.

Each gang is usually evolving during the execution of the workload. Each time a new application starts, an application finishes, or an application changes its requests, the gang accommodates more or less applications to fit the condition of having less than kP processors requested.

Step Sliding Window DSS (SSW–DSS) The Step Sliding Window DSS policy is designed to get the benefits of DSS, the time–sharing provided by SW–DSS and improve cache performance. In SSW–DSS the scheduling step is not a discrete new window, like in SW-DSS. Instead, it is the same window as in the previous quantum leaving out the first process and filling the gang with none, one or more processes to satisfy that the total requests does not exceed kP.

With the support of DSS, this policy ensures that in each scheduling step, all but the first applications will be executed again, and most of the processors will reuse the footprints in their cache memories.

Variable Time Quantum DSS (VTQ–DSS) The Variable Time Quantum DSS policy searches for equalizing the CPU time received by all the applications in the workload. This means that applications executed on more processors are going to receive such processors during a smaller amount of time than applications requesting less processors. The time quantum is different for each application.

In this policy, applications in the workload are again organized in gangs, which are executed like in the previous policies with the restriction of requesting less than kP processors. In VTQ, the applications at the end of the ready queue that do not compose a gang are enqueued in a repository queue.

When an application starts, it is assigned an initial quantum of 100ms. After execution, the quantum is updated to try to equalize the amount of CPU time received by all the applications in the gang. As a result, when the time quantum of an application expires, the application is stopped and another application from the repository queue is taken to use the processors up to the end of the gang. The same mechanism is used when an application finishes, leaving a hole in its gang.

4.4   Performance–Driven Processor Allocation

From the production point of view, it is interesting to ensure that applications getting a higher speedup should receive benefits compared to applications with poor performance. We propose the *Performance–Driven Processor Allocation* (PDPA) policy, which takes into account the speedup achieved at run–time in parallel regions. This feature avoids the assignment of physical processors to applications that are not able to take advantage of them. These processors can then be reassigned to other applications.

Traditionally, the speedup obtained by a parallel application has been computed doing several executions with 1 to P processors and the results have been provided to the scheduler.

We propose to dynamically compute the speedup and provide it to the scheduler in the same way the application informs about the number of requested processors. The speedup of an application is computed through the SelfAnalyzer library [7] which informs the CPU Manager at run–time. A similar approach is also used in [25] to compute the efficiency achieved by the applications.

The associated scheduling policy (*PDPA*) implements the state diagram presented in Figure 1. The state diagram is a search procedure, applied to each application and parameterized through three arguments: the number of processors assigned when the application starts (BASE), the increment / decrement on the number of processors applied when the application is performing well / bad (STEP), and the desired minimum efficiency level based on the performance got by the application with the current number of processors (MIN_EFFICIENCY). The definition of efficiency is taken from [12].

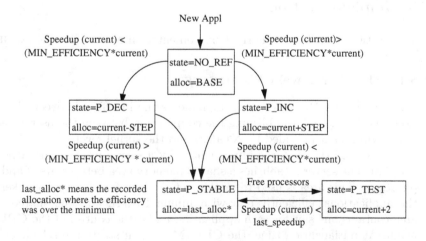

Fig. 1. State diagram used in the *PDPA* policy

An application can be found in five different states: speedup unknown (NO_REF), increasing the number of processors (P_INC), decreasing the number of processors (P_DEC), stationary (P_STABLE) and trying to improve the speedup due to free processors (P_TEST). When the application informs about the speedup achieved with BASE processors, the *PDPA* policy decides to increment or decrement the number of processors allocated to the application.

The four transitions showed in the figure are followed when the associated condition becomes true. An application performing badly in the NO_REF state, goes to the P_DEC state. Otherwise, if it performs well, it goes to the P_INC state. In both states, when the application reaches a sustained speedup, it goes to the P_STABLE state, where it remains for some time. In this state, the number of assigned processors remains constant.

At some point, for instance when there are free processors, the scheduler can decide to provide more processors to an application, testing several times whether the application is able to improve its efficiency. In the current implementation, this test is done three times.

By tuning the BASE, STEP, and MIN_EFFICIENCY parameters, it is possible to establish the aggressiveness of the policy. Sometimes it is also useful to consider two different levels of efficiency, one for increasing the number of processors and another one for decreasing it.

It is interesting to note that this policy can influence the long–term scheduler by changing the degree of multiprogramming at a given point. The policy can detect whether there are several idle processors because the actual applications can not take advantage of them. In this situation, the degree of multiprogramming can be increased to accommodate more applications. When the efficiency of applications increases, the policy can indicate to the long–term scheduler to reduce the degree of multiprogramming.

5   Implementation

This section describes the current implementation of the CPU MANAGER [8].

5.1   The User–Level CPU MANAGER

The user–level CPU MANAGER implements the interface between the applications and the kernel, establishing the cooperation between the user–level execution environment provided by NTHLIB and the kernel level.

The CPU MANAGER is implemented by a server process and a portion of NTHLIB. The server establishes a shared memory area between itself and the applications. This area is used to implement the interface between the kernel and the applications, efficiently and with minimal overhead. The shared–memory area contains one slot for each application under the control of the CPU MANAGER. At initialization time, the CPU MANAGER starts the scheduler thread. Its mission is to apply any of the user–selectable scheduling policies to the application workload, forcing the application threads selected to run on a specific physical processor. It also communicates all its decisions to the applications.

5.2   Implementation of the Kernel–Level Scheduling Framework

As it has been stated in Section 3, the NANOS kernel–level scheduling is application–oriented and takes applications as the scheduling target. As it is shown in figure 2, the knowledge of the applications is the central point in the design of the CPU MANAGER. All data structures and algorithms are oriented to manage applications as a whole through the interface implemented in shared memory.

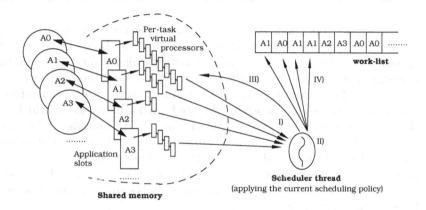

Fig. 2. CPU MANAGER environment

The kernel–level scheduling framework consists of two main data structures: the application slots shared with the applications and the work–list.

The left portion of the figure represents several applications attached to the shared–memory area. This area is divided in application slots, one slot for each application. The shared memory is readable and writable both from the applications and the CPU MANAGER. The information available in this area includes, inside each application slot, the number of processors requested, the number of processors assigned by the CPU MANAGER, whether the CPU MANAGER has preempted any thread of the application and other information useful for the scheduling policy, like the speedup obtained by the parallel application.

The right part of the figure represents the scheduler thread and the work–list structure. The scheduler thread is in charge of distributing processors every time quantum (100 ms.) The work–list is a list containing a reference to the applications which are requesting more processors than those allocated to them. It is used to maintain working during the current quantum all processors released by other applications running in the system due to some reasons (e.g., lack of parallel work inside the application). Processors, when released, go immediately to visit the work–list to find a new application where they can go to execute a ready virtual processor.

In this framework, physical processors are first assigned to an application, and then they choose a virtual processor belonging to that application for execution.

Figure 2 also presents the algorithm to apply the current scheduling policy. The scheduler thread starts executing the algorithm by collecting all the information about processor requests supplied by the applications (step I, in the figure). Then, the current scheduling policy decides how many processors each application is going to receive for the next time quantum (step II).

Next, the allocation results are communicated to the applications (step III), including the number of processors allocated and which virtual processors have been preempted, if any. Finally, the work list structure is used to indicate applications that want to receive more processors when any becomes available (step IV).

Applying the previous algorithm, some applications are going to loose processors. Physical processors that have to move, get from the work–list a new application and assign to it. Figure 3 details the algorithm by which a processor is assigned to an application *allocate_cpu*. The *application* parameter contains a descriptor for each virtual processor from the application point of view. The algorithm searches first for an unallocated virtual processor in which to assign the physical processor. If one is found, the virtual processor (thread) in this descriptor is bound to the physical processor, and unblocked (woken up), while updating the information shared with the application. In case there is no virtual processor available, this means that another free processor has filled the last one available, so the current processor remains unallocated and continues searching for work in the work–list.

In order to avoid that the IRIX operating system can disrupt the processor assignments, the CPU MANAGER uses system calls to block / unblock virtual processors and bind / unbind them to run on physical processors. Finally, the CPU MANAGER internal structure representing physical processors is updated accordingly.

This algorithm can be executed either by the CPU MANAGER to initially assign free processors to a running application or by NTHLIB, as part of the scheduler to transfer an application processor directly to another application.

Applications detect at user–level, through the shared–memory area, that some processors have been stolen and recover the work themselves using other processors already allocated. To implement this feature, the user–level idle loop of NTHLIB is slightly more complex than that of the other thread packages. Figure 4 shows how the idle code is responsible of freeing processors that are not going to be used by the application (through the primitive *cpus_release_self*).

After that, the idle code also checks whether the CPU MANAGER has preempted a virtual processor, and recovers the work stopped by transferring to it the current physical processor (through *cpus_processor_handoff*). This is implemented through the bind operating system primitive.

Finally, the idle code searches for work in the ready queues and executes it, if found.

The current implementation of the NANOS CPU MANAGER is equivalent in functionality with a pure kernel implementation. In this implementation, both the CPU MANAGER and NTHLIB participate in implementing the scheduling

```
int allocate_cpu (int cpu,
                  struct appl_info * application)
{
    int vp;

    /* Search for a virtual processor (vp) giving
       priority to (in this order) the vp used last
       time, a stolen vp, and any unallocated vp */
    vp = search_for_unallocated_vp (application);

    if (vp<application->n_cpus_requested) {
        /* Vp is valid, decrement number of preempted
           processors, when needed */
        if (application->cpu_info[vp].stat == CPU_STOLEN)
            --application->n_cpus_preempted;

        /* Assign thread/sproc to cpu through the OS */
        sys_bind_thread (
                application->cpu_info[vp].kthread, cpu);

        /* Assign cpu to the virtual processor vp and
           mark the vp running */
        application->cpu_info[vp].sys_sim_id = cpu;
        application->cpu_info[vp].stat = CPU_RUNNING;

        /* Unblock the associated thread/sproc */
        sys_unblock_thread (
                   application->cpu_info[vp].kthread);

        /* Update current number of processors */
        ++application->n_cpus_current;

        /* Update the processor structure */
        phys_cpus[cpu].status = CPU_ALLOCATED;
        phys_cpus[cpu].curr_appl = application->appl_no;

        /* Return succesfully */
        return 0;
    }
    /* Return indicating processor unallocated */
    return -1;
}
```

Fig. 3. Algorithm for allocating processors to applications

mechanisms. For this reason, the information shared among the applications and the CPU MANAGER is read/write for all the participating processors. This allows NTHLIB to transfer a physical processor to another application, when the CPU MANAGER requests to do so.

We have also implemented a different version of the CPU MANAGER, the MP CPU MANAGER, in which the design of the shared–memory areas enforces protection by using a different area for each application. This solution does not allow the transfer of a processor from an application directly to another one, and the CPU MANAGER itself has to intervene in each movement. The MP CPU MANAGER deals with IRIX application binaries running on top of the SGI–MP LIBRARY without neither recompiling nor relinking the source code.

```
struct nth_desc * nth_getwork (int vp)
{
    struct nth_desc * next;

    /* Dequeues work from the local ready queue */
    next = nth_lrq_dequeue (vp);

    if (next==NULL)
        /* The local queue is empty, tries to dequeue
           work from the global queue */
        next = nth_rq_dequeue ();

    return next;
}

void nth_idle (int vpid)
{
    struct nth_desc * next;
    work_t work;

    while (1) {
        if (cpus_asked_for ()) {
            /* The processor detects that the CPU
               Manager reclaims some processors
               and stops itself */
            cpus_release_self ();
            /* The processor returns here in case it is
               reassigned later */
        }
        else if (cpus_preempted_work () > 0) {
            /* Recovering preempted work (go & back) */
            work = cpus_get_preempted_work ();
            if (work!=NO_WORK) {
                cpus_processor_handoff (work);
                /* The processor returns here in case it is
                   reassigned later */
            }
        }
        /* Gets work from the ready queues */
        next = nth_getwork (vpid);
        /* Executes the work in the processor */
        if (next!=NULL) schedule (next);
    }
}
```

Fig. 4. Idle loop in the nano–threads environment

6   Evaluation

This section presents the evaluation of the scheduling framework developed for the NANOS environment. The environment is also evaluated in [29,30].

6.1   Experimentation Platform

The design and implementation of the NANOS CPU MANAGER has been carried on a Silicon Graphics Origin2000 machine [17,33], running the IRIX 6.5.5 operating system. The machine is located at the European Center for Parallelism of Barcelona (CEPBA [13]). It has sixty-four R10000 MIPS processors [16] running at 250 Mhz (chip revision 3.4). Each processor has separated 32 Kb. primary instruction and data caches and a common 4 Mb. secondary cache.

All benchmarks and applications used for the evaluation presented in this section have been compiled to run on both the native SGI–MP and NANOS environments. Input source programs were previously annotated with standard OpenMP directives. NANOS binaries have been obtained by preprocessing the applications through the NANOSCOMPILER [4].

The benchmarks are taken either from the NAS Benchmarks [5] or the SPEC95FP Benchmarks [35]. We have modified two of them to obtain two evolving benchmarks: EPD and ltomcatv. The EPD benchmark derives from EP (Embarrassingly Parallel) and consists of an external loop containing EP. At every iteration, the EPD benchmark requests a different number of processors, following the series: 2, 4, ... MAX-2, MAX, MAX, MAX-2, ...2, in order to give a variable (diamond shape) parallelism. The ltomcatv is a variation of the tomcatv from the SPEC95FP Benchmarks. In ltomcatv the main loop of the application is performed several times, generating a sequence of sequential and parallel regions. It requests one processor for the first I/O portion of the external loop and then it requests MAX processors for the parallel portion.

The NAS Benchmarks scale well up to 32 processors on a dedicated machine. The tomcatv, ltomcatv and swim SPEC95FP benchmarks scale also well, even achieving super–linear speedup with some number of processors. The turb3d scales well up to 16–20 processors. Its speedup decreases with more processors. And finally, the SPEC95FP apsi does not scale at all. The proportion of parallel code is very small and by the Amdhal's Law the speedup that it can achieve is less than two. Even more, when increasing the number of processors, apsi does not suffer an slowdown. It simply does not take advantage of the processors.

Compilation of all benchmarks in both environments has been done using the same command line options to generate machine code with the native MIPSpro F77 compiler: –64 –MIPS4 –R10000 –O3 –LNO:PREFETCH_AHEAD=1.

The following subsections present the results obtained through the execution of several workloads and policies.

6.2   Workload on 32 Processors (cpuset32)

This section presents the evaluation of a workload consisting of several NAS applications running on 32 processors. For this workload, the W class of each application is used. The EPD application is class S because class W is too large compared with the other applications. This workload was run inside a *cpuset* partition of 32 processors in our machine of 64 processors, while the other half of the processors in the machine were in production mode executing applications belonging to other users. Table 1 shows the applications participating in the workload, the number of processors requested by each one, and the total and system execution times of each application. Execution times are the arithmetic mean of the execution times obtained by the different instances of each application.

This workload shows the different behaviour between the SGI–MP environment and the NANOS Cluster policy. The largest difference is in CG. This is because CG requests 16 processors. Running in the SGI–MP environment, it

Table 1. Workload on cpuset 32

Benchmark	CPUS	Mean execution time (in s.)		Mean system time per thread (in s.)	
		SGI–MP LIBRARY	NANOS Cluster	SGI–MP LIBRARY	NANOS Cluster
sp.W	8	34.7	26.7	1.26	0.04
bt.W	12	18.8	7.51	2.01	0.01
epd.S	2-16	1.37	1.92	0.17	0.02
ft.W	8	1.03	1.04	0.10	0.03
cg.W	16	21.1	1.67	2.48	0.01

tries to use as many processors as possible, but the SGI–MP LIBRARY does not detect that the application performs bad. As a result the time spent in system mode for the CG application raises up to 2.48 seconds per thread. In the Cluster policy, the CG application receives only 4 processors (one cluster), and performs highly better without sharing processors with other applications.

EPD performs better in SGI–MP than using the Cluster policy because it is a dynamic application. In the SGI–MP LIBRARY environment, dynamic applications create and destroy processes at every request. It seems that this mechanism benefits execution time because new processes are created with their dynamic priority high in IRIX. We have to perform more experiments in this line to confirm this result.

SP and BT benchmarks are clearly better when using the NANOS Cluster Policy. And FT behaves the same, receiving only 4 processors with the Cluster Policy (given by the output trace generated by the CPU MANAGER) and up to 8 in the SGI–MP environment.

Figure 5 shows graphically the execution of 80 seconds of the workload using the PARAVER tool [28], recorded during the real execution. These plots present time in the x axis and applications in the y axis. The names of the applications are displayed on the left-hand side of the figure, along with the number of processors that they are requesting (enclosed in parenthesis). For each application, an horizontal line is displayed. For each instance of an application, a different color is used to fill the horizontal line. Different colors represent, thus, the execution of the different instances of the corresponding application. Also, a flag is displayed when an application starts. The reader can observe how the NANOS environment (bottom plot) manages better the execution of parallel applications and more instances of each one are executed in the same amount of time.

6.3   Workload on 64 Processors Using Dynamic Space Sharing

In this subsection, we present a workload running on 64 processors, with the machine in dedicated mode. Table 2 presents the workload, consisting of six class A NAS benchmarks, plus the class W EPD benchmark, and its results for three different policies (SGI–MP LIBRARY, NANOS SSWDSS and NANOS VTQ).

We want to highlight that the benchmark requesting more processors (SP, 32 processors) suffers a lot of performance problems in the SGI–MP LIBRARY

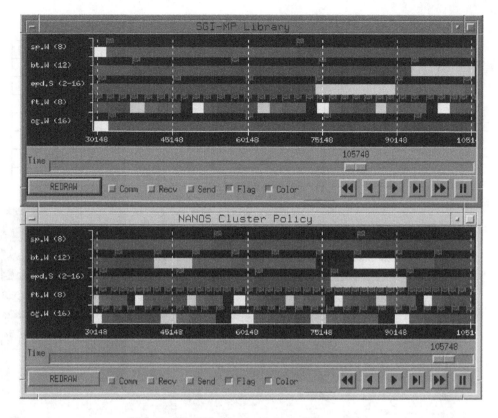

Fig. 5. Workload execution on 32 processors

environment due to resource sharing and preemptions. On the other hand, in the NANOS environment, all policies provide better response time for the SP benchmark. The differences in performance shown in the NANOS environment depend on the policy applied during execution.

FT and MG applications obtain also better performance in the NANOS environment, in general. CG and BT perform nearly the same and EPD is better in the SGI–MP environment.

The reasons for the better performance exposed by the NANOS environment are the better coordination between the user and kernel levels, solving synchronization problems earlier and allowing applications to work with a more stable number of processors.

Figures 6 and 7 show graphically the behaviour of the workload on the SGI–MP environment and under the VTQDSS policy. Up to four complete instances of the SP application are executed using the VTQDSS policy, compared with only two in the SGI–MP environment. This is a very good result that can be usually applied to applications with good scalability running in the NANOS environment and requesting a large number of processors.

Table 2. Execution times (in s.) in 64 processors

Benchmark	CPUS	SGI–MP LIBRARY	NANOS SSWDSS	NANOS VTQ
sp.A	32	236.6	98.5	101.1
bt.A	24	120.0	113.5	133.1
epd.W	2–8	70.8	128.7	110.2
cg.A	8	14.7	19.1	18.9
ft.A	8	65.2	35.9	37.1
mg.A	8	63.6	35.5	38.2
cg.A	8	14.7	18.6	18.1

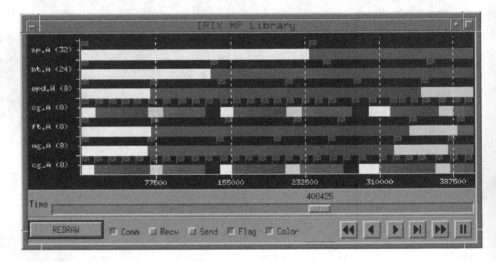

Fig. 6. Workload execution on 64 processors (SGI–MP LIBRARY)

6.4   Workloads on 64 Processors Using Dynamic Speedup Analysis

In order to evaluate the performance of the *PDPA* policy we have prepared three
different parallel workloads, trying to highlight different situations to see how
the policy adapts the environment to them.

All along the workloads, the applications request 32 processors in a 64–
processor machine. We have selected this number for two reasons: first, usually
the policy of supercomputing centers is to limit the number of processors that
can be used by an application. The second reason is that even when there are
no limits established, the users guess that applications will not scale well up to
the maximum number of processors and limit themselves to execute in a smaller
number of processors.

We have executed the three workloads in dedicated mode and under two
scheduling policies: the standard SGI–MP environment and the *PDPA* policy.
This policy was setup with the following parameters: the BASE number of pro-

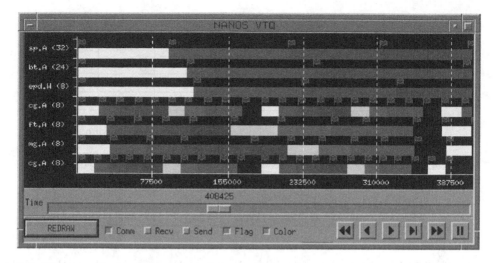

Fig. 7. Workload execution on 64 processors (NANOS VTQ POLICY)

Table 3. Results of the ltomcatv workload using Speedup Analysis

Policy	Mean execution time (in s.)		Total Speedup	Applications
	Ltomcatv	Total		
SGI–MP LIBRARY	165.9	606	1.0	15
Speedup Analysis	47.0	132	4.59	15

cessors is set to 4, the STEP is set to 2 and the MIN_EFFICIENCY is set to 0.7. These arguments were determined through experimentation.

In these experiments, the NANOS environment controls also the amount of applications that should be executed in parallel (the multiprogramming level). The CPU MANAGER is in charge of increasing the multiprogramming level when it detects that the current applications are not obtaining a good efficiency from the system. In this case, the CPU MANAGER can reduce the number of processors allocated to the applications and allow more applications to enter the system. Alternatively, when an application finishes, the CPU MANAGER can either test the performance of the remaining applications with more processors, thus decreasing the multiprogramming level, or allow another application to enter the system and maintain the multiprogramming level.

The first workload consists of five ltomcatv benchmarks. The degree of multiprogramming is set to five. Each instance of the ltomcatv is executed three times. The goal of this workload is to analyze what happens when the applications are highly dynamic. Table 3 shows the results.

This workload has the characteristic that the number of requested processors has a high variability since the applications change from sequential to parallel phases several times. The *PDPA* outperforms the SGI–MP policy. Several reasons can be given to this behaviour: first, since the applications enter the

Table 4. Results of the tomcatv/turb3d workload using Speedup Analysis

Policy	Mean execution time (in s.)			Total	Applications
	Tomcatv	Turb3d	Total	Speedup	
SGI–MP Library	33.36	48.69	251	1.0	18
Speedup Analysis	15.63	42.71	148	1.7	18

Table 5. Results of the swim/apsi workload using Speedup Analysis

Policy	Mean execution time (in s.)			Total	Applications
	Swim	Apsi	Total	Speedup	
SGI–MP Library	74.46	354	1082	1.0	18
Speedup Analysis	7.28	112	237	4.56	18

P_STABLE phase, their allocation does not change, even when other applications execute the I/O portion and release their processors. Second, in the SGI–MP environment, the MP Library is not able to track the different phases of the ltomcatv benchmark and this motivates synchronization problems. Although the speedup obtained by this benchmark can be quite good, the stable allocation with less processors avoids resource sharing and this improves overall performance.

The second workload is composed by three instances of the tomcatv and three of the turb3d, both from the SPECFP 95. In that case the multiprogramming level has been set to four, and each application is executed three times. The goal here is to show what happens when all the applications in the workload have good scalability up to 16–20 processors. Results are presented in Table 4. They show that the search procedure to determine the number of processors to achieve good efficiency is not introducing a noticeable overhead, although it is executed in several of the very first iterations of each application. The execution times obtained are competitive compared with the results obtained from the SGI–MP environment.

And finally, the last workload consists of three swim and three apsi, showing what happens when several applications do not scale at all and are sharing the machine with others that scale well. This scenario reproduces one of the situations where the *PDPA* policy can extract more benefits since the speedups achieved by the applications are very different. In this case the multiprogramming level has been set to four, and each application is executed three times. Table 5 shows the results.

As we expected, the *PDPA* policy outperforms the SGI–MP policy. *PDPA* is able to detect that all apsi benchmarks obtain a very poor speedup and reassigns their processors to swim benchmarks. The overall speedup achieved by the *PDPA* with respect to the SGI–MP environment reaches 4.5.

7   Conclusions and Future Work

In this paper, we have presented an execution environment to efficiently execute parallel applications in shared–memory multiprocessors, the NANOS environment. This paper has focused in the design and implementation of kernel–level scheduling inside the NANOS environment. A user–level scheduler has been presented, the CPU MANAGER, which efficiently cooperates with the applications. This tool has proven to be very powerful and useful to communicate the information the scheduler needs to distribute processors among the applications.

The CPU MANAGER also provides a good environment to implement and evaluate scheduling policies. In this paper, we have described a set of scheduling policies implemented in the CPU MANAGER, trying to cover a wide range of the possibilities that it offers. One of the major benefits of the CPU MANAGER is that it provides a real execution environment, and parallel applications can be executed on an actual system. This characteristic and the total control of the processor allocation provided by the CPU MANAGER, allows us a more accurate and realistic evaluation of the scheduling policies.

The scheduling policies have been evaluated comparing its performance with the SGI–MP LIBRARY. Results show that the NANOS environment is solid and flexible. Moreover, all the scheduling policies evaluated have outperformed the standard SGI–MP environment. When we compare the results achieved in individual applications, we see that some scheduling policies have outperformed the SGI–MP by a factor of more than two. And, when we compare the total execution times of some workloads, the NANOS environment achieves an speedup of 4 for some experimental workloads.

We are now working on porting this technology to run with native IRIX OpenMP applications. This means that we are developing an MP CPU MANAGER to deal with IRIX application binaries running on top of the SGI–MP LIBRARY without recompiling or relinking the source code. The high flexibility and tuning options offered by the SGI–MP environment allows to do that. The preliminary results indicate that the performance of these applications can also be improved through increasing the cooperation with the operating system scheduler represented by the MP CPU MANAGER.

We are also considering the design and implementation of some alternative kernel–level scheduling policies with memory locality considerations.

Acknowledgements

We want to acknowledge to all the NANOS Project partners, specially Toni Cortés for helping in the design of the NANOS kernel interface and Eduard Ayguadé, Marc Gonzàlez and José Oliver for the development of the NANOS-COMPILER.

This work has been supported by the European Community under the Long Term Research Esprit Project NANOS (E–21907), the DGR of the Generalitat de Catalunya under grant 1999 FI00554 UPC APTIND and the Ministry of Education of Spain (CICYT) under contracts TIC97-1445-CE and TIC98-0511.

References

1. T. Anderson, B. Bershad, E. Lazowska and H. Levy, "Scheduler Activations: Effective Kernel Support for the User–Level Management of Parallelism", Proceedings of the 13th. ACM Symposium on Operating System Principles (SOSP), October 1991.
2. E. Ayguadé, X. Martorell, J. Labarta, M. Gonzàlez and N. Navarro, "Exploiting Parallelism Through Directives on the Nano-Threads Programming Model", Proceedings of the 10th. Workshop on Language and Compilers for Parallel Computing (LCPC), Minneapolis, USA, August 1997.
3. E. Ayguadé, X. Martorell, J. Labarta, M. Gonzàlez and N. Navarro, "Exploiting Multiple Levels of Parallelism in Shared–memory Multiprocessors: a Case Study", Dept. d'Arquitectura de Computadors - Universitat Politècnica de Catalunya, Technical Report: UPC-DAC-1998-48, November 1998.
4. E. Ayguadé, M. Gonzàlez, J. Labarta, X. Martorell, N. Navarro and J. Oliver, "NanosCompiler: A Research Platform for OpenMP Extensions", Dept. d'Arquitectura de Computadors - Universitat Politècnica de Catalunya, Technical Report: UPC-DAC-1999-39, 1999.
5. D. Bailey, T. Harris, W. Saphir, R. Wijngaart, A. Woo and M. Yarrow, "The NAS Parallel Benchmarks 2.0", Technical Report NAS-95-020, NASA, December 1995.
6. A. Charlesworth, "STARFIRE: Extending the SMP Envelope", IEEE Micro, Jan/Feb 1998.
7. J. Corbalán, J. Labarta, "Dynamic Speedup Calculation through Self-Analysis", Dept. d'Arquitectura de Computadors - Universitat Politècnica de Catalunya, Technical Report: UPC-DAC-1999-43, 1999.
8. J. Corbalán, X. Martorell and J. Labarta, "A Processor Scheduler: The CpuManager", Dept. d'Arquitectura de Computadors - Universitat Politècnica de Catalunya, Technical Report: UPC-DAC-1999-69, 1999.
9. D. Craig, "An Integrated Kernel– and User–Level Paradigm for Efficient Multiprogramming Support", M.S. thesis, Department of Computer Science, University of Illinois at Urbana–Champaign, 1999.
10. M. Crovella, P. Das, C. Dubnicki, T. LeBlanc, E. Markatos, "Multiprogramming on Multiprocessors", Technical Report 385, University of Rochester, February 1991 (revised May 1991).
11. Digital Equipment Corporation / Compaq Computer Corporation, "AlphaServer 8x00 Technical Summary", http://www.digital.com/alphaserver/alphasrv8400/8x00_summ.html, 1999.
12. D.L. Eager, J. Zahorjan and E.D. Lazowska, "Speedup Versus Efficiency in Parallel Systems", IEEE Transactions on Computers, pp. 408-423, Vol. 38, No. 3, March 1989.
13. European Center for Parallelism of Barcelona (CEPBA), http://www.cepba.upc.es.
14. D. Feitelson, "Job Scheduling in Multiprogrammed Parallel Systems", IBM Research Report 19790, Aug. 1997.
15. A. Gupta, A. Tucker and S. Urushibara, "The Impact of Operating System Scheduling Policies and Synchronization Methods on the Performance of Parallel Applications", ACM SIGMETRICS Performance Evaluation Review, Vol. 19(1), pp. 120-132, May 1991.
16. J. Heinrich, "MIPS R10000 Microprocessor User's Manual", version 2.0, MIPS Technologies, Inc., January 1997.

17. J. Laudon and D. Lenoski, "The SGI Origin: A ccNUMA Highly Scalable Server", Proceedings of the 24th. Annual International Symposium on Computer Architecture, pp. 241-251, Denver, Colorado, June 1997.

18. S. T. Leutenegger, M. K. Vernon, "The Performance of Multiprogrammed Multiprocessor Scheduling Policies", Proceedings of the ACM SIGMETRICS Conference, pp. 226-236, May 22-25, 1990.

19. B. Marsh, M. Scott, T. LeBlanc and E. Markatos, "First–Class User–Level Threads", Proceedings of the 13th. ACM Symposium on Operating System Principles (SOSP), October 1991.

20. X. Martorell, J. Labarta, N. Navarro and E. Ayguadé, "Nano-Threads Library Design, Implementation and Evaluation", Technical Report, Universitat Politècnica de Catalunya, UPC-DAC-1995-33, Sep. 1995.

21. X. Martorell, J. Labarta, N. Navarro and E. Ayguadé, "A Library Implementation of the Nano–Threads Programming Model", Proceedings of the 2nd. Euro–Par Conference, Lyon, France, August. 1996.

22. C. McCann, R. Vaswani, J. Zahorjan, "A Dynamic Processor Allocation Policy for Multiprogrammed Shared–Memory Multiprocessors", ACM Transactions on Computer Systems, 11(2), pp. 146-178, May 1993.

23. V. K. Naik, S. K. Setia, M. S. Squillante, "Performance Analysis of Job Scheduling Policies in Parallel Supercomputing Environments", Proceedings of the Supercomputing '93, 1993.

24. V. K. Naik, M. S. Squillante, "Analysis of Cache Effects and Resource Scheduling in Distributed Parallel Processing Systems", Proceedings of the Seventh SIAM Conference on Parallel Processing for Scientific Computing, SIAM Press, 1995.

25. T.D. Nguyen, R. Vaswani, J. Zahorjan, "Using Runtime Measured Workload Characteristics in Parallel Processor Scheduling", Proc. of the workshop on Job Scheduling Strategies for Parallel Processing, Lecture Notes in Computer Science, vol. 1162, Springer–Verlag, 1996.

26. OpenMP Architecture Review Board, "Fortran Language Specification, v 1.0", www.openmp.org/openmp/mp–documents/fspec.ps, October 1997.

27. J.K. Ousterhout, "Scheduling Techniques for Concurrent Systems", Proceedings of the 3rd. International Conference on Distributed Computing and Systems, pp.22-30, 1982.

28. V. Pillet, J. Labarta, T. Cortés, S. Girona, "PARAVER: A Tool to Visualize and Analyse Parallel Code", WoTUG-18, pp. 17-31, Manchester, April 1995. Also as Technical Report UPC-CEPBA-95-03.

29. E.D. Polychronopoulos, X. Martorell, D. Nikolopoulos, J. Labarta, T. S. Papatheodorou and N. Navarro, "Kernel–level Scheduling for the Nano-Threads Programming Model", Proceedings of the 12th ACM International Conference on Supercomputing (ICS'98), Melbourne, Australia, July 1998.

30. E.D. Polychronopoulos, D.S. Nikolopoulos, T.S. Papatheodorou, X. Martorell, J. Labarta, N. Navarro, "An Efficient Kernel-Level Scheduling Methodology for Multiprogrammed Shared Memory Multiprocessors", Proceedings of the 12th International Conference on Parallel and Distributed Computing Systems (PDCS'99), Fort Lauderdale (Florida - USA), August 18-20, 1999.

31. E.D. Polychronopoulos, D. Nikolopoulos, T. Papatheodorou, X. Martorell, N. Navarro and J. Labarta, "TSDSS – An Efficient and Effective Kernel–Level Scheduling Methodology for Shared–Memory Multiprocessors", Technical Report HPISL-010399, High Performance Information Systems Laboratory, University of Patras, 1999.

32. C. Severance, R. Enbody, "Automatic Self–Allocating Threads (ASAT) on an SGI Challenge", Proc. of the International Conference on Parallel Processing (ICPP96), Vol.3, pp. 132-139, August 1996.

33. Silicon Graphics Computer Systems SGI, "Origin 200 and Origin 2000 Technical Report", 1996.

34. Silicon Graphics Computer Systems (SGI), "IRIX 6.4/6.5 manual pages: mp(3F) & mp(3C)", IRIX online manuals, also in http://techpubs.sgi.com, 1997-1999.

35. SPEC Organization, "The Standard Performance Evaluation Corporation", www.spec.org.

36. M. S. Squillante, R. D. Nelson, "Analysis of Task Migration in Shared–Memory Multiprocessor Scheduling", ACM SIGMETRICS Performance Evaluation Review, vol. 19, no. 1, 1991.

37. J. Torrellas, A. Tucker, A. Gupta, "Evaluating the Performance of Cache–Affinity Scheduling in Shared–Memory Multiprocessors", Journal on Parallel and Distributed Computing, 24(2), pp. 139-151, February 1995.

38. A. Tucker and A. Gupta, "Process Control and Scheduling Issues for Multiprogrammed Shared–Memory Multiprocessors", Proceedings of the 12th. ACM Symposium on Operating System Principles (SOSP), December 1989.

39. A. Tucker, "Efficient Scheduling on Multiprogrammed Shared–Memory Multiprocessors", Ph.D. Thesis, Stanford University, December 1993.

Over the years, researchers have developed parallel scheduling algorithms that can be loosely organized into three main classes, according to the degree of coordination between processors: *gang scheduling* (GS), *local scheduling* (LS) and *implicit or dynamic coscheduling* (DCS).

On the one end of the spectrum, GS [7] ensures that the scheduling of communicating jobs is coordinated by constructing a static global list of the order in which jobs should be scheduled. A simultaneous context-switch is then required across all processors. Unfortunately, these straightforward implementations are neither scalable nor reliable. Furthermore, GS requires that the schedule of communicating processes be precomputed, which complicates the coscheduling of client-server applications and requires pessimistic assumptions about which processes communicate with one another. Finally, explicit coscheduling of parallel jobs interacts poorly with interactive jobs and jobs performing I/O [18].

At the other end of the spectrum is LS, where each processor independently schedules its processes. This is an attractive time-sharing option due to its ease of construction. However, the performance of fine-grained communication jobs can be orders of magnitude worse than with GS because the scheduling is not coordinated across processors [11].

An intermediate approach developed at UC Berkeley and MIT is DCS [1] [27] [4] [28]. With DCS, each local scheduler makes independent decisions that dynamically coordinate the scheduling actions of cooperating processes across processors. These actions are based on local events that occur naturally within communicating applications. For example, on message arrival, a processor speculatively assumes that the sender is active and will probably send more messages in the near future. The main drawbacks of dynamic coscheduling include the high overhead of generating interrupts upon message arrival and the limited vision of the status of the system that is based on speculative information. Some aspects of these limitations are addressed in [19] with a technique called *Periodic Boost*. Rather than sending an interrupt for each incoming message, the kernel periodically examines the status of the network interface, thus reducing the overhead for communication-intensive workloads.

We recently proposed a new approach to job multitasking, called *buffered coscheduling* (BCS) [6]. BCS shows promise in integrating the positive aspects of GS, e.g., global coordination of jobs, along with positive aspects of DCS, e.g., increased resource utilization obtained by overlapping computation and communication of different jobs. The benefits of BCS include higher throughput, dramatic simplification of run-time support, reduced communication overhead, efficient global implementation of flow-control strategies and fault-tolerant protocols, and accurate performance modeling. Here, we focus on the performance of BCS in the presence of memory constraints.

Like DCS, BCS must address a couple of important problems. A first problem is the impact of the memory hierarchy: All the benefits obtained with job multitasking can be wiped out if the memory requirements of multiple jobs exceed the physical memory available and overflow in the swap space. Secondary memory can be orders of magnitude slower. A second problem is the impact of

Time-Sharing Parallel Jobs in the Presence of Multiple Resource Requirements

Fabrizio Petrini and Wu-chun Feng*

Computing, Information, & Communications Division
Los Alamos National Laboratory, NM 87544, USA,
`fabrizio@lanl.gov`, `feng@lanl.gov`

Abstract. Buffered coscheduling is a new methodology that can substantially increase resource utilization, improve response time, and simplify the development of the run-time support in a parallel machine. In this paper, we provide an in-depth analysis of three important aspects of the proposed methodology: the impact of the communication pattern and type of synchronization, the impact of memory constraints, and the processor utilization.

The experimental results show that if jobs use non-blocking or collective-communication patterns, the response time becomes largely insensitive to the job communication pattern. Using a simple job access policy, we also demonstrate the robustness of buffered coscheduling in the presence of memory constraints. Overall, buffered coscheduling generally outperforms backfilling and backfilling gang scheduling with respect to response time, wait time, run-time slowdown, and processor utilization.

Keywords: Parallel Job Scheduling, Distributed Operating Systems, Communication Protocols, Performance Evaluation.

1 Introduction

The scheduling of parallel jobs has long been an active area of research [8,9]. It is a challenging problem because the performance and applicability of parallel scheduling algorithms is highly dependent upon factors at different levels: the workload, the parallel programming language, the operating system (OS), and the machine architecture. The importance of job scheduling strategies stems from the impact that they can have on the resource utilization and the response time of the system.

Time-sharing scheduling algorithms are particularly attractive because they can provide good response time without migration or predictions on the execution time of the parallel jobs. However, time-sharing has the drawback that *communicating processes must be scheduled simultaneously to achieve good performance*. With respect to performance, this is a critical problem because the software communication overhead and the scheduling overhead to wake up a sleeping process dominate the communication time on most parallel machines [15].

* The work was supported by the U.S. Department of Energy through Los Alamos National Laboratory contract W-7405-ENG-36

D.G. Feitelson and L. Rudolph (Eds.): JSSPP 2000, LNCS 1911, pp. 113–136, 2000.
© Springer-Verlag Berlin Heidelberg 2000

the type of the job communication and synchronization on the overall through-put. This problem leads to another closely related problem: the choice of the time-slice length. While a long time-slice can hide the overhead and increase the scalability of BCS, it can also increase the processor idle time due to blocking communication.

In this paper, we analyze the above problems with a detailed simulation model driven by a real workload drawn from an actual supercomputing environment at Lawrence Livermore National Labs. By considering a simple job-scheduling algorithm that limits the access into the system of those jobs that exceed the memory requirements, we evaluate the system response time and utilization under various types of workloads and system parameters.

The rest of the paper is organized as follows. Section 2 motivates our work by analyzing the resource utilization of some scientifc parallel programs. Section 3 briefly introduces BCS. Section 4 describes the job access policy that takes into consideration the memory requirements, Section 5 the experimental framework and Section 6 the results of the simulations. Some considerations on the potential advantages on the development of system-level and user-level software are listed in Section 7, the relations between BCS and the Bulk-Synchronous Parallel model of parallel computation are described in Section 8, followed by a conclusion in Section 9.

2   Resource Utilization of Parallel Programs

In Figure 1, we show the *global* processor and network utilization (i.e., the number of active processors and the fraction of active links) during the execution of a transpose FFT algorithm on a parallel machine with 256 processors. These processors are connected with an indirect interconnection network using state-of-the-art routers [23]. Based on these figures, there is obviously an *uneven and inefficient use of system resources*. During the two computational phases of the transpose, the network is idle. Conversely, when the network is actively transmitting messages, the processors are not doing any useful work. These characteristics

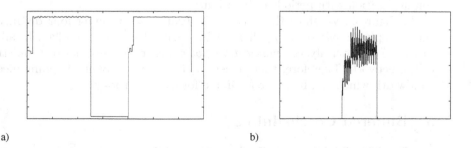

a)   b)

Fig. 1. Resource Utilization in a Transpose FFT Algorithm. a) Number of active processors (out of 256). b) Fraction of active communication links.

are shared by many SPMD programs, including Accelerated Strategic Computing Initiative (ASCI) application codes such as Sweep3D [13]. Hence, there is tremendous potential for increasing resource utilization in a parallel machine.

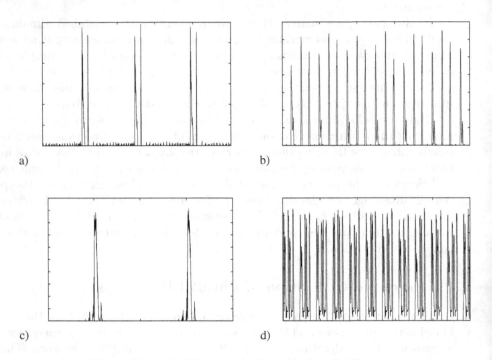

a)   b)

c)   d)

Fig. 2. Network Utilization in Scientific Parallel Programs.

Another important characteristic shared by many scientific parallel programs is their access pattern to the network. The vast majority of scientific applications display *bursty communication patterns* with alternating spikes of impulsive communication with periods of inactivity.

In Figure 2, we show the network utilization by running four distinct scientific applications over a parallel machine with 256 processors [20]. In all four cases, we can identify *communication holes*, i.e., periods of network inactivity, in the network. Therefore, there exists a significant amount of communication bandwidth which can be made available for other purposes.

3   Buffered Coscheduling

To implement job multitasking, BCS relies on two techniques. First, the *communication generated by each processor is buffered* and performed at the end of regular intervals (or time-slices) in order to amortize the communication and scheduling overhead. By delaying communication, we allow for the global scheduling of the communication pattern. Second, a *strobing mechanism performs a total exchange of control information* at the end of each time-slice in order to move from isolated scheduling algorithms [1] (where processors make decisions based solely on their local status and a limited view of the remote status) to more outward-looking or global scheduling algorithms. An important characteristic of BCS is that, instead of overlapping computation with communication and I/O within a *single parallel program*, all the communication and I/O which arises from a *set of parallel programs* can be overlapped with the computations in those programs.

This approach represents a significant improvement over existing work reported in the literature. It allows for the implementation of a global scheduling policy, as done in GS, while maintaining the overlapping of computation and communication provided by DCS.

3.1   Communication Buffering

Rather than incurring communication and scheduling overhead on a per-message basis, BCS accumulates the messages generated by each process and tries to amortize the overhead over a set of messages. Specifically, the cost of the system calls necessary to access the kernel data structures for communication is amortized over a set of system calls rather than being incurred on each individual system call. This implies that BCS can be tolerant to the potentially high latencies that can be introduced in a kernel call or in the initialization of the network interface card (NIC) that can reside on a slow I/O bus.

3.2   Strobing Heartbeats

Virtually all the existing research in parallel job scheduling use isolated algorithms, which speculatively make scheduling decisions based on a limited knowledge of the status of the machine, rather than algorithms which use non-isolated (or even global) knowledge. In order to provide the above capability, we propose a strobing mechanism to support the scheduling of a set of parallel jobs which share a parallel machine. Let us assume that each parallel job runs on the entire set of p processors, i.e., jobs are time-sharing the whole machine. Our goal is to synchronize the processors of the parallel machine at the end of a time-slice in order to perform a total exchange of information regarding their status. To amortize the overhead, all the communication operations are buffered and executed at the end of the time-slice. The strobing mechanism performs an optimized total-exchange of control information (which we call heartbeat or strobe) and triggers the downloading of any buffered packets into the network. At the start of the heartbeat, each processor downloads a personalized broadcast into network. After downloading the heartbeat, the processor continues running the currently active job. (This ensures computation is overlapped with communication.) When p heartbeats arrive at a processor, the processor will enter a phase where its kernel will download any buffered packets. Each heartbeat contains information on which processes have packets ready for download and which processes are asleep waiting to upload a packet from a particular processor. This information is characterized on a per-process basis, so that on reception of the heartbeat, every processor will know which processes have data heading for them, and which processes on that processor they are from.

Figure 3 shows how computation and communication can be scheduled over a generic processor. At the beginning of the heartbeat, t_0, the kernel downloads control packets into the network for a total exchange. During the execution of the heartbeat, another user process gains control of the processor; and at the end of the heartbeat, the kernel schedules the pending communication, accumulated in the previous time-slices (before t_0), to be delivered in the current time-slice $[t_0, t_2]$. From the control information exchanged between t_0 and t_1, the processor will know (at t_1) the number of incoming packets that it is going to receive in the communication time-slice as well as the sources of the packets and will start the downloading of outgoing packets. It is worth noting that the potentially high overhead of the strobing algorithm is simply removed from the critical path by running another process. Thus, we can tolerate the latency of a global exchange of information without experiencing performance degradation.

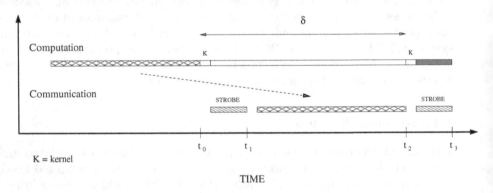

Fig. 3. Scheduling Computation and Communication. Communication accumulated in the time-slice up to t_0 is downloaded into the network between t_1 and t_2 (after the heart beat). $\delta \equiv$ length of a time-slice $= t_2 - t_0$.

4   Job Access Control

Scheduling parallel jobs by sharing processors not only spatially but also temporally provides an extra degree of flexibility and a considerable performance advantage. Unfortunately, this advantage can be limited by multiple resource requirements, e.g., memory hierarchy requirements. If the jobs mapped on a processing node exceed the physical memory available and use the virtual memory, the advantages of job multitasking can be nullified.

In order to avoid such problem we consider a very simple job access control policy, which allows jobs into the system only if their memory requirements

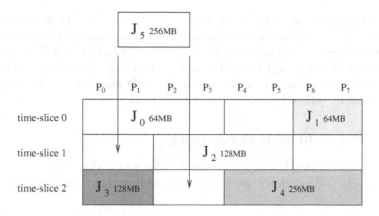

Fig. 4. Ousterhout Matrix of an 8-Processor System with 512-MB Memory/Processor and Multiprogramming Level of 3.

do not exceed the physical memory available. For instance, Figure 4 shows the Ousterhout matrix of an 8-processor system with a multiprogramming level of three and 512 MB of physical memory per processor P_i. Job J_5 requires 2 processors and 256 MB of memory per processor. Thus, it can only be mapped onto two of the four two-processor slots available due to memory constraints.

In our experiments, we combine the above access control policy with an aggressive backfill heuristic [26], which selects any job from the ready queue that does not interfere with the expected start time of the first blocked job. As shown in [30], this technique, when used with GS, can provide improvements over a wide spectrum of performance criteria. However, this greedy method does not look at the additional resource requirements of the jobs in the ready queue or the current state of the system resource loads, thus leaving room for future improvements.

GS can re-use some of the unused slots in the Ousterhout matrix if a job assigned to a given time-slice can atomically fit into one or more empty slots in another time-slice. This is the case of jobs J_1 and J_3 in Figure 4, which can be run on the two slots available in time-slice 1, as shown in Figure 5.

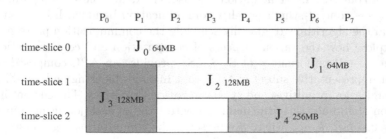

Fig. 5. Empty slot utilization with GS

While GS cannot fill in the two unused slots in the time-slices 0 and 2 with job J_2, BCS can potentially use their processing time, because the grain size of the resource allocation is the process and not the entire job. The communication pattern of the jobs, the local process scheduling algorithms, and many other factors can influence how the resources made available by the empty slots can be used by different jobs.

5   Experimental Framework

Before presenting the experimental results, we provide details on our simulation platform, the workloads used to drive the simulator, and the metrics of interest.

5.1   Simulation Model

In order to efficiently simulate and analyze different job scheduling strategies for parallel computers in depth, we developed a novel simulator called the *Job Scheduling Simulator* (JSS). With JSS, the user can explore the Cartesian product generated by different dimensions of the design space. A first dimension is machine scheduling: JSS provides space sharing and two basic forms of time sharing — gang scheduling (GS) and buffered coscheduling (BCS). A second dimension is the selection algorithm of the ready-jobs queue. Jobs can be selected in FCFS (First Come First Served) order or backfilled using a *conservative* or an *aggressive* policy. Conservative backfilling searches the ready queue for jobs that can be scheduled immediately, with the constraints that these jobs cannot interfere with the expected start time of the jobs which come before them in the ready queue. Aggressive backfilling is a weaker version of conservative backfilling, which selects any job from the queue which does not interfere with the expected start time of the first job in the ready queue. Both conservative and aggressive backfilling can dramatically improve the overall machine utilization and response time over FCFS but require a reasonably good estimate of the job run-time.

Both GS and BCS can have a parametric multiprogramming level (MPL) and times-slice length and can use the job access control policy described in Section 4. With GS, the user can also set the delay associated with job context-switch at the end of each time-slice.

In our BCS implementation, the user can define the system parameters as the process context-switch penalty, communication bandwidth between processors, and the algorithms to globally schedule the communication pattern. In order to explore how the various aspects of computation and communication influence the overall performance of BCS, JSS provides an API, composed of a limited but representative subset of MPI, that includes blocking and non-blocking communication primitives and synchronization primitives. The current implementation of JSS abstracts the main characteristics of each job using four parameters $\langle g, v, comm, sync \rangle$, where g represents the computational grain size, v the load imbalance, $comm$ the communication pattern, and $sync$ the type of synchronization. A parallel job consists of a group of P processes, and each process is mapped on a processor throughout the execution. Processes alternate phases of purely local computation with interprocess communication, as shown in Figure 6. Each process compute locally for a time uniformly selected in the interval $(g - \frac{v}{2}, g + \frac{v}{2})$. By adjusting g, we model parallel programs with different computational granularities. By varying v, we change the degree of load-imbalance across processors. The communication phase consists of an optional sequence of communication events. The parameter *comm* defines one of the three communication patterns: *Barrier*, *News* and *Transpose*. *Barrier* does not perform any communication and can be used to analyze how buffered coscheduling responds to load imbalance. The other two patterns consist of a sequence of point-to-point communications. The communication pattern generated by *News* is based on a stencil with a grid where each process exchanges information with its four neighbors. This pattern represents those applications that perform a domain decomposition of the data set and limit their communication pattern to a fixed set of partners. *Transpose* is a communication-intensive workload that emulates the communication pattern generated by the FFT transpose algorithm [12], where each process accesses data of all other processes. Finally, *sync* describes the type of synchronization in a job: we can have either blocking communication (B), where each point-to-point communication is implemented with blocking sends and receives or non-blocking communication (NB), where the communication primitives do not require an explicit handshake between sender and receiver and are terminated by a global barrier synchronization.

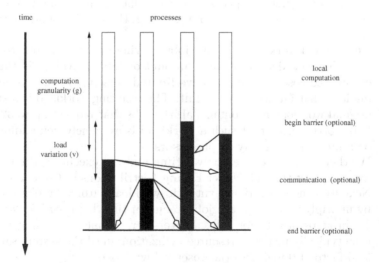

Fig. 6. Overlap of Computation and Communication

Table 1 describes some of the system parameters used during the experimental evaluation. We consider an architecture with 32 processors where each processor is equipped with 512 MB of main memory.

Table 1. Experimental System Parameters and Values.

Parameter	Value
Processors	32
Main memory per processor	512 MB
Job context-switch (GS)	1 ms
Process context-switch (BCS)	100 μs
Message size (BCS)	4KB
Communication Bandwidth (BCS)	100 MB/s

5.2   Workloads

A crucial aspect in the performance evaluation of job scheduling strategies is the availability of realistic workloads that can be represented with a compact mathematical formulation. Parallel workloads are often dispersive: job inter-arrival time distribution and job execution time distribution have a coefficient of variation that is greater than one, i.e., they are long tailed. These distributions can be fitted adequately with Hyper Erlang Distributions of Common Order [14]. Our experiments use a workload directly extracted from a real supercomputing environment, ASCI Blue-Pacific at Lawrence Livermore National Laboratory. Our modeling procedure involves the following steps.

1. The jobs are first grouped into classes, based on the number of processors they require. Each class is a bin in which the upper boundary is a power of two.
2. The original workload contains jobs varying in size from one to 256 processors. However, due to the large amount of details involved in the simulation of buffered coscheduling, we have limited ourselves to 32 processors, selecting jobs that fall within this limit. The resulting workload is a subset of the original workload and contains all the jobs that request up to 32 processors. It is worth noting that such a workload is extremely demanding, when run on a machine with only 32 processors.
3. We then model the inter-arrival time and the execution time distributions for each class through Hyper Erlang Distributions of Common Order.
4. Next we generate various synthetic workloads from the observed workload by multiplying the average job execution time by a *load factor* from 0.1 to 1.6 in steps of 0.1. For a fixed inter-arrival time, increasing job execution time typically increases resource utilization, until the system saturates. The load factor 1.0 identifies the observed workload.
5. Each job requires an amount of main memory which is exponentially distributed around a given mean value, which represents the maximum memory requirements over all processes belonging to a job.

When simulating buffered coscheduling, we need an extra degree of detail to characterize how computation, communication and synchronization are performed inside each job. Thus, the modeling procedure requires some extra steps.

1. Based on the workload characterization, we pick a job template for each job in a workload.
2. Based on the job template, we determine the computation and communication patterns of the job.

Table 2 outlines the five workload characterizations used in the experiments: each one is composed of three job templates, described using the notation defined in Section 6. Jobs in a workload can be assigned one of the three templates with equal probability. These characterizations display different communication and synchronization patterns. In the first one (workload 0) all the jobs perform an intensive communication pattern (Transpose) using blocking communication. The second workload uses the same communication pattern together with non-blocking communication. The same characteristics distinguish workloads 2 and 3. They use the same communication pattern, News, but a different type of synchronization. In the fifth workload, jobs do not perform any communication: the goal of this workload is to identify the impact of load imbalance.

Table 2. Five Workloads: Each with an equal mix of three job classes. The job granularity and skew are expressed in ms.

Workload	Job Template 0	Job Template 1	Job Template 2
0	$\langle 50, 25, Tra, B \rangle$	$\langle 100, 50, Tra, B \rangle$	$\langle 200, 100, Tra, B \rangle$
1	$\langle 50, 25, Tra, NB \rangle$	$\langle 100, 50, Tra, NB \rangle$	$\langle 200, 100, Tra, NB \rangle$
2	$\langle 50, 25, News, B \rangle$	$\langle 100, 50, News, B \rangle$	$\langle 100, 100, News, B \rangle$
3	$\langle 50, 25, News, NB \rangle$	$\langle 100, 50, News, NB \rangle$	$\langle 200, 100, News, NB \rangle$
4	$\langle 50, 25, Barrier, NB \rangle$	$\langle 100, 50, Barrier, NB \rangle$	$\langle 200, 100, Barrier, NB \rangle$

5.3 Metrics

The experimental evaluation considers metrics that are important from both the system's and user's perspectives.

- *Wait Time*: The time spent by a job waiting in the ready queue before it is scheduled.
- *Execution Time*: The actual job run time.
- *Response Time*: The sum between wait and execution time.
- *System Utilization*: The system utilization identifies the machine utilization at the job allocation level. Intuitively, the system utilization is the fraction of the scheduling matrix that is filled with jobs.
- *Processor Utilization*: The processor utilization is the fraction of time CPU spent is useful computation. It is worth noting that, in the general case, the processor utilization is always smaller than the system utilization, because the processors can be idle during the job execution.

- *Execution Time Slowdown*: The execution time slowdown is the ratio between the execution time and the job run time in a dedicated environment. The execution time slowdown is 1.0 with space sharing and a number larger than 1.0 in a time shared environment.

6   Experimental Results

The experimental results try to provide insight into three important aspects of buffered coscheduling: (1) the impact of the communication pattern and the time-slice length on the response time, (2) the impact of memory constraints with the job access control policy outlined in section 4 and the (3) the processor utilization. In all three cases we compare buffered coscheduling with aggressive backfilling (BF), a scheduling policy that can obtain excellent performance results with space sharing [26], and with backfilling gang scheduling (BGS), the extension of this technique to gang scheduling, recently proposed in [30].

6.1   Impact of Communication, Synchronization and Time-Slice Length

The choice of the time-slice for BCS is the result of a compromise between competing factors. On the one hand, a large time-slice could easily hide the overhead associated with the strobing algorithm and the process context-switches, thus allowing the scalability of BCS to architectures with a large number of processors. On the other hand, it increases the likelihood of having idle processors, due to blocking communication and global synchronization, thus limiting the potential increase in resource utilization.

Figure 7 shows how the response time is influenced by increasing the time-slice from 5 ms to 100 ms. All the experiments use a MPL equal to three. From the graphs, we can clearly see that workloads with a large amount of blocking communication (templates 0 and 2) can be efficiently supported only with small time-slices. This is particularly true for workload 0 which is extremely sensitive to the increase in the time-slice because it is communication intensive.

Looking at the graphs generated by templates 1 and 3 we can see that they almost overlap with all time-slices. These workloads share the same form of synchronization, obtained with a global barrier, though they have fairly different communication patterns. We explored this aspect in depth using many other communication patterns, workloads templates, number of processors, and architectural characteristics (not shown here for brevity), and we have found out that this is a strong property of BCS. With BCS, *the overall performance is relatively insensitive to the communication pattern when the communication is performed with non-blocking calls or, more generally, with a collective communication pattern*. The rationale behind this property is related to the fact that the run-time support cannot efficiently schedule blocking communication, while it can rearrange non-blocking primitives. This leads to a nearly optimal overlap between computation and communication when we use relative large MPLs. Also, there

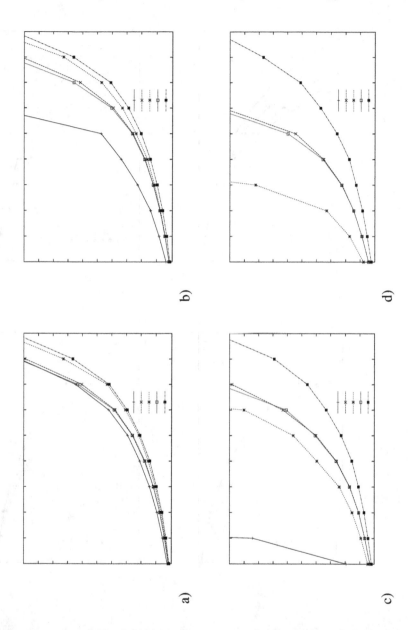

Fig. 7. Response time for various time-slices, communication and synchronization patterns. In all graphs the MPL is 3.

is an extra advantage in using collective communication patterns (e.g., broadcasts, scatter & gather, multicasts) because the information provided by the communication pattern can be directly passed to the run-time support, which can thus perform effective global optimizations. This is not true in the general

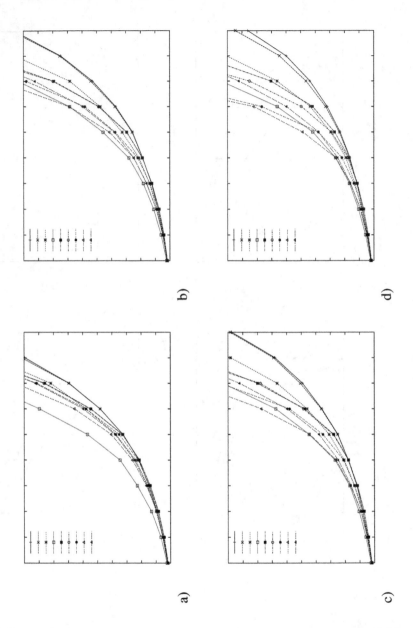

Fig. 8. Response time versus load for various MPLs. The graphs compare BCS with BF and BGS.

case; in fact, many parallel applications possess a well defined communication structure that is lost in the compilation process (e.g., because it is mapped in an unstructured communication graph of blocking calls).

6.2 Impact of Memory Constraints

This section analyzes the machine response time, the wait time, and execution time slowdown in conjunction with the memory-aware job scheduling policy described in Section 4. In all experiments we use the workload template number 3 and we consider workloads with increasing average memory requirements, ranging from 0 MB (i.e., no memory constraints), to 256 MB, half the size of physical memory available on each processor.

From Figure 8 we can draw the following considerations:

- BCS outperforms GS in all configurations. This is more pronounced at higher loads, because BCS can overlap computation with communication and can re-use computing resources at the process-level granularity rather than at the job level, as shown in Section 4.
- There is no penalty in using an arbitrarily large MPL with BCS. For a given average memory requirement, the system converges to a given state and does not experience any degradation when we further increase the MPL. That state is mainly determined by the ratio between the job average memory requirements and the actual physical memory available.
- When the memory requirements are high (e.g. 256 MB), BCS converges to backfilled space-sharing (BF). Intuitively, when the memory constraints do not allow job multitasking, the system converges to space sharing. This is not true for GS as it experiences sharp degradation in response-time performance, as shown if Figure 8 d) with 128 and 256 MB.

Figure 9 provides insight on the wait time for the same set of experiments of Figure 8. The graphs clearly show how time sharing can dramatically reduce the wait time over space sharing. BCS reduces the wait time further over backfilled gang scheduling (BGS), in particular with high MPLs.

The reduction of the wait time obtained increasing the MPL, usually implies an increase of the job execution time. In the worst case, the slowdown can be as high as the MPL. In Figure 10 we can see that BCS limits the slowdown when we increase the MPL and outperforms BGS in all configurations, again thanks to the re-use of empty slots in the scheduling matrix at the process level rather than the job level.

6.3 Processor Utilization

Most results on job scheduling strategies focus on system utilization rather than processor utilization and show that both BF and BGS can get more than 90% under many workloads. Figure 11 extends these results by analyzing the processor utilization obtained by BF, BGS and BCS.

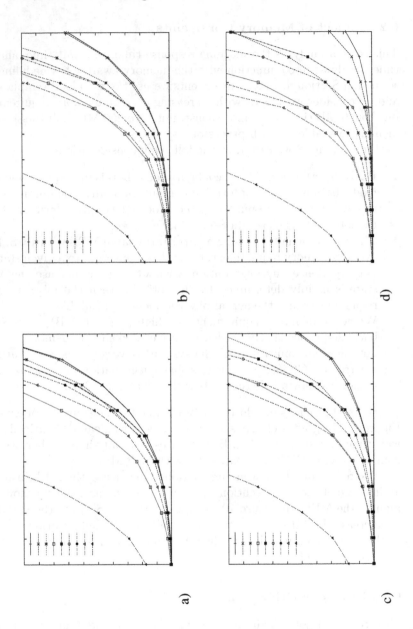

Fig. 9. Wait Time versus Load for Various MPLs.

We observe the following:

– Though BGS improves response time over BF, it does not improve system and processor utilization. The slight decrease in performance is due to the job context-switching overhead.

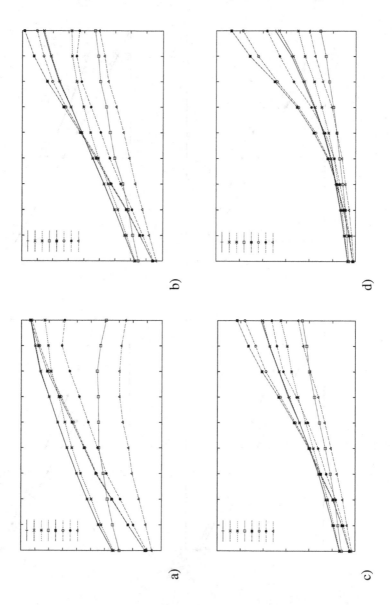

Fig. 10. Execution Time Slowdown versus Load for Various MPLs.

- With BCS, we can get a processor utilization that asymptotically reach 85%, while BGS and BF approach 60%. This is one of the main advantages of BCS over BGS and BF.
- Processor utilization is sensitive to a job's average memory request when we use time sharing: the higher the memory request, the lower the processor utilization.

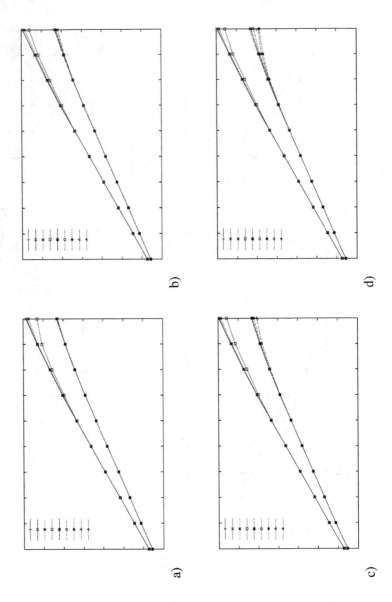

Fig. 11. Processor Utilization versus Load for BCS and BGS.

- The results address the overlapping of computation and communication only. We expect that the resource utilization gap between BF, BGS and BCS will increase further in the presence of I/O.

7   Discussion

The potential technical impact of BCS is significant for a large class of parallel machines and distributed systems, ranging from Linux clusters to the larger and more sophisticated massively parallel machines. To the best of our knowledge, this is the first methodological attempt to globally optimize the resources of a parallel machine rather than using the limited local knowledge available on each processor.

While BCS enhances overall system performance, particularly with respect to processor utilization and response time, BCS also naturally provides system-level and user-level advantages which we discuss in this section.

7.1   System-Level Advantages

First, the communication is optimized in several ways. The cost of the system calls necessary to access the kernel data structures is amortized over a set of user calls. This implies that the methodology is tolerant to the potential high latencies that can be introduced in a kernel call. BCS can obtain comparable performance to user-level network interfaces (e.g., FM [17] or ST [24]) without using specialized hardware.

Second, the global knowledge of the communication pattern provided by the total exchange allows for the implementation of efficient flow-control strategies. For example it is possible to avoid congestion inside the network by carefully scheduling the communication pattern and limit the negative effects of hot spots by damping the maximum amount of information addressed to each processor during a time slice. The same information can be used at kernel level to provide fault tolerance in the communication. For example the knowledge of the number of incoming packets greatly simplifies the implementation of receiver-initiated recovery protocols. By globally scheduling a communication pattern, it is also possible to obtain an accurate estimate of the communication time with simple analytical models. By knowing the maximum amount of information that can be delivered in a time-slice, it is possible to minimize the size of the communication buffers in each network interface. This is a crucial problem in a massively parallel architecture. Let's consider, for example, a machine with 10000 processors - the approximate number of processors expected to be in the next ASCI supercomputers. Given that each processor can potentially receive a message from all the remaining 9999 processors, it must reserve a proportional amount of network interface memory (typically few MB for each potential partner). This is infeasible with current network technology and poses a serious limit to the efficient implementation of large scale parallel machines.

Third, because communication is buffered and delayed to the beginning of the next time-slice, we can always implement zero- (or low-, if we desire fault tolerant communication) copy communication. Fault tolerance in general can also be enhanced by exploiting the synchronization point at the end of each time slice to incrementally take a snapshot of the status of the machine.

Fourth, an important advantage of time-sharing parallel jobs is a better utilization of the resources. When we consider I/O, there can be several orders of magnitude of difference between the computational grain of the parallel application and the access time of secondary storage. The usual approach of overlapping computation with I/O, for example using user-level threads, can only provide a limited return in the presence of a single parallel job. By overlapping the activities of multiple parallel jobs we can potentially hide most of the latency. The same argument can be applied to hide the non-uniform latencies of large clusters of SMPs. The higher latency of the inter-cluster communication can be overlapped with the execution of another parallel job.

Fifth, by time-sharing parallel jobs it is possible to obtain better response time and quality of service for critical applications. Time-slicing can be used to give good average completion times for dynamically changing workloads, while retaining fast response times for interactive jobs.

Sixth, because of the deep pipelines and wide out-of-order superscalar architectures of contemporary processors, an interrupt may need to nullify a large number of in-flight instructions [16]. Larger register files require existing system software to save and restore a substantial amount of process state. The reduction of the interrupt frequency provided by BCS can substantially improve the performance on these processors.

Seventh, BCS can also efficiently support future processor architectures, such as Simultaneous Multi-threading (SMT) [3] [5], that time-share multiple processes at hardware level.

7.2   User-Level Advantages

The typical approach to developing parallel software is by using low-level programming models such as MPI. At that level the user is exposed to a large number of details. The user must identify the form of parallelism in the application and decompose it in a set of parallel threads, partition the data set among these threads, map the threads and the data set on a parallel architecture, define communication and synchronization between these threads. This development process is typically specific to a particular application or class of user applications.

As a consequence, *it is extremely difficult and very expensive to build software using such programming models.* Because both correctness and performance can only be achieved by attention to many details, writing optimized MPI programs is a lengthy process, and the result is often machine-dependent[1].

The alternative of using high level programming models, for example automatic parallelization of legacy Fortran codes, is not mature yet and must trade generality in the parallelization process with efficiency, making conservative choices. *BCS has the potential of solving this tradeoff between high development costs and high efficiency vs. low development cost and low efficiency by tolerating several types of inefficiencies related to the parallelization process.*

---

[1] Though portable to other machines, MPI programs need to go through a non trivial re-optimization process, when moved from one parallel machine to another.

In a buffered coscheduled system, time-slicing a collection of bad programs (i.e., unbalanced computation or communication) may give the same behavior as a single well-behaved program. Therefore, programs running on a parallel machine need not be carefully balanced by the user to achieve good performance. Multiprogramming can provide opportunities for filling in the "spare communication, computation and I/O cycles" when user programs are sparse, by merging, for example, many sparse communication patterns together to produce a denser communication pattern.

This can have a huge impact on the parallelization of existing legacy codes. If successful, the implementation of BCS could provide a dramatic reduction in the development times and costs of parallel software. Also, *the proposed methodology is valid in general, and not specific to any particular class of applications* (e.g., molecular dynamics, linear solvers, simulations etc.), *nor to a particular machine architecture* (e.g., Cray T3E, SGI, IBM SP).

Finally BCS greatly simplifies the performance evaluation of a parallel application. With BCS the amount of work done by all processors, a metric very close to the sequential complexity of an algorithm, becomes as important as the critical path of the computation.

8   BCS vs BSP

One of the goals of BCS is to transform a collection of unstructured parallel jobs in a single, well-behaved Bulk-Synchronous Parallel (BSP) computation [29] [25].

A BSP computation consists of a sequence of parallel *supersteps*. During a superstep, each processor can perform a number of computation steps on values held locally at the beginning of the superstep and can issue various remote read and write requests that are buffered and delivered at the end of the superstep. This implies that communication is clearly separated from synchronization, i.e. it can be performed in any order, provided that the information is delivered at the beginning of the following superstep. However, while the supersteps in the original BSP model can be variable in length, BCS generates computation and communication slots which are fixed in length and are determined by the time-slice.

One important benefit of the BSP model is the ability to accurately predict the execution time requirements of parallel algorithms and programs. This is achieved by constructing analytical formulae that are parameterized by a few constants which capture the computation, communication, and synchronization performance of a p-processor system. These results are based on the experimental evidence that the generic collective communication pattern generated by a superstep called h-relation[2] can be routed with predictable time [10] [22]. This implies that the maximum amount of information sent or received by each processor during a communication time-slice can be statically determined and

---

[2] h denotes the maximum amount of information sent or received by any process during the superstep.

enforced at run time by a global communication scheduling algorithm. For example, if the duration of the time-slice is δ and the permeability of the network (i.e., the inverse of the aggregate network bandwidth) is g, the upper bound h_{max} of information, expressed in bytes, that can be sent or received by a single processor is

$$h_{max} = \frac{T}{g}.$$

Furthermore, by globally scheduling a communication pattern, as described in Section 3, we can derive an accurate estimate of the communication time with simple analytical models already developed for the BSP model [22] [2] [21].

Unfortunately, BSP computations are overly restrictive, and many important applications cannot be efficiently expressed using this model. *With BCS, we can inherit the nice mathematical framework of BSP, without forcing the user to write BSP programs.*

9   Conclusion and Future Work

In this paper, we presented buffered coscheduling (BCS), a new methodology for multitasking jobs in parallel and distributed systems. By leveraging the positive aspects of gang scheduling and dynamic coscheduling, this methodology can significantly improve resource utilization as well as reduce response and wait times of parallel jobs.

Using our Job Scheduling Simulator in the presence of memory constraints, we illustrated that backfilling in combination with space sharing or time sharing improves overall system performance. Furthermore, we showed that BCS generally outperformed backfilled gang scheduling and backfilled space sharing.

We also examined how BCS performed with respect to three parameters: type of job communication and synchronization, memory constraints, and processor utilization. We were pleasantly surprised to find that the performance of BCS was relatively insensitive to the communication pattern when the communication was non-blocking communication or, more generally, a collective-communication pattern. In addition, what we originally thought to be a weakness in BCS [6], i.e., memory constraints imposed by BCS, only results in the performance of BCS degrading to being comparable to BF and not significantly worse as with BGS. Finally, the processor utilization with BCS exceeds backfilling gang scheduling (BGS) and BF by as much as 40%.

References

1. Andrea C. Arpaci-Dusseau, David Culler, and Alan M. Mainwaring. Scheduling with Implicit Information in Distributed Systems. In *Proceedings of the 1998 ACM Sigmetrics International Conference on Measurement and Modeling of Computer Systems*, Madison, WI, June 1998.
2. Douglas C. Burger and David A. Wood. Accuracy vs. Performance in Parallel Simulation of Interconnection Networks. In *Proceedings of the 9th International Parallel Processing Symposium, IPPS'95*, Santa Barbara, CA, April 1995.

3. Keith Diefendorff. Compaq Chooses SMT for Alpha: Simultaneous Multithreading Exploits Instruction- and Thread-Level Parallelism. *Microprocessor Report*, 13(16), December 1999.

4. Andrea C. Dusseau, Remzi H. Arpaci, and David E. Culler. Effective Distributed Scheduling of Parallel Workloads. In *Proceedings of the 1996 ACM Sigmetrics International Conference on Measurement and Modeling of Computer Systems*, Philadelphia, PA, May 1996.

5. Susan J. Eggers, Henry M. Levy, and Jack L. Lo. Multithreading: A Platform for Next-Generation Processors. *IEEE Micro*, 17(5), September/October 1997.

6. Fabrizio Petrini and Wu-chun Feng. Buffered Coscheduling: A New Methodology for Multitasking Parallel Jobs on Distributed Systems. In *Proceedings of the International Parallel and Distributed Processing Symposium 2000, IPDPS2000*, Cancun, MX, May 2000.

7. Dror G. Feitelson and Morris A. Jette. Improved Utilization and Responsiveness with Gang Scheduling. In Dror G. Feitelson and Larry Rudolph, editors, *Job Scheduling Strategies for Parallel Processing*, volume 1291 of *Lecture Notes in Computer Science*. Springer-Verlag, 1997.

8. Dror G. Feitelson and Larry Rudolph. Parallel Job Scheduling: Issues and Approaches. In Dror G. Feitelson and Larry Rudolph, editors, *Job Scheduling Strategies for Parallel Processing*, volume 949 of *Lecture Notes in Computer Science*. Springer-Verlag, 1995.

9. Dror G. Feitelson and Larry Rudolph. Toward Convergence in Job Schedulers for Parallel Supercomputers. In Dror G. Feitelson and Larry Rudolph, editors, *Job Scheduling Strategies for Parallel Processing*, volume 1162 of *Lecture Notes in Computer Science*. Springer-Verlag, 1996.

10. Alex Gerbessiotis and Fabrizio Petrini. Network Performance Assessment under the BSP Model. In *International Workshop on Constructive Methods for Parallel Programming, CMPP'98*, Marstrand, Sweden, June 1998.

11. A. Gupta, A. Tucker, and S. Urushibara. The Impact of Operating System Scheduling Policies and Synchronization Methods on the Performance of Parallel Applications. In *Proceedings of the 1991 ACM SIGMETRICS Conference*, pages 120–132, May 1991.

12. Anshul Gupta and Vipin Kumar. The Scalability of FFT on Parallel Computers. *IEEE Transactions on Parallel and Distributed Systems*, 4(8):922–932, August 1993.

13. Adolfy Hoisie, Olaf Lubeck, and Harvey Wasserman. Scalability Analysis of Multidimensional Wavefront Algorithms on Large-Scale SMP Clusters. In *The Ninth Symposium on the Frontiers of Massively Parallel Computation (Frontiers'99)*, Annapolis, MD, February 1999.

14. Joefon Jann, Pratap Pattnaik, Hubertus Franke, Fang Wang, Joseph Skovira, and Joseph Riordan. Modeling of Workload in MPPs. In Dror G. Feitelson and Larry Rudolph, editors, *Job Scheduling Strategies for Parallel Processing*, volume 1291 of *Lecture Notes in Computer Science*, pages 95–116. Springer-Verlag, 1997.

15. Vijay Karamcheti and Andrew A. Chien. Do Faster Routers Imply Faster Communication? In *First International Workshop, PCRCW'94*, volume 853 of *LNCS*, pages 1–15, Seattle, Washington, USA, May 1994.

16. Stephen W. Keckler, Andrew Chang, Whay S. Lee, Sandeep Chatterje, and William J. Dally. Concurrent Event Handling through Multithreading. *IEEE Transactions on Computers*, 48(9):903–916, September 1999.

17. Mario Lauria and Andrew Chien. High-Performance Messaging on Workstations: Illinois Fast Messages (FM) for Myrinet. In *Proceedings of Supercomputing '95*, November 1995.

18. Walter Lee, Matthew Frank, Victor Lee, Kenneth Mackenzie, and Larry Rudolph. Implications of I/O for Gang Scheduled Workloads. In Dror G. Feitelson and Larry Rudolph, editors, *Job Scheduling Strategies for Parallel Processing*, volume 1291 of *Lecture Notes in Computer Science*. Springer-Verlag, 1997.

19. Shailabh Nagar, Ajit Banerjee, Anand Sivasubramaniam, and Chita R. Das. A Closer Look At Coscheduling Approaches for a Network of Workstations. In *Eleventh ACM Symposium on Parallel Algorithms and Architectures, SPAA'99*, Saint-Malo, France, June 1999.

20. Fabrizio Petrini. Network Performance with Distributed Memory Scientific Applications. Submitted to the Journal of Parallel and Distributed Computing, September 1998.

21. Fabrizio Petrini. Total-Exchange on Wormhole k-ary n-cubes with Adaptive Routing. In *Proceedings of the 12th International Parallel Processing Symposium, IPPS'98*, Orlando, FL, March 1998.

22. Fabrizio Petrini and Marco Vanneschi. Efficient Personalized Communication on Wormhole Networks. In *The 1997 International Conference on Parallel Architectures and Compilation Techniques, PACT'97*, San Francisco, CA, November 1997.

23. Fabrizio Petrini and Marco Vanneschi. Latency and Bandwidth Requirements of Massively Parallel Programs: FFT as a Case Study. *Future Generation Computer Systems*, 1999. Accepted for publication.

24. Ian R. Philp and Y. Liong. The Scheduled Transfer (ST) Protocol. In *Proceedings of Workshop on Communication, Architecture, and Applications for Network-based Parallel Computing*, January 1999.

25. D. B. Skillicorn, Jonathan M. D. Hill, and W. F. McColl. Questions and Answers about BSP. *Journal of Scientific Programming*, 1998.

26. Joseph Skovira, Waiman Chan, Honbo Zhou, and David Lifka. The EASY-LoadLeveler API Project. In Dror G. Feitelson and Larry Rudolph, editors, *Job Scheduling Strategies for Parallel Processing*, volume 1162 of *Lecture Notes in Computer Science*, pages 41–47. Springer-Verlag, 1996.

27. Patrick Sobalvarro, Scott Pakin, William E. Weihl, and Andrew A. Chien. Dynamic Coscheduling on Workstation Clusters. In Dror G. Feitelson and Larry Rudolph, editors, *Job Scheduling Strategies for Parallel Processing*, volume 1459 of *Lecture Notes in Computer Science*, pages 231–256. Springer-Verlag, 1998.

28. Patrick Sobalvarro and William E. Weihl. Demand-Based Coscheduling of Parallel Jobs on Multiprogrammed Multiprocessors. In *Proceedings of the 9th International Parallel Processing Symposium, IPPS'95*, Santa Barbara, CA, April 1995.

29. Leslie G. Valiant. A Bridging Model for Parallel Computation. *Communications of the ACM*, 33(8):103–111, August 1990.

30. Yanyong Zhang, Hubertus Franke, José Moreira, and Anand Sivasubramaniam. Improving Parallel Job Scheduling by Combining Gang Scheduling and Backfilling Techniques. In *Proceedings of the International Parallel and Distributed Processing Symposium 2000, IPDPS2000*, Cancun, MX, May 2000.

The Performance Impact
of Advance Reservation Meta-scheduling

Quinn Snell, Mark Clement, David Jackson, and Chad Gregory

Brigham Young University, Provo, Utah 84602
{snell, clement, gregory}@cs.byu.edu, jacksond@mhpcc.edu

Abstract. As supercomputing resources become more available, users
will require resources managed by several local schedulers. To gain access to a collection of resources, current systems require metajobs to
run during locked down periods when the resources are only available
for metajob use. It is more convenient and efficient if the user is able
to make a reservation at the soonest time when all resources are available. System administrators are reluctant to allow reservations external
to locked down periods because of the impact reservations may have on
utilization and the Quality of Service that the center is able to provide
to its normal users. This research quantifies the impact of advance reservations on and outlines the algorithms that must be used to schedule
metajobs. The Maui scheduler is used to examine metascheduling using
trace files from existing supercomputing centers. These results indicate
that advance reservations can improve the response time for metajobs,
while not significantly impacting overall system performance.

1 Introduction

Recently, there have been a number of research groups focusing their efforts on
utilizing the combined resources of multiple supercomputing facilities [1,2,3,4].
The motives for this avenue of research are obvious. First, and perhaps fore-
most, is the belief that the proper combination of resources and their aggregate
processing power will yield a system that is both scalable and potentially more efficient. A system such as the one proposed in this paper would provide enhanced
scheduling services for at least three kinds of jobs: those that require more resources than are available at any one site, jobs that require a combination of
resources that are not available at any one site, and finally, jobs from users that
desire a better overall response time than could be obtained by limiting their
jobs to using the resources found at any single site.

Regardless of the job type, using the combined resources of more than one
site requires cooperation that is not inherent in local resource scheduling systems. A system that coordinates and works with the local schedulers is required.
Such a system is often called a metascheduler. The metascheduler makes this
aggregation of resources available to what are termed throughout this paper as
'metajobs'. Each metascheduler maintains a job queue to which these metajobs
are submitted by users where they are stored until they complete. A metajob can

D.G. Feitelson and L. Rudolph (Eds.): JSSPP 2000, LNCS 1911, pp. 137–153, 2000.

be simply a normal batch job submitted to the meta scheduler or it may be modified to utilize special functionality that can only be found in a metascheduling environment. There are three key differences between a metajob and a standard batch job: 1) The machine or local scheduler under which the metajob will run is not known at job submit time. 2) The metajob may contain a utility function which instructs the metascheduler as to what aspects of the resources are most important to it. These aspects may include cost, machine speed, time until availability, etc. 3) The resources utilized by the metajob may span more than one machine or local scheduler.

Some current metascheduling systems work by dedicating a set of local resources to be used and scheduled by the metascheduler. With these metaschedulers, local management and administration staff determine both a maximum amount of resources allowed for metascheduled work and a set of timeframes during which these resources can be used. During each of these timeframes, the metascheduler assumes full control of all allowed resources, preventing their use by locally submitted jobs. These resources remain unavailable regardless of the metascheduled workload. Supercomputer system managers have reported average utilizations ranging between 5% and 25% on those nodes that are dedicated for metacomputing systems. Due to the fragmentation of resources, low utilizations occur even when there is a backlog of local jobs. A metascheduling system based on this model clearly wastes valuable resources, significantly lowering the overall system utilization and increasing the average job turnaround time for local jobs.

This dedicated resource metascheduler schedules resources as if it were a local scheduler, according to its own private set of policies and priorities. It does not leverage the knowledge or capabilities of the local scheduler. The local scheduler has, in reality, completely relinquished control of the resources that have been dedicated to the metascheduler. This brings up more issues. First, lower utilization can be expected since the local compute resources are now fragmented. Additionally, the resource fragments are exclusive of each other meaning that those resources dedicated for metascheduled jobs cannot be used by locally submitted jobs even if they are idle; the same holds true for metascheduled jobs and resources dedicated for local workload. Also, under existing 'dedicated resource' metaschedulers, each resource fragment is scheduled according to an independent, private set of policies. There is no cooperation between the local schedulers and metaschedulers, and there is no knowledge of each others policies, priorities, or workload. In consequence of these conditions, there is no opportunity for cross-fragment scheduling optimizations such as backfill or intelligent node allocation.

Ursala, a metascheduler developed at Brigham Young University and used for the research described in this paper, cooperates with the local schedulers and introduces metascheduled jobs into the locally-produced workload. A system capable of doing this can achieve better overall utilization of resources because full information *and* control are maintained at the local scheduler level. Local scheduling optimizations such as backfill can then occur. Instead of dedicating the maximum block of resources allowed by the administrator, Ursala intelligently reserves only those resources that are required for existing, queued metajobs.

Ursala operates by breaking up a metajob into a number of localized sub-jobs, each of which is submitted to a different local resource manager. With parallel jobs, it is imperative that all resources required by the entire job be made available at job start time. The metascheduler must be able to determine a time when all of the needed resources are available. Each local scheduler must also be able to guarantee the availability of the needed resources for the corresponding sub-job at that determined time.

The guarantee of providing specific resources at a specific time is typically termed an advance reservation. Foster *et. al* [5] report that currently there is "no widely deployed resource management system for networks, computers, or other resources" that supports advance reservations. This is no longer the case. The Maui scheduler[6,7] has extensive support for advance reservations and is the local scheduler used in this research.

Creating coinciding advance reservations on each of the needed systems is not as simple as using a block of dedicated resources. However, the advantages of using such a system are tremendous. First, there is no fragmentation and there are no resources sitting idle while the metascheduled workload is low. The metascheduler only reserves the resources it needs exactly when it needs them. Thus, the local scheduler is allowed to utilize these resources at all other times and the overall utilization of the system is consequently higher. Each local scheduler is also able to enforce its local policies for all jobs. There are still questions which must be answered about a metascheduler that uses advance reservations to launch jobs across multiple systems: "What effect does metascheduling using advance reservations have on overall system utilization?", "What problems arise when trying to create coinciding reservations?", and "What impact does this type of metascheduling have on both local and metajob turn around time?"

This paper will deal with the issues listed above. Sections 2 and 3 discuss advance reservations and metascheduling respectively. The issues that surround metascheduling based on advance reservations are then discussed in Section 4. Finally, we present our metascheduling system and the experimental results we have obtained to answer the questions posed above.

2   Advance Reservations

In the most general sense, an advance reservation is a scheduling object which reserves a group of resources for a particular timeframe for access only by a specified entity or group of entities. These configurable aspects of an advance reservation can be set to support a metajob. The settings required are listed below.

1. A reservation must reserve exactly the type and amount of resources requested by the job.

2. A reservation must reserve these resources for use at the requested start time.
3. A reservation must reserve these resources for the wallclock limit of the metajob.
4. A reservation must reserve these resources for use only by the specified metajob.
5. The local scheduler must guarantee that the metajob will only run in the job reservation even if resources exist elsewhere which would allow the job to run earlier.

Reservations which meet the above configuration are termed a *job* reservation. While local schedulers may support advance reservations with additional attributes and features, the attributes listed above are the minimal set required to properly reserve resources for a metajob.

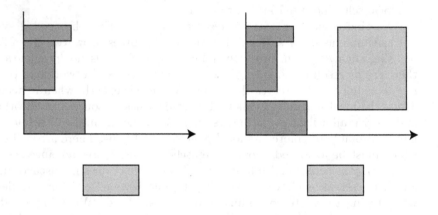

Fig. 1. Comparison of scheduling with and without advance reservations

Scheduling in the presence of advance reservations is significantly more complex than normal scheduling. Without advance reservations, a scheduler simply sets a policy of not scheduling any job that will delay the start time of the highest priority job in the queue. As long as that policy is maintained, the scheduler is free to take jobs from other parts of the queue and backfill the nodes. The scheduler need only consider if adequate resources exist at the present time to start a given job and need not determine if a job will fit on a given set of nodes in the time dimension.

Scheduling with advance reservations and guaranteed start time requires that the scheduler be capable of not only fitting jobs into the node space dimension, but also fitting them into the time dimension. This potentially involves analyzing resource dedication to other jobs both before and after the time of interest. Figure 1 compares scheduling with and without advance reservations. Note that without advance reservations, the future in the time dimension is open. With only a single advance reservation in place, the scheduler must now consider if a job will have enough resources available and if the resources will be available long enough for the job to complete before the resources are required by the future reservation. This is a much more complex decision.

Despite the added complexity, there are numerous advantages associated with advance reservations. Once reservations are incorporated, a scheduler can perform reservation-based deadline scheduling. The scheduler can guarantee the start time of a given job so that job start time can be coordinated with data availability. Schedulers can backfill around reservations to minimize the impact of dedicating resources to jobs, users, or projects. These functions yield a higher overall level of service to all users. This paper will show that while advance reservations can be utilized by the local scheduler to provide a number of local services, their greatest value may lie in their use in the metascheduling realm where they can be built upon to provide a new and powerful class of metascheduling services.

3   Meta-scheduling

Meta-scheduling can be loosely defined as the act of locating and allocating resources for a job on a metacomputer. Smarr and Catlett [8] define a metacomputer as the collection of resources that are transparently available to the user via the network. Thus a metascheduling system should make a collection of resources transparently available to the user as if it were a single large system. The key in this definition is that the user need not be aware of where the resources are, who owns the resources, or who administers the resources in order to use them. The scheduling issues that surround the creation of such a system is the focus of this section.

From the point of view of the metascheduler, metajobs fall into two basic categories: those that run on a single machine, and those that span multiple machines. The first category of jobs require less effort on the part of the metascheduler. The metascheduler simply locates which local scheduler can provide the greatest utility to the metajob and submits the metajob into that local scheduler's workload queue. The local scheduler takes care of the rest. Meta jobs that span multiple local schedulers introduce new issues that are not found in local scheduling systems.

The first step in developing a metascheduling system is to define the types of scheduling that will be performed. The following three classifications can be applied to metajobs.

1. Specified Co-Allocation: The user specifies all resource requirements including exactly which processors and resources are required. For example a user may specify that telescope X, 512 IBM SP2 processing nodes from site Y, and an SGI graphics pipe from site Z are needed. The metascheduler would then find a time when all of the resources were available for the user's priority. In this case, all requests are for particular resources and locations are

defined by the user. Reservations are made for each required resource at that time. This is the easiest kind of scheduling and little information need be passed between the scheduler and the metascheduler. Job initialization and resource management issues are all handled locally.

2. General Co-Allocation: This type of scheduling differs from specified co-Allocation in that the user does not specify where to run each part of the job. The user merely specifies the needed resource types and the metascheduler decides when and where the best resources are located, reserves those resources at that time and runs the requested job. For example, the user's specification of a SGI graphics pipe could yield any SGI graphics pipe known to the metascheduler.

3. Optimal Scheduling: The extreme case in scheduling is to determine the best location for every resource in the job. Using knowledge about machine and network performance, the metascheduler determines the placement that optimizes cost, performance, response time, throughput, and other factors. This type of metascheduling requires up to date performance knowledge from each part of the metacomputer as well as a characterization of the application's network and CPU requirements. For example, if a user simply requested 100 processors, the scheduler would determine the best 100 processors to use, even if that means fragmenting the job across supercomputer centers.

These three types of scheduling are ordered according to the level of intelligence that is required of the metascheduler. Specified Co-Allocation requires only that the metascheduler optimize in the time dimension, whereas the other categories require that the metascheduler make intelligent decisions in both time and space. Category 2 and category 3 scheduling can be performed by allowing the user to specify a utility function. The metascheduler then locates resources for the job such that the utility function is maximized. This type of scheduling will not be considered here, but is part of ongoing research.

Because all three categories of metascheduling are dependent upon advance reservations, it is critical to determine the impact of these reservations on local workload and their effectiveness in coordinating metajob components. The remainder of this paper will discuss Specified Co-Allocation using advance reservations and their effect on local and metascheduler performance.

3.1   Meta-scheduling Using Advance Reservations

As stated above, the goal of metascheduling is to reserve groups of resources from different resource management systems. To accomplish this goal, a metascheduler must create multiple, coinciding advance reservations. Creating these advance reservations can be reduced to the resource allocation problem in distributed algorithms research [9]. It is well known that such problems introduce possibilities of deadlock and livelock. Before discussing these issues, we consider the steps that a metascheduler must take to create coinciding reservations.

1. Determine available resources at each site.
2. Select the resources and time frame.
3. Create the advance reservations at each site.
4. Stage the appropriate job components to each local scheduler.

Determination of the available resources can be performed in many different ways. In the simplest sense, a query is performed on the local scheduler asking if resource set X is available at time Y. A much more flexible metascheduling system may be created if the metascheduler can ask 'what resources are available for job X in the time range A to B?' and the local scheduler responds with all ranges of acceptable times and resource sets that can be made available while still meeting local scheduler policies. For example, '8 nodes available from now until 8 hours out and 16 nodes available from 8 hours out until 24 hours out'. For metajobs which must span local schedulers, the metascheduler must perform an intersection of the returned start time ranges to determine the possible start times. The metascheduler could then automatically select the optimal metajob start time using the job's utility function or present the possibilities to the submitting user for a final decision.

For example, perhaps a scientist would like to allocate resources at three sites during working hours for interactive use. Referring to Figure 2, if the local schedulers can only answer yes or no to a proposed start time, the metascheduler must then propose a new start time if no appropriate times are available. This is shown in the first column of the figure. Flexibility is added when resource availability time ranges are returned as shown in the second column. Now the metascheduler can find the intersecting time ranges and present that to the scientist. However, there may be no appropriate intersecting time, thus forcing the scientist to propose a new start time. If a list of start time ranges is returned, the scientist may see that although there are no appropriate times today, there is a time the next day. This eliminates the need for the scientist to begin the process over again with a new proposed start time.

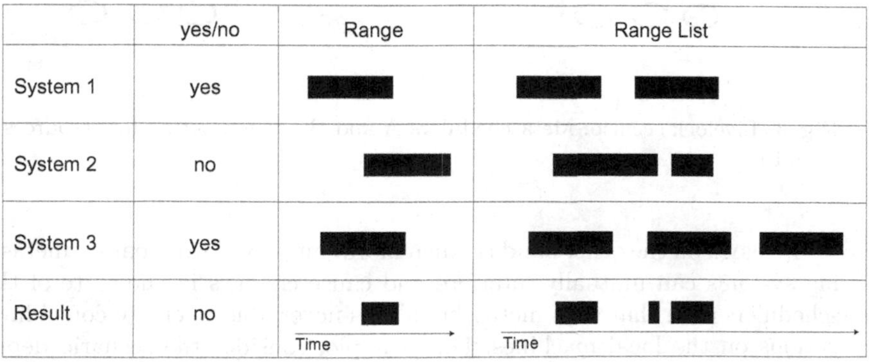

Fig. 2. Comparison of possible query results returned from local schedulers.

Deadlock and livelock issues are introduced because the metascheduler must gather resource information and make reservations on several local schedulers. The metascheduler receives available time ranges, then determines the appropriate start time and resources for the job before making the reservations. Because there is a brief delay between collecting the resource availability information and making the reservations, it is possible that the availability of the resources under the control of each local scheduler has changed. This could be due to local scheduling or due to reservations created by a competing metascheduler attempting to create advance reservations in the same time frame.

The potential for deadlock is brought about because all of the four deadlock conditions exist [10]. Eliminating one of the four conditions eliminates deadlock. Perhaps the easiest condition to eliminate is Hold and Wait. In a metascheduling environment, this means that as advance reservations are created, if any reservation cannot be made due to recent resource availability changes, all existing reservations for that job must be cancelled. This policy is logical in the case of metascheduling since the local reservations are for a specific time and the job must start on all resources at the same time. Thus deadlock situations are eliminated by forbidding Hold and Wait.

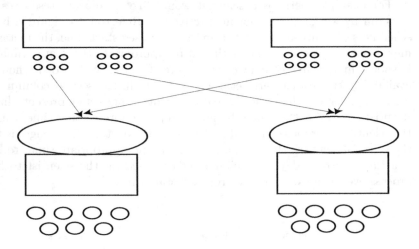

Fig. 3. Livelock scenrio. Metaschedulers A and B are competing for resources at sites A and B.

Livelock on the other hand is much more complex. Two separate metascheduling systems can mutually interfere and cause changes in the state of the local schedulers such that each metascheduler is never able to create coinciding reservations on the local machines. For example, consider the scenario depicted in Figure 3. Both metaschedulers need resources at sites A and B. If either site grants the needed resources to one of the metaschedulers, the needed resources will not be available for the other metascheduler. The resource query and reservation allocation are separate steps. If the metaschedulers proceed through the steps by approaching the local schedulers in opposing order, they will mutually interfere. Both metaschedulers will see that the needed resources are available, and will request reservations from their corresponding sites. However, when the metaschedulers request from opposing sites, they will both fail and release their other reservations. The process will then begin again. If the metaschedulers continue to request, they will most likely get out of sync eventually and one will succeed, thus breaking the livelock. The metaschedulers may go through many of these iterations though.

There are many research areas that have similar livelock characteristics. In particular, the Ethernet [11] CSMA/CD networking protocol has a random exponential backoff policy for dealing with collisions on a shared network. When utilization on the network is high, much of the network bandwidth is spent in collision detection and backoff, resulting in degraded performance. One major difference, however, is that the Ethernet possess only a single shared resource while the metascheduling problem has multiple shared resources, increasing the problem's complexity.

The main cause of the livelock problem is that the local system can change state between the metascheduler's resource query and reservation phases. The state changes can come from two sources, new resource manager information (i.e. a node going down) and new reservations created by competing metaschedulers. While nothing can be done to control actual resource state changes, steps can be taken to eliminate the possibility of resource state due to other metaschedulers. One solution is to have the resource query lock the reservation state of the local scheduler for a period of time preventing other metaschedulers from creating reservations during this time. The locked time would be just long enough to allow the locking metascheduler to process the resource information and make all needed reservations. This locking of reservation state is one form of a *courtesy* reservation. A timeout can be imposed to eliminate the case of a courtesy reservation locking out the entire machine for long periods of time. If the reservation is not made before the timeout, there is no guarantee that the resources will still be available. However, these courtesy reservations introduce several problems into local scheduling algorithms. It is hard to determine the potential effects of courtesy reservations on scheduler performance. Further research is being conducted to examine the tradeoffs between courtesy reservations and stateless reservations combined with a backoff policy.

3.2   The Maui Scheduler

The Maui scheduler is currently in use at many supercomputing facilities and is ideal for this research. The Maui scheduler supports advance reservations in the form previously described allowing the scheduler to guarantee a job's start time. A metascheduling interface allows very flexible resource availability queries to be performed. The metascheduler may specify the job in great detail or it may simply specify the number of resources and the amount of time required. Replies to these queries are returned as a list of start time ranges and associated resource sets. As discussed previously, this yields great flexibility in determining when and where to start a given metajob.

Perhaps the most important feature of the Maui scheduler with respect to this research is its ability to run in simulation mode. Given a trace file of an actual workload, the Maui scheduler can simulate the scheduling of the workload, allowing the administrator to experiment with different parameters and attempt to improve scheduler efficiency. The scheduler steps forward in discrete amounts of time. It can be told to single step through these discrete time blocks or to advance through a number of them. Another unique feature valuable to this research is the ability to externally insert new jobs and reservations into the simulated workload as the simulation is running.

3.3   Brigham Young University Meta-scheduler (Ursala)

At Brigham Young University, we have created Ursala, a metascheduling system which creates coinciding advance reservations on participating local schedulers. The metascheduler communicates with each local scheduler, for this research, Maui, using the following steps:

1. Ursala contacts each Maui scheduler requesting resource availability and cost information for a specific job and time frame.
2. Each Maui scheduler incorporates existing reservation, resource, policy, and priority information to determine when resources could be made available for the specified job.
3. Each Maui scheduler reports its finding to Ursala as a list of start time ranges, costs, and resource sets.
4. Ursala receives the lists of start time ranges from each Maui scheduler, computes the intersection of the range lists and determines a best start time and collection of resources.
5. Ursala attempts to create needed reservations for this job on each Maui scheduler. If any reservation attempt fails, Ursala releases all existing reservations for this job, and after a 'backoff' time, returns to step 1. If all reservations succeed, Ursala advances to step 6.
6. With all reservations made, Ursala submits the proper job components to each local resource manager.

The current design implements a reservation release and backoff algorithm to handle the livelock possibility described earlier. Figure 4 is a representation of the basic architecture. Ursala communicates with the local scheduler to obtain resource state information and to create advance reservations. It also interfaces to the local resource management systems for submitting metajob components. Ursala currently supports three scheduling modes described earlier: Specified Co-Allocation, General Co-Allocation, and Optimal Scheduling.

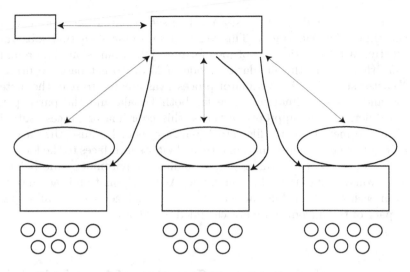

Fig. 4. Meta-scheduler architecture.

4   Experimental Results

The goal of this research is to determine what effects advance reservations have on local scheduling performance and system utilization. To accomplish this, a series of experiments were designed. In this section, we present the experimental environment and results.

In each experiment, the Maui scheduler was used in simulation mode as the local scheduler. Simulation traces were provided to simulate a 192 node IBM SP system with memory sizes ranging from 128 to 512 MB per node. Workload traces representing several weeks of actual workload were used for each simulation run. Each workload trace contains every scheduling aspect relevant to a job, including submit time, submitting user and group, resource requirements, wallclock limit, and actual run time. Using this information, the Maui scheduler is able to introduce the job into the queue at the recorded queue time as the submitting user allowing local scheduler throttling policies to be enforced (e.g. Max Jobs Per User). At that point, the job is scheduled according to the policies and algorithms that currently set for the Maui scheduler. If no changes are made to the configuration of Maui, the simulation of the trace will yeild the same resulting schedule as if the jobs were scheduled and run on the real system.

The job traces used for this experiment contained a mix of jobs requesting between 1 and 128 nodes and requiring between 2 minutes and 36 hours to run. The trace represents a period of 2 weeks at the Maui High Performance Computing Center. See [7] for more details about the job trace used. For each experiment, a simulation time period of 10 days was run and analyzed. Since every scheduling-relevant aspect of node resources and jobs is captured in the traces, differences between simulated and actual 'real world' runs are minimal.

To represent the metajobs, a random set of batch jobs were extracted from the simulation job traces. This yeilds a sampling of actual jobs rather than creating a hypothetical set of jobs for metajob submission. The remaining jobs were then run in the simulation mode of Maui to get baseline utilization and XFactor statistics. A coordinator process was created to read the metajob trace file and advance simulated time for both Ursala and the participating Maui schedulers. At the appropriate times, this coordinator process submitted jobs from the metajob trace file into Ursala's queue. Because Ursala only sees its metajob queue and information returned via its interfaces to the local schedulers, it cannot tell that it is running in a simulated environment and behaves exactly as it would if run in 'production' mode. As the simulation is advanced, statistics from each Maui scheduler are collected and analyzed to determine performance impact of the introduced metascheduled workload.

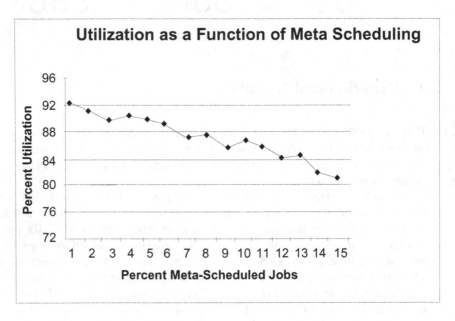

Fig. 5. The effect of advance reservations on system utilization.

The first experiment is a detailed examination of the effects of advance reservations. Ursala was used to insert metajobs requiring advance reservations into the Maui simulation. Initially, no metajobs were inserted, the entire simulation was run to completion, and statistics were gathered. The simulation was then run repeatedly, increasing the percentages of metajobs inserted into the workload mix in each run. Figure 5 shows the resulting system utilization graph for this experiment. Note that, as the percentage of metajobs increases, the overall system utilization declines. This is expected due to the added constraint of a guaranteed start time for each metajob. As a general rule, every added con-

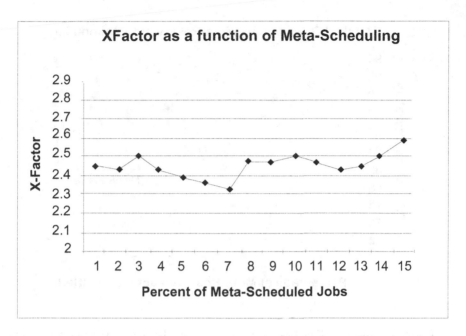

Fig. 6. The effect of advance reservations on expansion factor.

straint will decrease scheduling flexibility and thus decrease resource utilization. This constraint is no exception. Jobs requiring a dedicated start time fragment the scheduler's time space as well as its node space making it more difficult for the scheduler to utilize idle resources. In addition, due to inaccuracies in user's wallclock limit estimations, most jobs will complete early. While normal workload can take advantage of the now available resources by being started earlier than originally planned, metajob components cannot since doing so would cause this component to start before the metajob's other components. Consequently, these resources may go unused.

As previously shown in Figure 1, when advance reservations are added to the workload mix, the scheduler must fit jobs into a two-dimensional mapping. The optimal placement of jobs into this mapping can be reduced to a two-dimensional bin packing problem which is NP-complete[12]. As more advance reservations are added to the mix, placing backfill jobs into the map becomes more difficult. Thus, holes are created and the system utilization goes down. If the accuracy of job run-time estimates were improved, backfill job placement would also be more accurate and somewhat alleviate this effect, but not eliminate it.

The average job expansion factor was also recorded in this experiment, and the resulting graph is shown in Figure 6. The expansion factor is a measure of job turnaround time. While the canonical definition of expansion factor is $(1 + (QueueTime/WallClockLimit))$, Maui scheduler uses a modified version of this to incorporate the affect of wallclock limit inaccuracies, namely, $(QueueTime + RunTime)/WallClockLimit$. Regardless, the expansion factor calculation scales

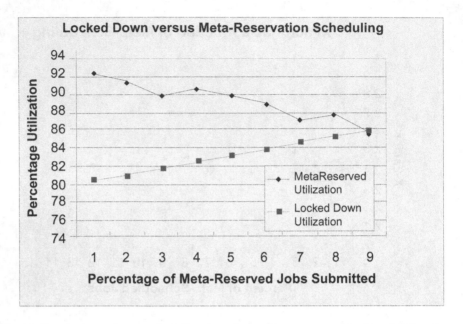

Fig. 7. Comparison of metascheduling based on advance reservations vs. locking down the resources.

the job's actual turnaround time by the job's requested length. Since metajobs increase the number of holes in the two-dimensional node-time map, it becomes harder to backfill. This decreases utilization and increases the average expansion factor, as is reflected in the graph. As the percentage of metascheduled jobs increases, the average expansion factor also increases because QueueTime is increased.

Experiment two is a direct comparison between advance reservation and dedicated resource based strategies for metascheduling. As described before, current 'dedicated resource' metascheduling systems lock down a set of resources to be used by the metascheduler for a specified time frame each day. The findings of this research suggest that scheduling advance reservations for metajobs is more efficient than the blocked dedicated resource approach. The graph in Figure 7 shows the system utilizations of the two approaches. In this experiment, the system in question controlled 192 nodes. For the locked down node metascheduling strategy, 48 of the nodes were blocked out for 8 hours each day for the metascheduled jobs. This was compared to a system using Ursala to schedule advance reservations for the same jobs. The number of metascheduled jobs increased in each simulation such that 1% metascheduled jobs corresponds roughly to 10% utilization of the dedicated nodes. Since we are using 25% of the nodes for 1/3 of each day, 8.3% metascheduled load would be roughly 100% utilization of the locked down nodes. With a small percentage of metajobs, advance reservation metascheduling yields much higher utilization. Larger percentages of metascheduled jobs bring the two curves closer together, and finally, the dedicated node strategy will result in slightly higher overall utilization. However, it should be noted that the utilization assigned to the block of dedicated metascheduler resources was assigned arbitrarily in this experiment, i.e. the utilization on the blocked nodes was increased rather than attempting to schedule an increased metascheduling workload onto these resources. This removed the issues of fragmentation and packing metascheduled workload. In reality, since both the local workload and the metascheduled workload contained a similar mix of jobs, but the metascheduled resources were relatively smaller, the metascheduler would be able to obtain a system utilization which approached but did not exceed that obtained by the local scheduler. Also, since average system utilization is generally proportional to (average job size) / (total resources available), neither the local scheduler nor the metascheduler would be able to obtain the level of utilization obtained when the resources were not fragmented.

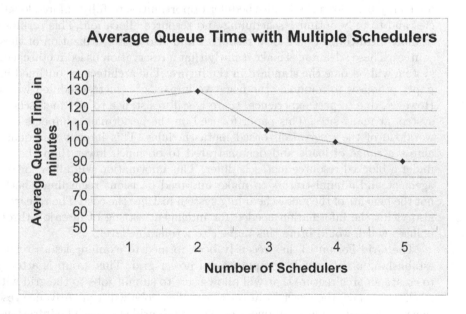

Fig. 8. Meta-scheduled job queue time comparison using a single local scheduler vs. using multiple local schedulers.

The final experiment is set up to show the benefits of metascheduling using the resources at multiple sites. In this case, Ursala was connected to multiple Maui schedulers; each running a different simulation trace file. Ursala processed a job trace using a simple 'ASAP' utility function. Each metajob in this experiment only required resources at a single site. This allowed Ursala to minimize queue time for each metajob and showcase the benefits of such an approach.

The graph in Figure 8 shows the average queue time for the metajobs as more local systems are added to the simulated metacomputer. It is clear that as more systems are added, the probability of finding an earlier start time for a metascheduled job increases even though each local system maintains a high local system utilization. This is due to the fact that there is a greater probability of finding an appropriate sized hole for the metascheduled job earlier on one of the local systems. Thus the queue time for the metajobs decreases.

5   Conclusion

An advance reservation based metascheduling system provides significant advantages over a metascheduler based on blocked resources dedicated to metajob usage. Such a system allows metajobs to run at any time and not be limited to dedicated resource blocks and time frames. The 'integrated' approach of allowing the local scheduler to determine when and which resources are available for metajobs, allows the local scheduler opportunities to fully enforce local policies and to fully optimize scheduling and resource allocation. This results both in more local control over local resources and also better utilization of these resources. These advantages make it likely that a reservation based metascheduling system will become the standard in the future. The architecture outlined in this paper promises to minimize the negative impact of a metascheduled workload. However, due to past experience, there is still resistance to any metascheduling system at many sites. This paper focused on the performance impacts on local workload of the reservation based metascheduler. This impact was quantified across a range of loads and demonstrated to be much lower than that found under a blocked resource metascheduler. This information will allow local management and administrators to make informed decisions regarding whether or not the benefits of the metascheduling system justifies the cost. The research here also yields the information needed for intelligent setting of metajob throttling policies which would bring this impact to a tolerable level.

The Grid Forum[13] has recently been formed to examine issues related to establishing a nationwide computational power grid. This group is attempting to create an architecture that will allow users to submit jobs to the grid without needing to know the exact location where their jobs will run. Advance reservations are an important component of the overall grid system. The infrastructure created for this research will enable investigators to answer questions about several design decisions that must be made in creating the grid. This paper indicates how varying metascheduled workloads affect the quality of service delivered to local jobs thus allowing scheduler administrators and management to determine acceptable impacts and set appropriate policies to throttle such external workload.

Future research will compare stateless reservation creation vs. courtesy reservations. Additional research will also be conducted in the area of 'Optimal' job scheduling and in ways of utilizing current performance information in deciding optimal metajob fragmentation and resource allocation. Answering these questions in a quantitative way is important as a step towards validating the feasibility of a wide-spread metascheduling environment. Such research is vital in the effort to persuade local system administrators to make their systems available for use by metajobs and demonstrate that an advance reservation metascheduler will increase the utility and availability of computational resources in the supercomputing and cluster community.

References

1. P. Chandra *et. al.* Darwin: Resource management for value-added customizable network service. In *Sixth IEEE International Conference on Network Protocols*, 1998.
2. K. Czajkowski, I. Foster, N. Karonis, C. Kesselman, S. Martin, W. Smith, and S. Tuecke. A resource management architecture for metacomputing systems. In *The 4th Workshop on Job Scheduling Strategies for Parallel Processing*, 1998.
3. I. Foster and C. Kesselman. Globus: A metacomputing infrastructure toolkit. *IJSA*, 11(2):115–128, 1997.
4. Andrew S. Grimshaw and William A. Wulf. The legion vision of a worldwide virtual computer. *Communications of the ACM*, 40(1), 1997.
5. I. Foster, C. Kesselman, C. Lee, R. Lindell, K. Nahrstedt, and A. Roy. A distributed resource management architecture that supports advance reservations and co-allocation. In *International Workshop on Quality of Service*, 1999.
6. Maui High Performance Computing Center. The maui scheduler. In *http://www.mhpcc.edu/maui/*, 1999.
7. Mark Clement, Quinn Snell, David Jackson, and David Ashton. High performance scheduling for windows nt. In *Proceedings of the 1999 International Conference on Parallel and Distributed Techniques and Applications*, pages 525–531, 1999.
8. Larry Smarr and Charles E. Catlett. Metacomputing. *Communications of the ACM*, 35:45–52, June 1992.
9. Nancy A. Lynch. *Distributed Algorithms*. Morgan Kaufmann Publishers, Inc., 1996.
10. Abraham Silberschatz and Peter Baer Galvin. *Operating System Concepts*. Addison-Wesley, 1998.
11. R. Metcalf and D. Boggs. Ethernet: Distributed packet switching for local computer networks. *Communications of the ACM*, 19(7):395–403, 1976.
12. M. R. Garey and D. S. Johnson. *Computers and Intractability – A Guide to the Theory of NP-completeness*. W.H. Freeman, 1979.
13. The Grid Forum. The grid forum. In *http://www.gridforum.org/*, 1999.

The Influence of the Structure and Sizes of Jobs on the Performance of Co-allocation

Anca I.D. Bucur and Dick H.J. Epema

Parallel and Distributed Systems Group
Faculty of Information Technology and Systems
Delft University of Technology, P.O. Box 356, 2600 AJ Delft, The Netherlands
anca@pds.twi.tudelft.nl, epema@pds.twi.tudelft.nl

Abstract. Over the last decade, much research in the area of scheduling has concentrated on single cluster systems. Less attention has been paid to multicluster systems, although they are gaining more and more importance in practice. We propose a model for scheduling rigid jobs consisting of multiple components in multicluster systems by pure space sharing, based on the Distributed ASCI Supercomputer. Using simulations, we asses the influence of the structure and sizes of the jobs on the system's performance, measured in terms of the average response time and the maximum utilization. We consider three types of requests, total requests, unordered requests and ordered requests, and compare their effect on the system's performance for two scheduling policies, First Come First Served, and Fit Processors First Served, which allows the scheduler to look further in the queue for jobs that fit. These types of job requests are differentiated by the restrictions they impose on the scheduler and by the form of co-allocation used. The results show that the performance improves with decreasing average job size and when fewer restrictions are imposed on the scheduler.

1 Introduction

Much work has been done in the area of scheduling in parallel computer systems, but most of it is related to single-cluster systems (i.e., single multiprocessors and single clusters of uniprocessors) with identical processors connected by links of the same speed. Much less research has been dedicated to multicluster systems, although many such systems are in use. We study the performance of co-allocation, that is of scheduling jobs that can be spread on more than one cluster, in multicluster systems such as the Distributed ASCI Supercomputer (DAS) [5], depending on the structure and size of jobs and on the scheduling policy. In particular, we provide a performance comparison between a single-cluster system and a multicluster system of the same total size.

Multiprocessor systems gained popularity during the last years. The increase in computational power of the existing sytems encouraged people to design larger and larger parallel applications. The sequential solutions to many problems were replaced by parallel ones in order to become faster.

Being expensive, large parallel systems are in general not dedicated, but shared by large numbers of applications designed by many different users. For this reason, many scheduling strategies have been developed, giving solutions for how applications should

D.G. Feitelson and L. Rudolph (Eds.): JSSPP 2000, LNCS 1911, pp. 154–173, 2000.

be structured, how they should be chosen for being processed, and how they should be mapped to the resources.

One of the simplest ways to solve these problems, and yet often used in practice due to its simplicity, is to allow only rigid jobs, scheduled by pure space sharing. This means that at execution, each job requires some number of processors and is executed on those processors until its completion. The advantages are that the implementation of the application is not restricted by the system, so the users can design their applications the way they consider the best performance is obtained, and that each application can have exclusive access to and control of the assigned processors. There is also the economical advantage that the providers of service can easily and fairly charge the users for the employed resources.

Compared to single-cluster systems, multicluster systems can provide a larger computational power (more nodes). They can be geographically spread, and instead of smaller groups of users with exclusive access to single clusters, larger groups of users can share the multicluster consisting of the total of the initial single clusters. Of course, the fact that the resources are spread will entail that the connections between clusters will be slower than the ones inside the clusters. Another reason for building multicluster systems is that very large single-cluster systems are hard to manage by single schedulers.

The necessity of dividing the processors into pools in order to simplify the scheduling decisions is discussed in the literature [3]. In the case of multiclusters, the division is natural and is imposed by the architecture of the system, and not by the scheduler. The nodes cannot be treated as identical anymore because their relative position inside the clusters influences the performance of the communications between them, and this must be taken into account by the application and the scheduler.

This paper concentrates on real multicluster systems such as the DAS. We provide a model of the system and study by simulations the influence of the structure and size of the jobs on the performance of the multicluster system. We also take into account the effect of the scheduling policy on the system's performance, being aware of the modifications the policy brings to the order of the requests. The scheduling schemes implemented are First Come First Served and Fit Processors First Served, which can look further in the queue for jobs that fit. The scheduler provides co-allocation, meaning that a job can ask for the simultaneous allocation of processors in multiple clusters. The performance is measured in terms of the maximal utilization and of the response time as a function of the system's utilization.

2   The Model

Our model is a simplification of a real system, a multicluster distributed system called the Distributed ASCI Supercomputer, the performance of which we intend to evaluate, depending on the scheduling scheme and on the structure and the distribution of the requests of the incoming jobs.

2.1   The Structure of the System

We model a multicluster distributed system consisting of C clusters of processors, cluster i having N_i processors, $i = 1, \ldots, C$. The system has a single central scheduler, with one global queue (see Fig. 1).

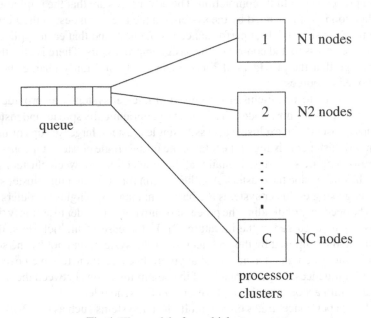

Fig. 1. The model of a multicluster system.

We assume that all processors have the same service rate. For both interarrival times and service times we use exponential distributions.

By job we understand a parallel application requiring some number of processors. A job can simultaneously ask for processors in more than one cluster (co-allocation). We will call a task the part of an application which runs on a single processor. Jobs are rigid, meaning that the numbers of processors requested by and allocated to a job are fixed, and cannot be changed during its execution. All tasks start and end at the same time, which implies that all the processors allocated to a job are being simultaneously occupied and released. Preemption is not admitted, nodes being released only when the tasks running on them end. We also assume that jobs only request processors and we do not include in the model any other types of resources.

In our simulations we make the simplification that all the clusters have an equal number N of processors. Clusters of different sizes would not change the results significantly, but would make them harder to be evaluated. Besides, factors of another nature, such as the users' preference for the larger clusters, would become relevant. When $C = 1$, the system is a single cluster. We compare the performance of the multicluster system with a single-cluster system with CN processors.

2.2   The Structure of Jobs

We consider three cases for the structure of jobs, differentiated by the structure of the system and of the job's request:

1. A request of a job is represented by a tuple of C values $(r_1, r_2, \ldots, r_C)$, each of them uniformly distributed on the interval $[n_1, n_2]$, with $0 < n_1 \leq n_2 \leq N$. By these values, the job only specifies how many nodes it needs in separate clusters, but not the precise clusters where the nodes must be allocated. We will further call this type of request "unordered request".
2. The request is again given by a tuple of C values $(r_1, r_2, \ldots, r_C)$, each uniformly distributed on the interval $[n_1, n_2]$, with $0 < n_1 \leq n_2 \leq N$, but here their positions in the tuple specifies the clusters from which the processors must be allocated. This will be called an "ordered request".
3. Here, there is only a single cluster with size CN, and a request only specifies the single number of processors it requires. An instance of this case is characterized by a number of clusters C and an interval $[n_1, n_2]$. The distribution of the numbers of processors required by jobs is the sum of C copies of the uniform distribution on the interval $[n_1, n_2]$. In this case, the requests are called "total requests". We include this case in order to compare the ordered and unordered multicluster cases above with a single-cluster case in which the job sizes have the same distribution.

As long as we do not take into account the characteristics of the applications (e.g., the amount of communication between processors), the case of total requests amounts to the same as would a case with a multicluster when the requests are given as single values and the users do not impose restrictions on the clusters they will receive processors from. In order to be able to compare the results, we choose the intervals for the uniform distributions in such a way as to have equal mean values for the request sizes, in all three cases. Ordered requests are used in practice when the user has enough information about the system, to take full advantage of the characteristics of the different clusters, for example of the data availability. Unordered requests (especially the case when grouping request components on the same cluster is allowed) model applications like FFT, where tasks in the same request component share data and need intensive communication, while tasks from different components exchange little or no information.

We also did simulations for the situation when requests are unordered and the scheduler tries to group as many components as possible on the same cluster. For the value ranges we chose the results were not much different from the case when only distinct clusters are used. However, in general this choice can much influence the performance (see also Sect. 3).

2.3   The Scheduling Policies

To observe the contribution of the scheduling scheme to the system's performance, apart from the First Come First Served (FCFS) policy, the Fit Processors First Served (FPFS) policy explained below was implemented as well.

For ordered and total requests, it is clear when a job fits on the system, either the total number of processors requested are idle, or all job components fit in the clusters they request.

When requests are unordered, for both FCFS and FPFS, the algorithm that checks whether a job fits first orders the values inside the request, and then tries to schedule them in decreasing order of their size. This ensures the maximum success for the individual job, whatever way of placement such as First Fit, Best Fit or Worst Fit, is chosen (if our placement would not succeed, no other one would—the request cannot be served for that configuration). Clusters are checked in the same order each time and the components of the request are placed into the clusters in decreasing order of their size, in the First Fit manner.

We do not consider the influence each placement has on the jobs following in the queue, although it can affect performance, especially for the FCFS policy (a placement according to Worst Fit could give better results than First Fit because it would leave in each cluster as much room as possible for the next job). Our focus is on the influence of the structure and sizes of the requests on the system's performance and less on the impact of the scheduling schemes. FCFS is the simplest scheduling scheme, processors being allocated to the job at the head of the queue. When the job at the head of the queue does not fit, the scheduler is not allowed to choose another job, further in the queue. Because of this restriction, FCFS results in a low maximal processor utilization.

In FPFS the scheduler searches further in the queue, from head to tail, and schedules the jobs which fit. It is similar to the backfilling policy [1], but the duration of jobs is not taken into account, so the requirement that the job at the head of the queue should not be delayed is not enforced. In order to avoid starvation (a job is never scheduled) we introduce counters as aging mechanism. Each job counts the number of times it was jumped over by jobs which were behind it in the queue, but were scheduled before it. When a job's counter reaches a chosen limit MaxJumps, the scheduler is not allowed to overpass that job anymore. In this way, the effectiveness of scheduling is preserved. Of course, when MaxJumps is equal to zero, FPFS becomes FCFS. FPFS has the potential advantage of an increased maximal utilization of the system compared to FCFS.

2.4   The Distributed ASCI Supercomputer

The DAS [5] is a wide-area distributed computer, consisting of four clusters of work-stations located at four Dutch universities, amongst which Delft. One of the clusters contains 128 nodes, the other three contain 24 nodes each. All the nodes are identical Pentium Pro processors. The clusters are interconnected by ATM links for wide-area communications, and for local communication inside the clusters Myrinet LANs are used. The operating system employed is RedHat Linux. The system was designed by the Advanced School for Computing and Imaging (ASCI, in the Netherlands) and is used for research on parallel and distributed computing. On single DAS clusters a local scheduler called prun is used; it allows users to request a number of processors bounded by the cluster's size, for a time interval which does not exceed an imposed limit (15 minutes).

Using the Globus toolkit [10] which we installed in the DAS system, a job can simultaneously and transparently require processors on distinct clusters. However, this form of co-allocation has not been used enough so far to let us obtain statistics on the sizes of the jobs' components.

3   The Maximal Utilization

In the model described in Sect. 2, it may happen that some processors are idle while at the same time there are waiting jobs. Of course, this phenomenon already occurs in single clusters, but in multiclusters we can expect it to occur more often or with a larger fraction of the processors remaining idle. As a consequence, if ρ_m is the traffic intensity such that the system is stable (unstable) at traffic intensities ρ with $\rho < \rho_m$ ($\rho > \rho_m$), we have $\rho_m < 1$. We will call the quantity $1 - \rho_m$ the (maximal) *capacity loss*, which we denote by L.

In this section we first discuss some important reasons for capacity loss, and then we present a very simple approximation for the capacity loss in single-cluster systems. We validate this approximation with simulations when the job sizes have a uniform or a (truncated) geometric distribution. Finally, we assess the capacity loss in multiclusters with simulations.

3.1   Reasons for Capacity Loss

The problem of unutilized processor capacity when space sharing is employed for rigid jobs in single clusters has of course been recognized before. In [8], gang scheduling is proposed as a solution to this problem. However, for multiclusters such as the DAS, gang scheduling may not be a viable solution for technical reasons and because of the distributed ownership of such systems. Even if the cluster schedulers support gang scheduling (and our local DAS scheduler does not), the separate cluster schedulers would have to synchronize and agree on the number and size of the time slices, and on the jobs that run in each time slice. Because of the wide-area latencies, the context-switching overhead will be larger than in single clusters. Clusters in a multicluster may have different systems administrators or different owners, who want to determine for themselves how their own systems are used. Setting aside some number of processors for some amount of time for (components of) foreign jobs (i.e., space sharing) does interfere much less with local jobs than gang scheduling.

There are at least three reasons for the phenomenon of capacity loss. First, it may be due to the job-size distribution, and, in multiclusters, to the jobs' structures. For instance, when in a single cluster with N processors all jobs have size $\lceil (N + 1)/2 \rceil$, for large values of N the capacity loss L is close to 0.5. In multicluster systems in which ordered requests are used, much higher fractions of the capacity may be lost if many jobs have mutually conflicting requirements in one specific cluster while they do not require many processors in the remaining clusters.

Second, the scheduling policy employed may cause capacity loss. It is possible that the job at the head of the queue does not fit, while some job further down in the queue does fit, which means that the capacity loss when FCFS is employed is larger than when a policy like FPFS is used instead. In the case of total requests, this only occurs when not enough processors are idle, while in the cases of unordered and ordered requests, even when the total number of idle processors is large enough, a job may still not be accommodated because its components do not fit in the separate clusters.

A third reason for having $\rho_m < 1$ is that we are considering an *on-line* problem, which means that we take scheduling decisions without knowing when jobs will arrive in the (near) future and what their sizes and service times are. We may expect that in multiclusters, having knowledge of the structure of jobs and the sizes of their components would be even more important to reduce capacity loss.

3.2   An Approximation of Capacity Loss in Single Clusters

We now present a procedure for computing an approximation to L in a single cluster of size N for the FCFS policy. Subsequently, we simplify this approximation, and show this simplification to yield good results for different job-size distributions. We assume that there is no correlation between the job sizes (number of processors requested) and the job service times.

When in a single cluster the traffic intensity approaches ρ_m, the job queue will be very long. This means that we can assume that whenever a job leaves the system, new jobs from the head of the queue can be started until the next job does not fit. So in fact, we can find an approximation to L by computing the average number of processors that remain idle when we put jobs one by one on a single cluster of N processors that is initially completely idle until the next job does not fit. If there was a correlation between job size and service time—for instance, when larger jobs run for a longer period of time, as has been observed in some systems [9]—the mix of the sizes of the jobs in service would be different from the general job-size distribution, and the approximation would in general not be valid.

To find the approximation, let N be the number of processors, and let F be the job-size distribution, which is a discrete distribution on the set $\{1, 2, \ldots, N\}$; $F(n)$ is the probability that a job's size does not exceed n. We assume F to be non-degenerate, for otherwise, if all jobs are of size say d, we have $L = (N \bmod d)/N$. Let f be the density of the job sizes, so $f(n) = F(n) - F(n-1), n = 1, 2, \ldots, N$, is the probability that a job is of size n. For an N-tuple $v = (v_1, \ldots, v_N)$ of jobs of sizes $1, 2, \ldots, N$, respectively, we denote by $s(v)$ the sum $\sum_n v_n n$, which is the total number of processors these jobs require. Now let

$$V = \{(v_1, \ldots, v_N) | v_n \geq 0, n = 1, \ldots, N, s(v_1, \ldots, v_N) \leq N\}$$

be the set of N-tuples of numbers of jobs that fit on N processors, and let

$$W = \{v \in V | \text{ there exists a } n \text{ with } f(n) > 0, \text{ such that } s(v) + n > N\}$$

be the subset of V of N-tuples of jobs such that an additional job may not fit. Then the set I of numbers of processors that can remain idle is

$$I = \{i | i = N - s(w), w \in W\}.$$

We are interested in the probabilities $P(i)$ that i processors remain idle, for all $i \in I$. The probability $P(i)$ is made up of the probability that when adding jobs we reach a level of $N - i$ processors, and the probability that the next job is larger than i processors. A general expression for these probabilities is (the first factor in the summation below is a multinomial coefficient)

$$P(i) = (1 - F(i)) \cdot \sum_{w = (v_1, \ldots, v_N) \in W, s(w) = N - i} \binom{\sum_n v_n}{v_1, \ldots, v_N} \cdot \left(\prod_{n=1}^{N} f(n)^{v_n} \right). \quad (1)$$

The capacity loss L can now be approximated by

$$L = \frac{1}{N} \sum_{i \in I} P(i)i. \tag{2}$$

The reason that this is an approximation rather than an exact result is that we assume that the fractions of time that i processors are idle for $i \in I$, are equal.

Equations (1) and (2) give a procedure for computing the approximation of the capacity loss, but for large values of N and a large number of possible job sizes this procedure is time-consuming. Therefore, we now present a simple approximation of L in the case of a single cluster with the FCFS scheduling scheme.

The approximation simply consists in assuming that the $P(i)$ are proportional to the first factor, $1 - F(i)$, in (1), which amounts to assuming that the value of the summation in (1) is the same for all $i \in I$. The approximated capacity loss is then given by

$$L = \frac{1}{N} \cdot \frac{\sum_{i \in I}(1 - F(i))i}{\sum_{i \in I}(1 - F(i))}. \tag{3}$$

Let's now assume that the job size is uniformly distributed on the interval $[n_1, n_2]$, with $0 < n_1 < n_2 \leq N$. Then we have $I \subset \{0, 1, \ldots, n_2 - 1\}$. When the interval $[n_1, n_2]$ is large or n_2 is much smaller than N, the set I will not be much different from $\{0, 1, \ldots, n_2 - 1\}$, and we assume equality below. A straightforward computation shows that (3) can then be written as

$$L = \frac{1}{N} \cdot \frac{n_2^3 - n_1^3 + 3n_1^2 - n_2 - 2n_1}{3n_2^2 - 3n_1^2 + 3n_2 + 3n_1}. \tag{4}$$

In particular, when $n_1 = 1$, (4) yields

$$L = \frac{n_2 - 1}{3N}, \tag{5}$$

and so

$$\rho_m = \frac{3N - n_2 + 1}{3N}. \tag{6}$$

We have validated the approximation of (3) with two different kinds of simulations. The first kind consists of filling a single bin of size N with items of sizes drawn from the job-size distribution in the order they are drawn, until the next job does not fit. All results for simulating bin filling reported in this section give averages for $10,000$ simulation runs. The second kind is by simulating the queueing model defined in Sect. 2 and finding the utilization when the average response time is at least $1,500$ time units (the average service time is put to 1 time unit; for more on the simulations see Sect. 4). Of course, simulating bin filling is much easier than trying to simulate a queueing model close to its maximal utilization. In the latter case, it is very difficult to find out whether the simulation is still in its transient phase, and programming difficulties like running out of space for datastructures such as job queues may arise.

In Table 1 we compare the approximation and the two sets of simulation results for a cluster of 32 processors and for different uniform job-size distributions. Overall, the results agree very well, except when the interval of job sizes is rather small and the job sizes are large relative to 32. Figure 2 shows the results of simulating the queueing model for uniform job sizes on $[1, 16]$ in a 32-processor cluster, with 95% confidence intervals, and may be compared with the entry for $n_1 = 1, n_2 = 16$ in Table 1.

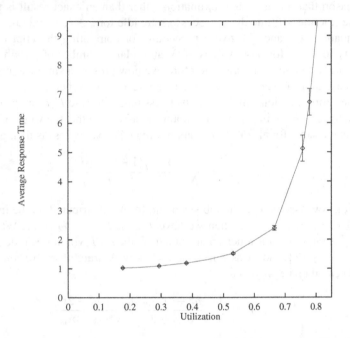

Fig. 2. The response time for a 32-processor single cluster, with job requests uniformly distributed in [1,16], for the FCFS policy.(The bars show the 95% confidence intervals)

In Table 2 we compare the approximation with only bin-filling simulations when the job sizes have a (truncated) geometric distribution on the interval $[1, 32]$ in a 32-processor cluster. In this distribution, $f(n)$ is proportional to q^n for some value q with $0 < q < 1$. This distribution gives a larger proportion of small jobs, a phenomenon that has been observed in actual systems [9], [13].

3.3 Capacity Loss in Multiclusters

For multiclusters, we have only performed a few bin-filling simulations for uniform distributions of the size of job components, for both ordered and unordered requests. It is not generally true that a multicluster performs better with unordered requests than with ordered requests. In fact, when the different job components of unordered requests all have to go to distinct clusters, First Fit may cause a much larger capacity loss than ordered requests experience because the first cluster fills up more rapidly than the last, until at some point it cannot accommodate any component of the next job. In all our

Table 1. The capacity loss in a cluster with 32 processors and with a uniform job-size distribution on the interval $[n_1, n_2]$.

job size		capacity loss		
n_1	n_2	approximation	simulation bin filling	simulation queueing model
1	4	0.031	0.031	0.033
1	5	0.042	0.042	0.044
1	13	0.125	0.124	0.138
1	16	0.156	0.154	0.166
4	5	0.056	0.049	0.052
4	13	0.132	0.132	0.145
4	16	0.163	0.159	0.175
5	13	0.137	0.137	0.150
5	16	0.166	0.163	0.178
13	16	0.212	0.094	0.095

Table 2. The capacity loss in a cluster with 32 processors and with a (truncated) geometric job-size distribution on the interval $[1, 32]$ with parameter q.

	capacity loss	
q	approximation	simulation bin filling
0.95	0.272	0.254
0.90	0.215	0.211
0.85	0.163	0.161
0.80	0.122	0.123
0.75	0.093	0.091
0.70	0.073	0.074
0.65	0.058	0.058
0.60	0.047	0.046
0.55	0.038	0.039
0.50	0.031	0.032

queueing-model simulations in Sect. 4 (in which First Fit is used) the performance with unordered requests is better than with ordered requests, which is in agreement with the results of the bin-filling simulations shown in Table 3, which presents the maximal utilization ρ_m for sets of parameters that are also used in Sect. 4.

When we use Worst Fit instead of First Fit for unordered requests (job components in decreasing order of size go to distinct clusters in decreasing order of the numbers of idle

Table 3. The maximal utilization in a multicluster with 4 clusters of 8 processors each with a uniform job-component-size distribution on the interval $[n_1, n_2]$, for ordered (O) and unordered (U) requests (First Fit, distinct clusters). These results are obtained with bin-filling simulations.

job size		maximal utilization	
n_1	n_2	O	U
1	4	0.685	0.722
1	8	0.578	0.608

Table 4. The capacity loss in a multicluster with C clusters of 32 processors each with a uniform job-component-size distribution on the interval $[n_1, n_2]$, for ordered (O) and unordered (U) requests (Worst Fit, distinct clusters). These results are obtained with bin-filling simulations.

job size		capacity loss				
n_1	n_2	$C = 1$	$C = 4$		$C = 10$	
			O	U	O	U
1	4	0.031	0.146	0.049	0.198	0.053
1	5	0.042	0.172	0.063	0.229	0.067
1	13	0.124	0.326	0.177	0.411	0.177
1	16	0.154	0.363	0.219	0.444	0.229
4	5	0.049	0.106	0.041	0.146	0.029
4	13	0.132	0.282	0.181	0.363	0.199
4	16	0.159	0.329	0.230	0.371	0.282
5	13	0.137	0.270	0.164	0.358	0.158
5	16	0.163	0.317	0.242	0.342	0.303
13	16	0.094	0.094	0.094	0.094	0.094

processors), we can expect that the performance for unordered requests is always better than for ordered requests. In Table 4 we present some results of bin-filling simulations that confirm this expectation.

4 Simulating Co-allocation

In order to estimate the performance of multicluster systems such as the DAS, for different structures and sizes of requests, we modeled the corresponding queuing systems and studied their behaviour using simulations. The simulation programs were implemented using the CSIM simulation package [4]. Simulations were performed for a single-cluster system with 32 processors and for a multicluster system with 4 clusters of 8 nodes each. We varied the distribution of the number of processors requested by jobs by changing the interval from which it was generated, in order to study the influence it has on the performance. Simulations were made for job component sizes uniformly distributed on the intervals $[1, 4]$ and $[1, 8]$ for the multicluster system. The sizes of the total requests in the single-cluster system with 32 processors we use for comparison, are the sum of 4 numbers uniformly distributed on these intervals.

In all the simulations, the mean of the service time was maintained constant, equal to 1, and the interarrival time was varied in order to determine the response time as a function of the utilization of the system, and to approximate the saturation point (see also Sect. 3.3).

The main goal is to evaluate the performance of the model depending on the structure and distribution of the requests. We consider the performance to be better when for the same utilization the average response time is smaller, and when the maximum utilization is larger.

In Sects. 4.1 and 4.2, the scheduling policy used is FCFS. In Sect. 4.3 the two scheduling policies, FCFS and FPFS are compared. Section 4.4 presents the simulation results for a system composed of 4 clusters with 8 processors each, using ordered requests with component sizes obtained from a job-size distribution presented as being more realistic in [9] and [13].

4.1   The Influence of the Structure of the Requests

Figure 3 compares the average response time for the three types of requests, for two different distribution intervals of their component sizes. As expected, the case of total requests gives the best results from the point of view of the maximal utilization of the system and of the response time, because whenever the number of requested processors does not exceed the number of idle ones, it will be possible to accept the job for service. Less good results are given by the case with unordered requests. Still, because of the fact that it gives more freedom to the scheduler than the one with ordered requests, its performance is better than in the ordered case, in all our simulations.

When requests are ordered the results are the worst because the user imposes both the number of nodes received from distinct clusters and the actual cluster for each of those numbers. It causes a lower maximum utilization and a larger average of the response time. Because of the low utilization, the system becomes saturated faster and gets instable for a lower utilization than in the other cases. However, in general there are situations when unordered requests determine a lower maximal utilization than ordered requests (see Sect. 3.3). The saturation point can be estimated in the graphs by the fast growth of the response time depending on the utilization, as the maximum utilization is being reached.

4.2   The Influence of the Size of the Requests

We may expect that the distribution intervals of the request sizes influence the probability of having multiple jobs served simultaneously. When the upper limit of the distribution interval is decreased, the average size of the requests decreases which means that more jobs can be simultaneously admitted for service. As Fig. 3 and Fig. 4 show, this has a positive impact on the maximum utilization of the system, and on the average response time.

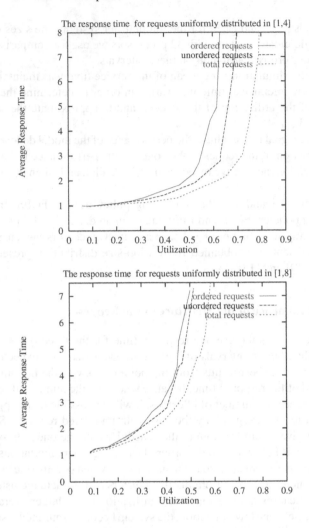

Fig. 3. The influence of the structure of the requests, for the FCFS policy.

Figure 3 shows that for each type of requests, smaller request sizes generate a decrease in the response time. For the distribution in $[1, 8]$, the mean value of the job components sizes is larger than half of the cluster's size, which makes the probability to have more jobs served simultaneously small, especially in the ordered case. Then, on average there is little more than one job in service at a time, which allows a comparison with the M/M/1 queueing model. For the ordered requests case with job components sizes in $[1, 8]$, the system behaves like a single processor, as Fig. 5 indicates. The simulation results prove the comparison to be accurate, the maximum throughput being similar to that of the M/M/1 system.

Figure 4 compares the results for the two distributions of sizes in the cases of ordered and total requests.

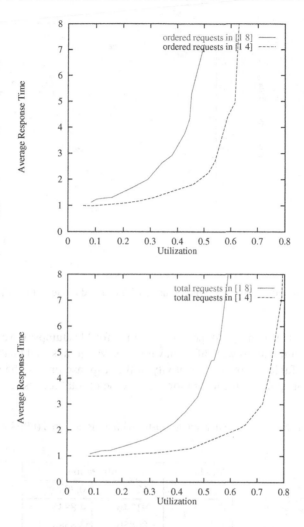

Fig. 4. The influence of the size of the requests for the FCFS policy.

4.3 The Impact of the Scheduling Policy

Another factor which influences the performance of the system is the scheduling policy. As expected, FPFS improves the maximal utilization and the response time compared to FCFS, because it can schedule jobs in an order different from the arrival order. Figure 6 also shows that the influence on performance of the distribution of jobs sizes and of the structure of the requests observed for FCFS is maintained for the FPFS scheme.

For FPFS, increasing the maximum number of times a job can be jumped over, MaxJumps, improves the performance up to a point. When this number is too large, the performance of individual jobs is negatively influenced, and even the effectiveness of the scheme can be affected (MaxJumps $\rightarrow \infty$ would cause starvation, being the same as

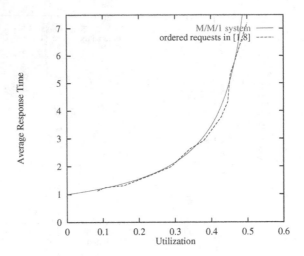

Fig. 5. A comparison between a multicluster with ordered requests in [1,8] and a M/M/1 system.

FPFS without a counter). At the other extreme, for MaxJumps=0 we return to FCFS. We performed simulations with different values for Maxjumps, and finally chose MaxJumps equal to 7. Table 5 show the sensitivity of the response time to the value of MaxJumps for different values of the utilization, in the case of total requests.

Table 5. The response time in a single cluster with 32 Processors (FPFS policy) as a function of MaxJumps.

MaxJumps	utilization	
	0.62	0.78
0	1.91246	4.8845
1	1.80850	3.8588
3	1.80102	3.3412
7	1.70349	2.9125
12	1.69023	2.8249
20	1.68996	2.7771

It can be noticed that for low utilizations, far from the saturation point, improvements given by the scheduling scheme or the distribution and the structure of the requests are very small if any. The differences show only for heavy traffic, when the arrival rate is reasonably high and the job queue is long. For a low arrival rate, under all circumstances we obtain the same results because jobs can be served immediately upon arrival.

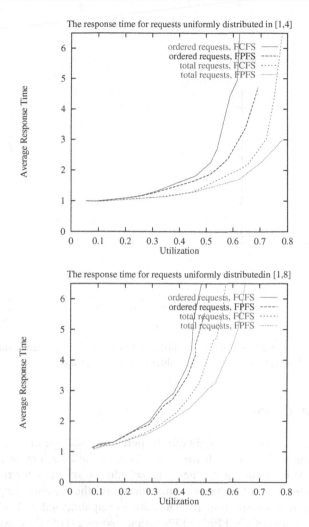

Fig. 6. The influence of the scheduling policy.

4.4   A Realistic Job-Size Distribution

The simulations described in this section use a distribution of the job component sizes that favours small values and powers of 2.

In order to achieve this, with probability $p = 0.7$ the component-size distribution on [1,8] is the normalization of $(q, 3q^2, q^3, 3q^4, \ldots, 3q^N)$, where $N = 8$ and $q = 0.90$. With probability $1 - p$ a job with components uniformly distributed in $[1, 4]$ is generated. Figure 7 shows the variation of the response time for the composed distribution together with the confidence intervals, for a confidence level of 95%.

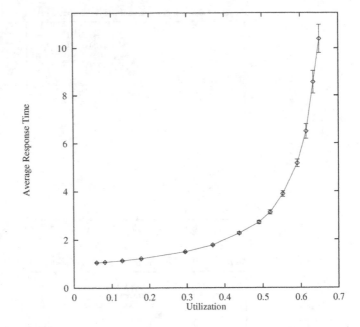

Fig. 7. The response time for a multicluster with ordered requests and with job sizes generated from a distribution that favours small values and powers of 2.

5   Related Work

The problem of scheduling rigid jobs by pure space sharing in a multiprocessor system was also the subject of [1]. It was pointed out that although more complex scheduling schemes are presented in the literature, scheduling schemes for rigid jobs using pure space sharing are still important since these are the schemes implemented on most existing multiprocessor systems. The authors implemented and compared scheduling strategies such as FCFS, FPFS, FPFS with job sorting (both decreasing and increasing), and backfilling. In order to avoid starvation in FPFS and its variations, a time limit is used rather than the maximal number of times a job can be overtaken. Simulation results were combined with performance analysis and experiments in order to verify the effectiveness and the practicality of the schemes. The performance was analysed in terms of processor utilization and stability, using queueing models and the one-dimensional bin-packing problem. As a result of the simulations, the mean response time and the utilization were represented as a function of the system's load. It was concluded that the most effective and the most practical from the schemes analysed are FPFS and Fit Processors Most Processors First Served (FPMPFS). Backfilling can improve performance as well, but it requires a-priori knowledge of the execution times of jobs, which makes it less practical. The performance of the scheduling schemes proved to be sensitive to the distribution of the number of processors requested by a job.

In [13], the optimizations of sorting the job queue according to increasing numbers of processors requested, and of backfilling, are studied with trace-driven simulations. The traces were derived from the logs of three supercomputer installations, amongst which an SP2, and showed relatively large numbers of short jobs and of jobs with sizes that are small or powers of 2. On the SP2, for a sorted job queue, increasing the Maximum Allowable Skipping Count (MASC), a parameter with the same meaning as our MaxJumps, to a large value (simulations were presented with MASC=10, 100, 1000) yielded a considerable decrease of the average turnaround time. This contrasts with our result that the performance of FPFS in a single cluster is not very sensitive to increasing MaxJumps beyond 7. However, on the Paragon, the sensitivity to the MASC was much smaller than on the SP2, so this sensitivity is very dependent on the job mix.

The influence of splitting the processors into groups on the performance of the system was also studied in [3]. A technique for operating system schedulers called processor pool-based scheduling, designed to assign the processes of parallel applications in multiprogrammed, shared-memory NUMA multiprocessors, is presented and evaluated. It is assumed that a job starts as a single process, and that it may grow by starting additional processes. Different policies for the initial placement of the jobs and for the placement of its additional processes when it expands were studied. Since it was assumed that the number of processors required by each job is not known when the application starts, the best strategy for initial placement was found to be Worst Fit, because it leaves the largest room for the growth of jobs inside the pool. The author noted that when the number of processors required is known by the time of the arrival, the problem of choosing which processors to allocate is similar to a bin-packing problem with multiple bins. He studied the importance of application parallelism in determining the pool size, and also the influence of the architectural configuration. The results show that although application parallelism should be considered, the optimal pool size is a function of the system's architecture.

Whereas we approach the problem of the maximal utilization from a more theoretical perspective, in [11] a study of the utilizations as observed in existing supercomputing installations is presented. Experience with a large range of machines over more than a decade shows that employing FCFS results in a $40\% - 60\%$ utilization, that more sophisticated policies such as backfilling give an improvement of about 15 percentage points, and that reducing the maximal job size allowed increases utilization.

Finally, let us briefly mention some of the other research that is being performed in the context of the DAS. Whereas the research presented in this paper is at the operating systems level, the other research on the DAS is done at the level of the run-time system [12] and of the applications [2]. In [12], a library is presented which optimizes the collective communication primitives of MPICH, a widely used version of MPI, in order to achieve fast communications in wide-area systems. Because collective communication algorithms are usually designed for LANs, they do not take into account the high latencies of wide-area links, which negatively influence their performance. The authors designed algorithms which are wide-area optimal in that an operation includes only one wide-area latency, and every data item is sent at most once across each wide-area link. They modified 14 collective operations of MPI and obtained substantial performance improvements over MPICH. As an example, in the case of the MPI_Bcast primitive, the completion time was reduced to 50% for 32 processors divided into 4 clusters and a message size of one byte. This was obtained by sending the message only once to each cluster over the wide-area links, and then broadcasting it inside each cluster on the fast local links.

In [2], several nontrivial algorithms on a multilevel communication structure (LAN clusters connected by a WAN, such as the DAS) were analyzed and several optimization techniques were used to improve their performance. The optimizations either reduced intercluster traffic or masked the effect of intercluster communications and caused a significant improvement. The authors concluded that many medium-grain applications could be optimized to run well on a multilevel, wide-area cluster. One of the optimized applications solves the Traveling Salesman Problem. It was improved by replacing the dynamic work distribution through a centralized queue with a static distribution over the clusters, each of them having its own local queue. For 32 processors divided into 4 clusters, the speedup was 24, compared to 15 for the unoptimized solution.

6   Conclusions

We have proposed a model for scheduling rigid jobs in multicluster systems based on our DAS system, and assessed its performance for different structures and sizes of jobs in terms of average response time as a function of utilization.

We simulated two scheduling schemes, First Come First Served and Fit Processor First Served, and three types of requests. As expected, for both scheduling schemes, the average response time is smaller and the maximum utilization is larger when the requests are more flexible. The best performance was obtained for total requests, when only the total number of processors needed is provided, and when the problem is similar to a single bin-packing problem. For unordered requests, when the numbers of processors to be allocated in separate clusters is specified, the problem is similar to a set of related bin-packing problems, and because there are more restrictions, the performance decreases. It can be improved by changing the policy from FCFS to FPFS, because then the scheduler gets freedom to look further in the queue for jobs which fit, but it will still be below the total requests case. In all our simulations, ordered requests, when the exact clusters from which to satisfy the components of the requests are provided, cause even larger response times, and an even lower maximum utilization. This latter result is not universally valid using First Fit, as we did.

Decreasing the maximal size of the requests improves the performance of the system. This fact is again related to the bin-packing problem, because it is easier to schedule small jobs than large ones.

We derived an approximation for the maximal utilization in single-cluster systems and checked its validity against simulation results.

We plan future work on the effect of communication on the performance of multicluster systems (and of the applications) in comparison with single-cluster systems, because inter-cluster communication is much slower than communication inside the same cluster (in [2] a factor of 50 between these communication speeds was reported). We also intend to do simulations and performance measurements using traces from real multicluster systems (the DAS) instead of theoretical distributions.

References

1. Aida, K., Kasahara, H., Narita, S.: Job Scheduling Scheme for Pure Space Sharing Among Rigid Jobs. Job Scheduling Strategies for Parallel Processing, Lecture Notes in Computer Science **1459** (1998) 98–121
2. Bal, H.E., Plaat, A., Bakker, M.G., Dozy, P., Hofman, R.F.H.: Optimizing Parallel Applications for Wide-Area Clusters. Proceedings of the 12th International Parallel Processing Symposium (IPPS'98) (1998) 784–790
3. Brecht, T.B.: An Experimental Evaluation of Processor Pool-Based Scheduling for Shared-Memory NUMA multiprocessors. Job Scheduling Strategies for Parallel Processing, Lecture Notes in Computer Science **1291** (1997) 139–165
4. The CSIM18 Simulation Engine, User's Guide. Mesquite Software, Inc.
5. The Distributed ASCI Supercomputer's site. Http://www.cs.vu.nl/das/
6. Feitelson, D.G., Rudolph, L.: Toward Convergence in Job Schedulers for Parallel Supercomputers. Job Scheduling Strategies for Parallel Processing, Lecture Notes in Computer Science **1162** (1996) 1–26
7. Feitelson, D.G., Rudolph, L.: Theory and Practice in Parallel Job Scheduling. Job Scheduling Strategies for Parallel Processing, Lecture Notes in Computer Science **1291** (1997) 1–34
8. Feitelson, D.G., Jette, M.A.: Improved Utilization and Responsiveness with Gang Scheduling. Job Scheduling Strategies for Parallel Processing, Lecture Notes in Computer Science **1291** (1997) 238–261
9. Feitelson, D.G.: Packing Schemes for Gang Scheduling. Job Scheduling Strategies for Parallel Processing, Lecture Notes in Computer Science **1162** (1996) 89–110
10. The Globus site. Http://www.globus.org
11. Patton Jones, J., Nitzberg, B.: Scheduling for Parallel Supercomputing: A Historical Perspective of Achievable Utilization. Job Scheduling Strategies for Parallel Processing, Lecture Notes in Computer Science **1659** (1999) 1–16
12. Kielmann, T., Hofman, R.F.H., Bal, H.E., Plaat, A., Bhoedjang, R.A.F.: MagPIe: MPI's Collective Communication Operations for Clustered Wide Area Systems. ACM SIGPLAN Symposium on Principles and Practice of Parallel Programming (PPoPP'99) (1999) 131–140
13. Subhlok, J., Gross, T., Suzuoka, T.: Impact of Job Mix on Optimizations for Space Sharing Schedulers. Supercomputing '96 (1996)

Load Balancing for Minimizing Execution Time of a Target Job on a Network of Heterogeneous Workstations

S.-Y. Lee and C.-H. Cho

Department of Electrical and Computer Engineering
Auburn University
Auburn, AL 36849
sylee@eng.auburn.edu

Abstract. A network of workstations (NOWs) may be employed for high performance computing where execution time of a target job is to be minimized. Job arrival rate and size are "random" on a NOWs. In such an environment, partitioning (load balancing) a target job based on only the first order moments (means) of system parameters is not optimal. In this paper, it is proposed to consider the second order moments (standard deviations) also in load balancing in order to minimize execution time of a target job on a set of workstations where the round-robin job scheduling policy is adopted. It has been verified through computer simulation that the proposed static and dynamic load balancing schemes can significantly reduce execution time of a target job in a NOWs environment, compared to cases where only the means of the parameters are used.

Key Words: Dynamic load balancing, Execution time, Network of workstation, Round-robin job scheduling, Standard deviation, Static load balancing, Stochastic model

1 Introduction

A network of workstations (NOWs), or computers, is being employed as a high performance distributed computing tool in an increasing number of cases [1] [2]. Accordingly, using a NOWs efficiently for speeding up various applications has become an important issue. In particular, load balancing has a significant effect on performance one can achieve on a NOWs environment. The issue of load balancing in general is not new. Many researchers have investigated various aspects of load balancing for quite long a time [3][4][5][6][7][8][9][10].

There were many parameters and characteristics considered in load balancing. They include processor speed, job arrival rate and size, communication among jobs (or subtasks), homogeneity (or heterogeneity) of system, load balancing overhead, specific characteristics of a job, etc. In most of the previous work [11][12], only the *means* of such parameters were used in load balancing. However, a parameter may have the same mean for all workstations, but quite

D.G. Feitelson and L. Rudolph (Eds.): JSSPP 2000, LNCS 1911, pp. 174–186, 2000.

different a variance on a different workstation in a heterogeneous environment. Also, in many cases [13][14][15], the emphasis was on balancing job distribution rather than minimizing execution time of a *target* job.

There is a feature of NOWs, which distinguishes it from other high performance computing platforms, especially dedicated tightly-coupled multiprocessor systems, i.e., *randomness of job arrival* on an individual workstation. This is mainly due to the fact that each workstation is usually shared by multiple independent users who submit their jobs at any time. Also, the size of a job is random. This randomness in job arrival and size makes the number of jobs sharing (the processor on) a workstation time-dependent. That is, the number of jobs on a workstation is to be modelled as a random variable. When the processor is shared among jobs in a round-robin fashion, the amount of work completed in each job during a time interval depends on (e.g., inversely proportional to) the number of jobs (sharing the processor) in that interval. On a network of such workstations, distributing (load balancing) a target job considering only the mean of the number of jobs on each workstation does not achieve the minimum possible execution time. As will be shown later, not only the mean but also the standard deviation of the number of jobs affects execution time of a job on a workstation. Therefore, in order to minimize execution time of a target job, it is necessary to take into account the standard deviation of the number of jobs on each workstation in addition to its mean in load balancing.

In this paper, as a first step toward developing an efficient load balancing scheme, it is shown analytically and demonstrated via simulation that the second order moments as well as the first order moments of parameters are to be used to minimize execution time of a target job on a network of heterogeneous workstations. Workstations are considered to be heterogeneous when the mean and standard deviation of the number of jobs vary with workstation. Each workstation is time-shared by multiple jobs, i.e., multitasking. In this early study, it is assumed that a target job can be arbitrarily partitioned for load balancing and communication is not required among subtasks.

The main contributions of this work are (i) derivation of analytic formulas of performance measures used in load balancing, (ii) design of static and dynamic load balancing schemes for minimizing execution time of a target job, and (iii) showing that a load balancing scheme utilizing the standard deviations as well as the means of parameters can outperform those considering the means only.

In Section 2, a stochastic model of workstations is described. In Section 3, a set of measures is derived analytically on a single workstation, which are to be used for load balancing on multiple workstations. In Section 4, the proposed static and dynamic load balancing strategies are described. In Section 5, early results from computer simulation are discussed to validate the proposed strategies. In Section 6, a conclusion is provided with remarks on the future directions.

2   A Stochastic Model of Workstations

Glossary
The following notations are adopted in this paper.

W the number of workstations
W_i workstation i
X the size of a target job to be distributed
X_i the portion of X assigned to W_i
a_i the number of jobs (random variable) arrived in an interval on W_i
A_i the mean of a_i
σ_{a_i} the standard deviation of a_i
n_i the number of jobs (random variable) in an interval on W_i, excluding those arriving in the current interval
N_i the mean of n_i
σ_{n_i} the standard deviation of n_i
s_i the size of job (random variable) arriving at W_i
S_i the mean of s_i
σ_{s_i} the standard deviation of s_i
μ_i the service rate (computing power) of W_i
t_i execution time (random variable) measured in intervals on W_i
T_i the mean of t_i
σ_{t_i} the standard deviation of t_i
O_c overhead involved in checking load distribution
O_r overhead involved in redistributing load
$E[Z]$ expectation of Z

When a variable is to be distinguished for each time interval, a superscript with parentheses will be used, e.g., $a_i^{(j)}$ denotes a_i for the *jth* interval. The subscript of a random variable, which is used to distinguish workstations, is omitted when there is no need for distinction, e.g., a single workstation or when it does not vary with workstation.

Service Policy
A time *interval* is a unit of time for scheduling jobs (sharing the processor) on a workstation. All time measures are expressed in intervals. It is assumed that each workstation adopts a round-robin scheduling policy. A workstation (processor) spends, on each job in an interval, an amount of time which is inversely proportional to the number (n_i) of jobs sharing the workstation in that interval. That is, $\frac{\mu_i}{n_i}$ is allocated for each job in an interval on workstation i (denoted by W_i) where μ_i is *the service rate* of W_i. Those jobs arrived in an interval start to be serviced (processed) in the following interval without any distinction depending on their arrival times (as long as they arrive in the same interval). It is to be noted that n_i includes all jobs arrived but not completed by I_{i-1}.

Job Arrival

Jobs are submitted at random time instances and, therefore, the number of jobs arriving at a workstation in an interval may be modelled by a random variable denoted by a_i. *The mean and standard deviation* of a_i are denoted by A_i and σ_{a_i}, respectively.

Job Size

The size of a job varies with job and may have a certain distribution with a mean (S_i) and a standard deviation (σ_{s_i}). It is assumed that the job size is independent of the job arrival rate.

Overheads

Loads on workstations are checked to determine if load balancing is to be done. It is assumed that, given a number of workstations, there is a fixed amount of overhead, O_c, for checking information such as the remaining portion of X_i on W_i, and also a constant overhead, O_r, for redistributing the remaining X over workstations when it is decided to perform load balancing.

The job arrival rate and job size will be referred to as *system parameters*. The distributions of the system parameters may be known in some cases. Or their means and standard deviations can be estimated from a given network of workstations. Also, n_i can be directly monitored in practice. It needs to be noted that the proposed load balancing schemes do not assume any particular distribution of each of the system parameters.

In the model adopted in this paper, workstations are independent of each other in terms of the system parameters, as in most of real networks of workstations. The issue addressed is how to distribute a target job over a certain number of such workstations in order to minimize its parallel execution time.

3   Performance Measures on a Workstation

In this section, certain (performance) measures on a single workstation, to be used in the proposed load balancing schemes for multiple workstations, are derived.

The job of which execution time is to be minimized is referred to as *target job*. When the load characteristics (more specifically, the means and standard deviations of the system parameters) do not vary with time on a workstation, it is said that the workstation is in "steady state". When they vary with time, the workstation is said to be in "dynamic state".

3.1   Number of Jobs

The number of jobs, $n^{(j)}$, may be related to the job arrival rate, $a^{(j)}$, as follows.

$$n^{(j)} = 1 + a^{(j-1)} + (n^{(j-1)} - 1)p^{(j-1)} \tag{1}$$

where $p^{(j-1)}$ is the probability that a job in the $(j-1)th$ interval is carried over to the jth interval and the first term (of 1) corresponds to the target job.

Noting that $E[n^{(j)}] = E[n^{(j-1)}] = N$, and letting P denote the steady state value of $p^{(j)}$ which depends on μ and the distributions of $a^{(j)}$ and $s^{(j)}$, from Equation 1,

$$N = 1 + \frac{A}{1 - P} \tag{2}$$

Also, the standard deviation of $n^{(j)}$ can be derived as follows.

$$\sigma_n = \sqrt{E[(n^{(j)} - N)^2]} = \frac{\sigma_a}{1 - P} \tag{3}$$

3.2   Execution Time

In the jth interval, the target job (any job) is processed by the amount of $\frac{\mu}{n^{(j)}}$ for all j. If it takes t intervals to complete the target job,

$$\sum_{i=1}^{t} \frac{\mu}{n^{(i)}} = X. \tag{4}$$

Let's express $n^{(j)}$ as $N + \Delta n^{(j)}$. Then, $E[\Delta n^{(j)}] = 0$ since $E[n^{(j)}] = N$, and $E[(\Delta n^{(j)})^2] = \sigma_n^2$. Then, $\frac{1}{n^{(j)}}$ can be approximated by ignoring the higher order terms beyond the second order term as follows.

$$\frac{1}{n^{(j)}} = \frac{1}{N + \Delta n^{(j)}} \approx \frac{1}{N}\left(1 - \frac{\Delta n^{(j)}}{N} + \left(\frac{\Delta n^{(j)}}{N}\right)^2\right) \tag{5}$$

By taking $E[\ ]$ (expectation) on both sides of Equation 4 with Equation 5 incorporated into, the mean of execution time of the target job, T, can be derived.

$$T = \frac{NX}{\mu\left(1 + \frac{\sigma_n^2}{N^2}\right)} \tag{6}$$

Note that T depends on not only N but also σ_n both of which in turn depend on the standard deviations as well as the means of the system parameters, A, σ_a, S, and σ_s (and of course μ). Note that execution time of a target job on a workstation with a round-robin job scheduling decreases as variation (σ_n) in the number of jobs increases.

In order to derive the standard deviation of execution time, let $\Delta X^{(j)}$ denote a portion of X that is processed (completed) in the jth interval. Then $\Delta X^{(j)} = \frac{\mu}{N + \Delta n^{(j)}}$. Following the similar approximation used to obtain T, the standard deviation, $\sigma_{\Delta X}$, of ΔX can be shown to be $\frac{\mu \sigma_n}{N^2}$. Now, assuming "uncorrelatedness" of $\Delta X^{(j)}$ between intervals, the standard deviation, σ_X, of the amount of target job processed over T intervals (which is the mean execution time of the target job) can be easily shown to be $\sqrt{T}\sigma_{\Delta X}$. Finally, the standard deviation of execution time of a target job may be derived (approximated) by dividing σ_X by the mean processing speed which is $\frac{X}{T}$ and using Equation 6. That is,

$$\sigma_t = \frac{\sigma_X T}{X} = \sqrt{T} \frac{\frac{\sigma_n}{N}}{1 + \frac{\sigma_n^2}{N^2}} \tag{7}$$

4 Load Balancing over Heterogeneous Workstations

4.1 Static Load Balancing

In the proposed static load balancing scheme, a target job is partitioned such that the fraction of X assigned to W_i for $i = 1, \cdots, W$ is inversely proportional to the expected execution time of X on W_i where W is the number of workstations available for X. Let T_i denote execution time of the target job on W_i (i.e., when W_i only is employed for the entire X). Then,

$$T_i = \frac{N_i X}{\mu_i \left(1 + \frac{\sigma_{n_i}^2}{N_i^2}\right)} \quad \text{for } i = 1, \cdots, W. \tag{8}$$

Let X_i denote the size of the portion of X to be assigned to W_i. Then, X_i is determined as follows.

$$X_i = \frac{\frac{X}{T_i}}{\sum_{i=1}^{W} \frac{1}{T_i}} \tag{9}$$

Note that, even when N_i is the same for all i, X would not be distributed evenly unless σ_{n_i} is constant for all i. This load balancing strategy assigns more work to a workstation with a larger variation in the number of jobs on it when the average number of jobs is the same for all workstations. Suppose that $N_1 = N_2 = 2$, $\sigma_{n_1} = 0$, and $\sigma_{n_2} > 0$ (say, n_2 alternates between 1 and 3). Then, a target job would be processed at the average rate of $\frac{\mu}{2}$ on W_1 while at the average rate of $\frac{\mu}{1} + \frac{\mu}{3} = \frac{2\mu}{3}$ on W_2. Therefore, a larger portion of the target is to be assigned to W_2 which has a larger variation in the number of jobs.

4.2 Dynamic Load Balancing

Two essential issues in dynamic load balancing are how load should be redistributed (redistribution of a target job) and how frequently load distribution is to be checked (determination of checking point).

Redistribution. Let $X_{i.rem}$ denote the size of the remaining portion of a target job on W_i before load balancing at a checking point. If load balancing (redistribution) is not done at the checking point, the expected completion time of the target job would be $max_i\{\ T_{i.rem}\ \}$ where $T_{i.rem}$ is computed using Equation 6. That is,

$$T_{i.rem} \;=\; \frac{N_i X_{i.rem}}{\mu_i \left(1\ +\ \frac{\sigma_{n_i}^2}{N_i^2}\right)} \qquad \text{for}\ \ i = 1, \cdots, W \qquad (10)$$

Now, if load balancing is to be done at the checking point, the total remaining job, of which size is $X_{rem} = \sum_I X_{i.rem}$, is redistributed over W_i according to Equation 9. That is, $X'_{i.rem} \;=\; \dfrac{\frac{X_{rem}}{T_{i.rem}}}{\sum_{i=1}^{W} \frac{1}{T_{i.rem}}}$ where $X'_{i.rem}$ is the size of target job (portion) to be assigned to W_i after load balancing. The expected execution time of $X'_{i.rem}$ on W_i is denoted by $T'_{i.rem}$. Then, note that $T'_{i.rem} = T'_{j.rem}$ for all i, j since load has been balanced.

The expected reduction, ΔT, in execution time of the target job can be expressed as

$$\Delta T \;=\; max_i\{\ T_{i.rem}\ \} \;-\; T'_{1.rem} \;-\; O_r \qquad (11)$$

where O_r is the overhead for redistribution.

Load balancing (redistribution) is carried out only when the expected benefit (reduction in execution time, ΔT) exceeds a certain threshold.

Determination of Checking Point. In order to minimize execution time of a target job, it is necessary to minimize the duration in which any W_i is idle (does not work on the target job) before the target job is completed on all W_i. Hence, the load distribution is to be checked before any of W_i becomes idle while the others still work on the target job.

The standard deviation, $\sigma_{t'_{i.rem}}$, of execution time to complete $X'_{i.rem}$ can be derived using Equation 7. A reasonable estimate of the "highly likely" earliest completion time on W_i may be approximated to be $T'_{i.rem} \;-\; h\sigma_{t'_{i.rem}}$ where h is a tuning factor close to 1.

Then, the next checking point, T_{check}, measured with respect to the current checking point is set as follows.

$$T_{check} \;=\; min_i\{\ T'_{i.rem} - h\sigma_{t'_{i.rem}}\ \} \qquad (12)$$

That is, in the proposed dynamic load balancing scheme, it is attempted to check load distribution before any of W_i completes its execution of target job ($X'_{i.rem}$). Note that once a W_i completes $X'_{i.rem}$ it will not be utilized for the target job at least until next checking point.

5   Simulation Results and Discussion

A computer simulation has been carried out in order to verify the reduction in execution time of a target job, which can be achieved by considering the second order moments (standard deviations) as well as the means of system parameters for load balancing on a network of heterogeneous workstations. Some of the early results are provided in this paper.

5.1   Simulation

In this simulation, three different distributions, i.e., exponential, uniform, and truncated Gaussian distributions, have been considered for each of the job inter-arrival time and the job size. Since similar trends have been observed for all three distributions, only the results for the (truncated) Gaussian distribution are provided in this paper. The proposed load balancing schemes have been tested for a wide range of each parameter. The program was run multiple times in each test case, each with a different seed, and then results (execution time of a target job) were averaged.

The proposed static and dynamic load balancing schemes ("S_P" and "D_P" which reads "static proposed" and "dynamic proposed", respectively) are compared to other approaches, i.e., "S_E" (Static_Even) which distributes a target job *evenly* in the static load balancing and "S_M" (Static_Mean) and "D_M" (Dynamic_Mean) which use only the means (N_i) of the number of jobs in the static and dynamic load balancing, respectively.

In the cases of dynamic load balancing, the overhead, O_c, for checking load distribution is added to the execution time for each checking point. If load is redistributed, O_r (redistribution overhead) is also added (for each redistribution).

5.2   Results and Discussion

Execution time is measured in intervals. In addition to execution time of a target job, the measure of "relative improvement" is used in comparison, which is defined as $RI\_S = \frac{T_{S\_M} - T_{S\_P}}{T_{S\_M}}$ for the static load balancing where T_{S_M} and T_{S_P} are execution times of a target job achieved by S_M and S_P, respectively. Similarly, the relative improvement is defined for the dynamic load balancing as $RI\_D = \frac{T_{D\_M} - T_{D\_P}}{T_{D\_M}}$ where T_{D_M} and T_{D_P} are execution times of a target job achieved by D_M and D_P, respectively.

Results for cases where workstations are in the steady state are discussed first.

In Figure 1, execution time of a target job on a single workstation is plotted as a function of σ_n for different N in a steady state. Obviously, T increases as N increases. More importantly, as discussed in Section 3.2, T clearly shows its dependency on σ_n and decreases as σ_n increases.

In Figure 2, (parallel) execution time of a target job in steady states on two workstations is compared among the five load balancing schemes mentioned above. First, it can be seen that, as expected, the proposed load balancing schemes (S_P and D_P) work better than the other schemes, confirming that the second order moments of the system parameters are to be considered in load balancing in order to minimize the execution time of a target job. Second, it needs to be noted that S_P achieves shorter execution times than D_P. This

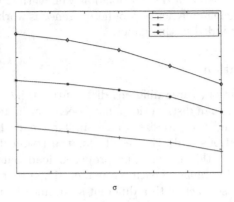

Fig. 1. Execution time of X on one workstation where $\mu=100$ and $X=1000$.

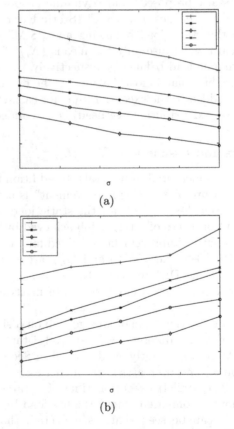

Fig. 2. Parallel execution time on two workstations where $\mu=100$, $A_1=1$, $A_2=2$, $S_1=10$, $S_2=20$, and $X=2000$. (a) $\sigma_{a_1}=53\%$, $\sigma_{s_1}=30\%$, $\sigma_{s_2}=48\%$, (b) $\sigma_{a_1}=53\%$, $\sigma_{a_2}=45\%$, $\sigma_{s_1}=30\%$

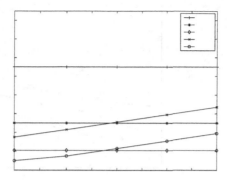

Fig. 3. Parallel execution time on two workstations where $\mu=100$, $A_1=1$, $A_2=2$, $S_1=20$, $S_2=30$, $X=2000$, $\sigma_{a_1}=90\%$, $\sigma_{a_2}=0\%$, $\sigma_{s_1}=96\%$, $\sigma_{s_2}=96\%$.

is due to the fact that in a steady state the load characteristics do not vary in the long term and therefore the one-time initial load balancing (by S_P) is good enough, and that D_P pays the overhead of checking and balancing during execution. Third, an increase in σ_a leads to a shorter execution time (Figure 2-(a)) while that in σ_s to a longer execution time (Figure 2-(b)). This is because an increase in σ_a causes a larger increase in σ_n than in N, leading to a shorter execution time (refer to Equation 6). However, increasing σ_s has an opposite effect.

In Figure 3, dependency of execution time on the load checking and redistribution overheads is analyzed in a steady state. As shown in the figure, when the overheads are relatively low, D_P can still achieve a shorter execution time than that by S_P. However, as the overheads become larger, they start to offset the gain by the dynamic load balancing and eventually make D_P perform worse than S_P.

The relative improvement by S_P over S_M is considered in Figure 4-(a), and that by D_P over D_M in Figure 4-(b). It can be seen in both cases that the relative improvement increases as the difference in σ_a or σ_s between two workstations becomes larger. This is due to the fact that the larger the difference is, the less accurate the load balancing by S_M becomes.

Effects of the number of workstations, W, are analyzed for steady states in Figure 5 where σ_{a_gi} and σ_{s_si} are σ_a and σ_s of the ith group of workstations. It can be observed that the relative improvement by S_P over S_M increases with the number of workstations. It increases more rapidly when the difference in either σ_a or σ_s is larger. Again, these observations stem from the fact that the load balancing by S_P becomes more (relatively) accurate than that by S_M as the difference in the second order moments between groups of workstations grows.

Now, a case where a system parameter varies with time is considered, i.e. dynamic state. In Figure 6, σ_{a_1} varies with time such that its deviation from the

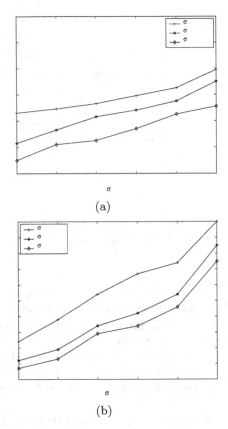

Fig. 4. (a) Relative improvement, RI_S, by S_P over S_M on two workstations. $\mu=100$, $A_1=0.5$, $A_2=0.5$, $S_1=40$, $S_2=40$, $X=3000$, $\sigma_{a_1}=0\%$, $\sigma_{s_1}=100\%$, (b) Relative improvement, RI_D, by D_P over D_M on two workstations. $\mu=100$, $A_1=2$, $A_2=2$, $S_1=20$, $S_2=20$, $X=16000$, $\sigma_{a_1}=0\%$, $\sigma_{s_1}=96\%$, $O_c=0.1$, $O_r=0.1$.

value used by S_P is changed (larger for Case i with larger i). As expected, the dynamic schemes (D_P and D_M) perform better than the static schemes (S_P and S_M). Also, it is noted that D_P which takes σ_{a_1} into account achieves a shorter execution time compared to D_M. The improvement by D_P over D_M tends to increase with the deviation.

6 Conclusion and Future Study

In this paper, it has been proposed that the second order moments (standard deviations) as well as the first order moments (means) of system parameters be taken into account for load balancing on a time-shared heterogeneous parallel/distributed computing environment. These load balancing schemes which attempt to minimize execution time of a target job have been tested via computer simulation. It has been verified that considering the second order moments also

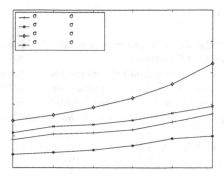

Fig. 5. Relative improvement, RI_S, by S_P over S_M on multiple workstations where $\mu{=}100$, $A_{g1}{=}0.5$, $A_{g2}{=}0.5$, $S_{g1}{=}40$, $S_{g2}{=}40$, $X{=}1500$, $\sigma_{a\_g1}{=}50\%$, $\sigma_{s\_g1}{=}96\%$.

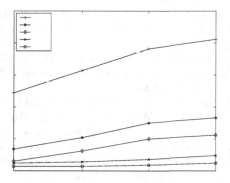

Fig. 6. Parallel execution time on two workstations where $\mu{=}100$, $A_1{=}1$, $A_2{=}2$, $S_1{=}20$, $S_2{=}30$, $X{=}2000$, $\sigma_{a_1}{=}24\%$, $\sigma_{a_2}{=}0\%$, $\sigma_{s_1}{=}0\%$, $\sigma_{s_2}{=}20\%$. σ_{a_1} varies with time where its deviation from the value used by S_P is larger for Case i with larger i.

in both static and dynamic load balancing can lead to a significant reduction in execution time of a target job on a NOWs with a round-robin job scheduling policy adopted in each workstation. The improvement (reduction in execution time of a target job) becomes larger as the difference in the second order moments between workstations or groups of workstations increases. The similar observations have been made for all of the three distributions considered for each system parameter. The proposed schemes are simple and general, and therefore are believed to have a good potential for wide application.

The future study includes consideration of communication among subtasks and job granularity, performance analysis for real workloads, application of the proposed schemes to scheduling multiple (or all) jobs on a NOWs, etc.

References

1. D. Culler, "Parallel Computer Architecture", Morgan Kaufman, 1999.
2. Pf, "In Search of Clusters".
3. G. Cybenko, "Dynamic Load Balancing for Distributed Memory Multiprocessors", *J. Parallel and Distributed Computing*, vol. 7, pp279-301, 1989.
4. C. Polychronopoulos and D. Kuck, "Guided Self-Scheduling Scheme for Parallel Supercomputers", *IEEE Transactions on Computers*, vol. 36, no.12, pp1,425-1,439, December 1987.
5. S. Ranka, Y. Won, and S. Sahni, "Programming a Hypercube Multicomputer", *IEEE Software*, pp69-77, September 1988.
6. M. Maheswaran and H. Siegel, "A Dynamic Matching and Scheduling Algorithm for Heterogeneous Computing Systems", *Proc. Heterogeneous Computing '98*, pp57-69, 1998.
7. M. Cierniak, W. Li, and M.J. Zaki, "Loop Scheduling for Heterogeneity", *Proc. of the 4th IEEE International Symposium High-Performance Distributed Computing*, pp78-85, August 1995.
8. A. Gerasoulis and T. Yang, "On the Granularity and Clustering of Directed Acyclic task graphs", *IEEE Transactions on Parallel and Distributed Systems*, vol. 4, no.6, pp686-701, 1993.
9. S. M. Figueira and F. Berman, "Modeling the Slowdown of Data-Parallel Applications in Homogeneous Clusters of Workstations", *Proc. Heterogeneous Computer Workshop*, pp90-101, 1998.
10. J.C. Jacob and S.-Y. Lee, "Task Spreading and Shrinking on Multiprocessor Systems and Networks of Workstations", *IEEE Transactions on Parallel and Distributed Systems*, vol. 10, no. 10, pp1082-1101, October 1999.
11. E.P. Makatos and T.J. Leblanc, "Using Processor Affinity in Loop Scheduling on Shared-Memory Multiprocessors", *IEEE Transactions on Parallel and Distributed Systems*, vol. 5, no.4, pp379-400, April 1993.
12. S. Subramaniam and D.L. Eager, "Affinity Scheduling of Unbalanced Workloads", *Proc. Supercomputing '94*, pp214-226, 1994.
13. M.-Y. Wu, "On Runtime Parallel Scheduling for Processor Load Balancing", *IEEE Transactions on Parallel and Distributed Systems*, vol. 8, no.2, pp173-186, February 1997.
14. X. Zhang and Y. Yan, "Modeling and Characterizing Parallel Computing Performance On Heterogeneous Networks of Workstations", *Proc. of the 7th IEEE Symp. Parallel and Distributed Processing*, pp25-34, October 1995.
15. B.-R. Tsai and K. G. Shin, "Communication-Oriented Assignment of Task Modules in Hypercube Multicomputers", *Proc. of the 12th International Conference on Distributed Computing Systems*, pp 38-45, 1992.

Adaptive Selection of Partition Size
for Supercomputer Requests

Walfredo Cirne and Francine Berman

Computer Science and Engineering
University of California San Diego
http://apples.ucsd.edu

Abstract. In this paper, we show how application scheduling can be used to reduce the turn-around time of supercomputer jobs. Our approach focuses on the use of **SA**, an AppLeS application scheduler, to adaptively craft the request to be submitted to the supercomputer based on the current state of the system. We demonstrate that **SA** significantly improves a job's turn-around time in a variety of scenarios. We also identify how the state of the system, the characteristics of the job, and the quality of the information made available to **SA** influence its performance.

1 Introduction

In the last decade, parallel supercomputers have emerged as a key platform for high performance computation. In order to promote the performance of fine-grained parallel applications, such machines are almost always space-shared. Each job has dedicated access to some number of the processors that compose the supercomputer. We therefore say that each job runs on its own *partition*.

In such an environment, an arriving job may not find enough processors to execute immediately. When this happens, the arriving job waits until enough resources become available. More precisely, jobs that cannot start immediately are placed in a wait queue, which is controlled by the *supercomputer scheduler*. The supercomputer scheduler's main task is to decide which job in the wait queue is the next to run. In order to make this decision, it typically requires each job to specify n, the number of processors it needs, and t_r, the time requested for execution of the job.

However, many parallel jobs are *moldable*, i.e. they can run over partitions of different sizes. When a moldable job j is to be submitted, the user has to decide which n (out of the set of possible partition sizes) is to be used. The choice of n is important because it affects j's *turn-around time*, i.e. the time elapsed between j's submission and its completion. The turn-around time is calculated by adding *wait time* and *execution time*. In principle, the user is able to evaluate the effect of n on the execution time. It typically diminishes as n grows (at least until a certain value n_{limit}). However, the user cannot in general estimate the wait time because it depends on n, t_r, the supercomputer scheduler, and the current load of the system.

D.G. Feitelson and L Rudolph (Eds.): JSSPP 2000, LNCS 1911, pp. 187-207, 2000.
© Springer-Verlag Berlin Heidelberg 2000

In this paper, we introduce a performance-efficient strategy for choosing n, the number of processors a job requests. This strategy is implemented by **SA**, an AppLeS [2] application scheduler that adaptively crafts the request that submits a given job to the supercomputer. **SA** uses knowledge of how the supercomputer scheduler works, together with information that describes the current state of the system, to adaptively choose which partition size to request. We show that **SA** significantly improves a job's turn-around time, and identify the factors that influence the performance achieved by **SA**. We also establish the maximum improvement that can potentially be achieved by adaptively selecting which request to submit to the supercomputer. Under most scenarios, **SA** delivers a performance improvement that is close to such a maximum.

This paper is organized as follows: Section 2 describes supercomputer scheduling and the **SA** application scheduler. It also states the research questions we intend to address in this paper. Section 3 describes the models and metrics used to investigate these research questions. Section 4 presents and analyzes the results. Section 5 sketches directions for future research, Section 6 discusses related work, and Section 7 concludes this paper by summarizing its results.

2   Scheduling Jobs on Supercomputers

In order to run a job j on a parallel supercomputer, the user submits a request to the supercomputer scheduler that specifies the resources to be allocated to j. Such a request includes n, the number of processors to be allocated to j, and t_r, an upper bound on the execution time of j. Job j runs for $t_e \leq t_r$. The supercomputer scheduler kills j if it runs longer than t_r, therefore enforcing the upper bound.

Job j runs with dedicated access to n processors for t_r time units. However, it might have to wait until such resources become available. Let t_w denote the time elapsed between j's submission and its start (i.e., the time j waits in the system's queue). Define j's *turn-around time*[1] as $t_t = t_w + t_e$. Note that t_t corresponds to the time elapsed between j's submission and its completion. It thus captures the user's view of how long the system takes to run j. Reducing the turn-around time t_t results in faster response to the user and hence is a natural performance optimization goal. In fact, reducing t_t is normally seen as a key goal for supercomputer schedulers. Here we take the complementary approach of trying to reduce the turn-around time t_t at the application level.

The turn-around time t_t depends on the current state of the system, but it can be influenced by the request (n, t_r) that submits j for execution. Jobs frequently are *moldable*, i.e. they can run on partitions of different sizes. This paper explores how to select which partition size to request in order to improve a moldable job's turn-around time.

---

[1] Other authors sometimes refer to turn-around time as *service time* or *response time*.

The execution time t_e generally decreases with the number of processors n allocated to the job. Of course each job has a limit n_{limit} of how many processors it can effectively use, i.e. t_e levels off or even increases for $n > n_{limit}$. But since there is no advantage in requesting $n > n_{limit}$, we don't consider such requests here. Note that increasing n might result in a larger wait time t_w, because more resources have to be available for the job to start. Since t_w depends on the current state of the supercomputer, the best request to submit cannot be statically determined.

We use **SA** (Supercomputer AppLeS) to select which n (and corresponding t_r) should be used to submit a moldable job to the supercomputer. **SA** is based on the AppLeS (Application-Level Scheduling) methodology [2] [3]. AppLeS schedulers use application-specific and dynamic information to craft an adaptive application schedule that can leverage current and forecasted resource capability.

SA determines the partition size n to be requested based information about the algorithm used by the supercomputer scheduler, the current state of the system, and estimates for the execution times of all jobs in the system. Using this information, **SA** *simulates* the submission of all possible requests and then selects the one that delivers the smallest turn-around time. When (i) the execution time estimates of all jobs are perfect, and (ii) the supercomputer scheduler does not allow arriving jobs to affect existing ones, this approach optimally selects the partition size for a given job. However, while assumption (ii) may be true, in practice assumption (i) is not. **SA** uses requested times as estimates for the jobs' execution times, making it usable in practice, but without the guarantee of optimality.

This work investigates, under common supercomputer usage scenarios:

- The performance achieved by **SA**.
- The *maximum improvement* that can be achieved by adaptively selecting the partition size.
- What factors influence **SA** and the maximum improvement.

3   Models and Metrics

We use simulations to tackle the questions stated above. This section describes (i) the models used for the supercomputer and the job, (ii) the information made available to **SA**, and (iii) our performance criteria. Our goal is to reproduce a realistic environment, while capturing enough detail to answer our research questions. To ensure the realism of the environment, we rely as much as possible on real-life submission logs.

3.1 The Supercomputer Model

In order to simulate a supercomputer, we need to define its scheduler, its size (how many processor it has), and its workload (the stream of jobs it is going to process). Consider a supercomputer that uses *conservative backfilling* [10]. Conservative backfilling uses an *allocation list* to maintain, for any given time, which processors are already committed to which jobs. Arriving jobs are put in the first "slot" in which they fit. Whenever an application finishes using less time than it requested, conservative backfilling traverses the wait queue (in submission order) and "promotes" the first job that fits in the just-made-available slot. Of course, this may create another available slot that is backfilled in the same way. The process stops only when no more backfilling can be done. For a more detailed description of conservative backfilling, we refer the reader to [10] and [4].

We employ conservative backfilling as an idealized representative of today's supercomputer schedulers. In practice the behavior of supercomputer schedulers varies from machine to machine. Even when the same scheduling software is used (e.g., Easy [15], Maui [16], and LSF [19]), each site establishes its own policies, causing the behavior of their schedulers to differ. However, almost everywhere backfilling is used to reduce unnecessary idle time. In addition, previous research has shown conservative backfilling to be a good scheduling approach [10]. Note also that conservative backfilling guarantees that arriving jobs don't affect existing ones.

The state of a conservative backfilling scheduler can be summarized by the *availability list*. An availability list contains the number of free processors a machine has over time. For example: [(from time 0, to time 10, 15 processors are available), (from time 10, to time 50, 80 processors are available), (from time 50, to time 210, 0 processors are available), (from time 210, to ∞, 128 processors are available)]. The availability list allows for a very fast implementation of **SA**, which doesn't simulate all possible requests to choose the best, but achieves the same result. Such an implementation evaluates all possible requests by traversing the availability list. Due to space limitations and the fact that both implementation of **SA** produce the same result, we refer the reader to [4] for a thorough description of **SA** based on the availability list.

For the size of the supercomputer and the workload it processes, we use the size of real-life supercomputers as well as the logs of the jobs submitted to them. We decided to use logs because supercomputer behavior is difficult to characterize [9]. The drawback of this approach is that we might be misled by some phenomenon that is particular to the site a log originates. We minimize this risk by using four distinct supercomputer logs. Table 1 summarizes the logs used in this research. The fact that all logs come from an SP2 machine is not significant. The results presented here apply for any distributed-memory parallel computer that serves multiple users via space-sharing.

SA makes its scheduling decisions based on the performance it achieves. We summarize the state of the supercomputer by its *relative load* current state of the system, and thus we expect the system state to influence the $N = J / P$, where J is the number of jobs currently in the system (both running and waiting), and P is the total number of processors in the supercomputer (see Table 1). J is a simple way to gauge the load of the supercomputer. Dividing it by P factors in the size of the supercomputer.

Table 1. Workloads used in this research

Name	Machine	Processors	Jobs	Period
ANL	Argonne National Laboratory SP2	120	5921	Nov 1996 Dec 1996
CTC	Cornell Theory Center SP2	430	60196	Jul 1996 Feb 1997
KTH	Swedish Royal Institute of Technology SP2	100	25954	Nov 1996 Aug 1997
SDSC	San Diego Super-computer Center SP2	128	19405	Jan 1999 May 1999

3.2   The Job Model

SA targets moldable jobs. For each job it schedules, **SA** receives from the user multiple requests that could be used to submit the job. From the set of possible requests, **SA** determines which is the best one to submit according to the current state of the supercomputer. Unfortunately for our study, the submission logs contain only one request per job (namely, the one submitted by the user).

We cope with this limitation by using a model of the speed-up of parallel jobs developed by Downey [7]. Speed-up measures how much faster a job j that uses n processors executes than execution using only one processor. Symbolically: $S(n) = t_e(1) / t_e(n)$. If we know the speed-up function $S(n)$ for our jobs, we can generate multiple possible requests for them. Downey's speedup model uses two parameters: A (the *average parallelism*) and σ (an approximation of the *coefficient of variance in parallelism*). The speed-up of a job is then given by:

$$S(n,A,\sigma) = \begin{cases} \dfrac{An}{A+\sigma(n-1)/2} & (\sigma \leq 1) \wedge (1 \leq n \leq A) \\[2ex] \dfrac{An}{\sigma(A-1/2)+n(1-\sigma/2)} & (\sigma \leq 1) \wedge (A \leq n \leq 2A-1) \\[2ex] A & (\sigma \leq 1) \wedge (n \geq 2A-1) \\[2ex] \dfrac{nA(\sigma+1)}{\sigma(n+A-1)+A} & (\sigma \geq 1) \wedge (1 \leq n \leq A+A\sigma-\sigma) \\[2ex] A & (\sigma \geq 1) \wedge (n \geq A+A\sigma-\sigma) \end{cases}$$

Intuitively speaking, A establishes how many processors a job can use. The larger the value of A, the more processors the job can use. Fig. 1 exemplifies how A affects the speed-up of a job. It fixes $\sigma = 1$ and shows speed-up curves for different values of A.

σ, on the other hand, determines how close to linear the speed-up is. The smaller the σ, the closer to linear the speed-up is. explores the effect of σ on the speed-up behavior. It fixes $A = 60$ and displays speed-up curves for different values of σ.

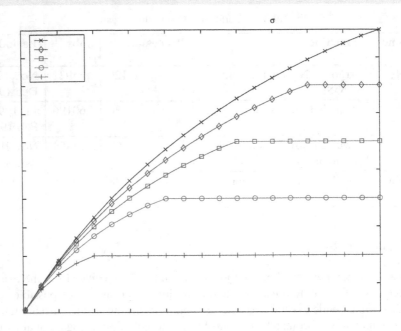

Fig. 1. Downey's speed-up function $S(n, A, \sigma)$ for different values of A (with $\sigma = 1$)

Since we are interested in understanding the performance of **SA** in a variety of conditions, we vary the values of A and σ. We uniformly choose A in the interval [2, 200] and σ in the interval [0, 2]. This gives large coverage over a wide range of parallel jobs. Moreover, experimental determination of values for A and σ have produced values in these ranges [7].

From the workload we can obtain n_u, the number of processors requested by the user, and $t_e(n_u)$, the job's execution time with n_u processors. Note that A, σ, n_u, and $t_e(n_u)$ uniquely determine the sequential execution time of the job $L = t_e(1) = t_e(n_u) \cdot S(n_u, A, \sigma)$. L represents how "large" a job is. The greater the L, the more processing is required to complete the job.

With A, σ and L, we can determine the execution time of the job running over an arbitrary number of processors n by $t_e(n) = \dfrac{L}{S(n, A, \sigma)}$. A, σ, and L therefore characterize the job being scheduled by **SA**.

3.3   Information Available to SA

Many jobs have constraints on how many processors they can use. For example, jobs that process bidimensional data many times require a perfect square number of processors. Moreover, the user has to come up with the submission choices to feed **SA**. These factors suggest that oftentimes **SA** will have only a small number of choices to

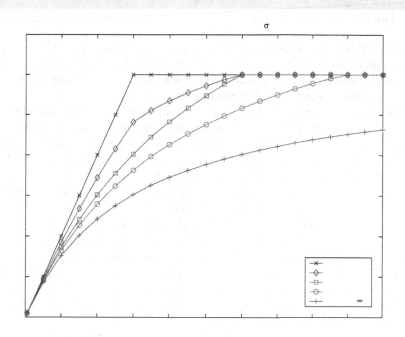

Fig. 2. Downey's speed-up function $S(n, A, \sigma)$ for different values of σ (with $A = 60$)

choose from. Therefore, we focus on the cases in which jobs are presented to **SA** with 3, 5, or 7 possible requests.

Another important aspect of the information available to **SA** is how far apart the choices are. Considering possible partition sizes of 40, 41, and 42 may be very different than having 10, 40, and 70. Hence we also investigate the impact of the *range of choices* on **SA**. We consider choices equally spaced in the range $[n_{min}, n_{max}]$, where n_{min} is uniformly chosen between 1 and n_u, and n_{max} is uniformly chosen between n_u and n_{limit}. n_{limit} is the largest number of processors a job can use, defined to be the smaller of (i) the number of processors in the machine, and (ii) the largest n before the Downey's speed up curve levels off.

Finally, *accuracy* represents a qualitative aspect of the information **SA** receives. Users' estimates are not perfect. We define the accuracy a as the fraction of the requested time that was indeed used by a job. That is, $a = t_e / t_r$. Since jobs cannot run longer then the time they've request, a is always a number between 0 and 1. In our simulations, a is uniformly distributed between 0 and 1, allowing us to investigate the impact of both good and poor information.

The number of choices, the size of their range ($n_{max} - n_{min}$), and the accuracy a are the factors that characterize the information made available to **SA**.

3.4   The Performance Criteria

Turn-around time is a useful metric for a single execution of a job. However multiple executions are necessary to draw statistically valid conclusions, as well as to cover the space of parameters we are investigating. Hence, we need a performance metric that summarizes turn-around times over multiple experiments.

Many researchers have used the *mean* to combine multiple turn-around times into a single metric [1] [4] [11] [14]. However, the *mean turn-around time* can be dominated by large jobs [11]. For example, improving a job's turn-around time from 20000 seconds to 18000 seconds (a 10% improvement) reduces the mean by $2000 / T$, while improving another job's turn-around time from 200 seconds to 100 seconds (a 50% improvement) reduces the mean by $100 / T$, where T is the total number of jobs.

Some authors have addressed this problem by using the *slowdown* $s = t_t / t_e$ instead of the turn-around time [10] [11] [23]. Slowdown provides a measure that is relative to the job's execution time and hence large jobs are not overemphasized in the mean slowdown. However, slowdown is not a metric that adequately represents the user's notion of performance. In our case, in which there are multiple possible requests to submit, one can often improve the slowdown by selecting n_{min}. This results in a large t_e, which often leads to a small slowdown s. The problem is that such a strategy can (and often does) **increase** the turn-around time.

The *geometric mean* equally rewards the improvement in the turn-around time of any job. In fact, recall that $\text{geomean}(x_1,...,x_n) = \sqrt[n]{x_1 \cdot ... \cdot x_n}$ and thus $\dfrac{\text{geomean}(x_1,...,x_n)}{\text{geomean}(y_1,...,y_n)} = \text{geomean}(\dfrac{x_1}{y_1},...,\dfrac{x_n}{y_n})$. Unlike the arithmetic mean, the geometric mean does not favor large jobs. For this reason, the geometric mean is used to aggregate the execution time of the programs that compose the Spec benchmark [22]. We hence use the geometric mean of the turn-around times as our performance criteria.

4   Results

We ran 56000 simulations: 14000 per workload. In each simulation, we randomly chose one job j, generated A, σ, n_{min}, n_{max}, and a as described above, and simulated five strategies for submitting j:

- Using the user's request, i.e. without **SA**.
- Using **SA** with 3 choices for partition sizes.
- Using **SA** with 5 choices for partition sizes.
- Using **SA** with 7 choices for partition sizes.
- Best choice, i.e. we simulate the submission of all 7 choices offered to **SA** and report the best turn-around time among them.

While it is not generally possible to determine the best choice in practice, strategy v establishes the **best** performance **SA** can achieve in our experiments, offering a bound on the *maximum improvement* achievable by adaptively crafting requests to a supercomputer. In order to better assess the maximum improvement, we define the *relative performance* for strategies *ii* to *v* as the ratio of the turn-around obtained by the user's request to the turn-around time achieved the strategy in consideration. The relative performance depicts how many times **SA** improved on the turn-around time. In particular, the relative performance of the best choice expresses the maximum improvement possible in our experiments.

Table 2 shows the overall results for the 56000 simulations. Notice the high maximum improvement of adaptively selecting supercomputer requests: The turn-around time of best choice is around a third of the turn-around time attained by the user's choice, yielding a relative performance of 2.98. Furthermore, **SA** is able to deliver turn-around times close to the best choice: With 7 choices, **SA**'s relative performance reaches 2.78. Even with 3 choices, **SA** delivers a substantial improvement: Its turn-around time is less than half of the turn-around time of user's choice.

Table 2. SA overall results

	User's choice	SA with 3 choices	SA with 5 choices	SA with 7 choices	Best choice
Geometric Mean of the Turn-Around Time (secs)	1259.9	600.2	525.3	453.3	423.6
Relative Performance	-----	2.10	2.40	2.78	2.98

In the following subsections, we investigate how **SA** and the maximum improvement are affected by the various parameters that describe the system, the job, and the information received by **SA**.

4.1   Results by the State of the System

Fig. 3 shows the impact of the relative load N on the results. The experiments are grouped in deciles according to N. Therefore, each data point in the graph averages around 5600 experiments. The values of N on the x-axis show the boundaries of the deciles. That is, the values that surround a given data point establish the range of values averaged by such a point. Unless stated otherwise, the following graphs display the data in the same way.

As expected, the turn-around time increases with N. This is because the more jobs there are in the system, the longer an arriving job has to wait in the queue. The relative performance provides a less intuitive result. It decreases as N increases for both best choice and **SA**. This suggests that adaptively selecting which request to submit becomes less useful as the load in system grows.

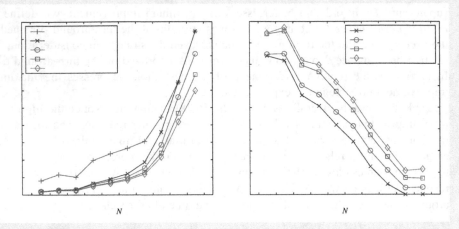

Fig. 3. Results by N, the relative load of the system

4.2 Results by Characteristics of the Job

The job scheduled by **SA** can be characterized by three parameters: the sequential execution time L, the average parallelism A, and the coefficient of variance in the parallelism σ. Recall that L measures the amount of computation j carries, A indicates how many processors j can effectively use, and σ denotes the slope of j's speed-up (the closer σ is to 0, the closer to linear the speed-up is). Fig. 4, Fig. 5, and Fig. 7 show how such parameters affect the performance of **SA** and the maximum improvement achieved by adaptively generating requests.

As one can expect, the larger the L (i.e., the more computation a job carries), the greater the turn-around time. But the wide distribution of L makes it hard to visualize any other patterns in the turn-around time graph. Relative performance provides a more insightful picture. Notice that the relative performance decreases for large values of L, those in 10th decile. For those jobs, the execution time represents a large fraction of the turn-around time, giving less latitude for **SA** to improve the job's performance. Consequently, one would think that the greatest relative performance must occur for small values of L. Somewhat surprisingly, however, this is not the case. As can be seen in the graph, medium values of L (say in the [2000, 50000] range) provide the best relative performance. A closer look at the jobs with small L reveals that most of them have very small turn-around times (up to 300 seconds). We conjecture that small jobs are easier to schedule in the presence of backfilling and thus get through the system quickly, minimizing the benefits of **SA**. Another interesting result is that the smaller the L, the more advantageous it is to have more choices. We are not sure why that is the case.

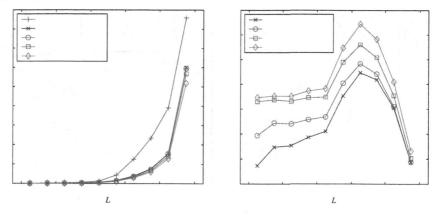

Fig. 4. Results by L

As Fig. 5 shows, the larger the A (i.e., the greater the potential for parallelism in the job), the greater the relative performance achieved by **SA** and the best choice. This behavior seems reasonable because the greater the average parallelism A, the more flexibility **SA** has in selecting a good request, which translates to a greater improvement in the job's turn-around time. Also, the utility of having more choices available to **SA** grows with A.

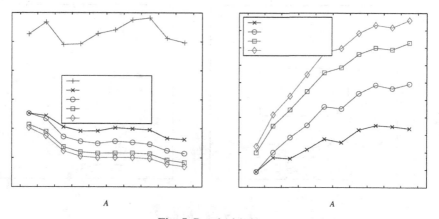

Fig. 5. Results by A

Note that in these experiments the increase in the relative performance slows down for $A \geq 100$. Similarly, the benefit of having more choices available to **SA** grows slower for $A \geq 100$. We believe this is related to the fact the three out of the four supercomputers we simulated have only slightly more processors than this value (see Table 1). To expand on this, consider the CTC results in isolation (the SP2 used there had 430 nodes), as shown in Fig. 6. As can be seen, the relative performance keeps increasing steadily beyond $A = 100$.

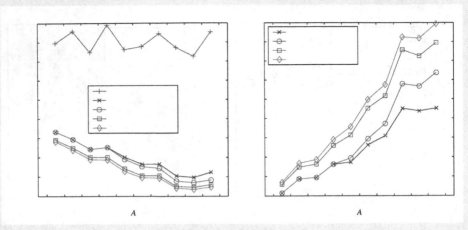

Fig. 6. CTC results by *A*

The results by the coefficient of variance of parallelism σ are very surprising. As Fig. 7 shows, **SA** seems to be completely indifferent to σ. We expected **SA** to perform better with smaller values of σ since these imply a speed-up closer to linear. Further investigations are required to determine why **SA** exhibits such robust performance regarding σ.

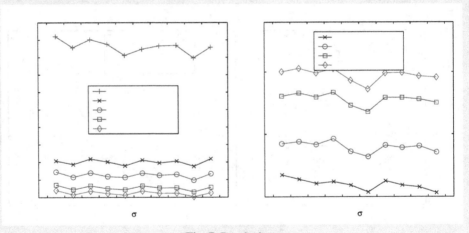

Fig. 7. Results by σ

4.3   Results by Information Available to SA

The information made available to **SA** also impacts its performance. We characterize the amount and quality of such information by (i) the number of choices available to **SA**, (ii) the size of the range of such choices, and (iii) the accuracy of the users' estimates *a*.

The number of choices available to **SA** is an especially important parameter because this information must be provided by the user. We therefore treated the number of choices independently of the other simulation parameters. This allows for the evaluation of the impact of the number of choices as a function of the other parameters. Fig. 3 through Fig. 9 present our results.

Fig. 8 contains the results by a, the accuracy of the users' estimates. Recall that $a = t_e / t_r$. Therefore a small a implies that the request asked for much more time than the job actually used. Note that a large request is harder to fit in the availability list and also harder to backfill (compared to a smaller one). We thus expected a to strongly impact the results. However, a shows almost no impact on the maximum improvement and little impact on the performance actually attained by **SA**. While it is true that small values of a (say $a \leq 0.2$) result in greater turn-around times for all strategies, we expected this to happen more intensely. Similarly, very small values of a (say $a \leq 0.1$) reduce the relative performance of **SA**, but again to a lesser degree than we expected. Our results seem to corroborate other studies that have found inaccurate user's estimates not to significantly hurt performance [10] [23].

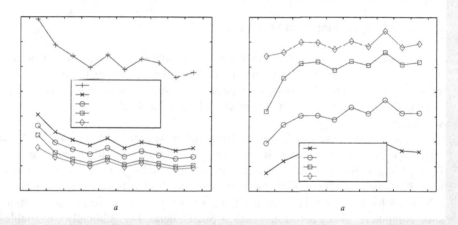

Fig. 8. Results by a (accuracy of the requests)

Fig. 9 shows results by varying the size of the range of choices. As before, the results were grouped into deciles. However, 29.2% of the experiments had range size equals 7 (this happened so often because many jobs have small n_u or n_{limit}). For that reason, the first data point in the graph averages the first three deciles of experiments, and the graphs contain seven data point instead of ten.

As expected, the maximum improvement grows with the size of the range. The greater the size of the range, the more leverage **SA** has in finding a good request to submit. In particular, large ranges (say above 100) seem to provide a substantial boost in the relative performance of both **SA** and best choice.

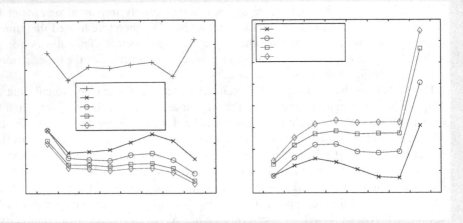

Fig. 9. Results by the size of the range of choices

4.4   Simulations Using Real Speedups

Simulations are an important research tool. They allow us to explore issues that are not tractable analytically or experimentally. However, they can produce invalid results due to a number of reasons, from poor modeling of reality to undetected bugs in the simulator. Consequently, it is important to double-check the results obtained via simulations.

A crucial part of our simulation model is the job speedup function. In this Section, we show the results of experiments designed to investigate whether using the Downey's model of parallel speed-up skewed our results. For these experiments, we used NAS benchmarks (which have known speed-up behavior) as the jobs to be scheduled by **SA**. NAS benchmarks have known execution times for a variety of supercomputers and partition sizes. Such data is publically available at `http://www.nas.nasa.gov/Software/NPB/`. Moreover, since they are used to evaluate performance, they are representative of real jobs. Finally, some of the NAS benchmarks are constrained with respect to the number of processors they can use. For some, the number of processors must be a perfect square. For others, it must be a power-of-two. This represents another real-world constraint for **SA**.

In the experiments, we replaced one job in the workload by a NAS benchmark (which has known speed-up). We then compared the performance of this NAS benchmark (i) when **SA** decides which request to submit, versus (ii) when we request the same number of processors for the NAS benchmark as the job we replace. We use five NAS benchmarks: MG, LU, SP, BT, and EP. MG and LU require a power-of-two partition size and thus are the most constrained jobs. `http://www.nas.nasa.gov/Software/NPB/` contains execution time information of MG and LU over 8, 16, 32, 64, 128, and 256 processors for the SP2. Consequently, for MG and LU, **SA** had 4 to 6 choices depending on the number of processors of the supercomputer being used (see Table 1). SP and BT require perfect-square partition size. The execution time data contains information for 9, 16, 25, 36, 64, 121, and 256 processors; providing 5 to 7 choices available to **SA**. There are no restrictions for EP. It can run over any number of processors and thus there are as many choices as processors in the supercomputer. We performed 10000 simulations in total: 2000 per NAS benchmark.

Table 3 shows the overall results of using NAS benchmarks as the job **SA** schedules. The results are consistent with those found when Downey's model is used to generate speed-up information (see Table 2). As before, **SA** gets relatively close to results obtained by the best choice. Furthermore, **SA** improves the turn-around time of the NAS benchmarks by a factor of 4.19 compared to the user's choice, a result even better than the one achieved using Downey's model. We attribute this better performance to the fact that EP provides **SA** with many more choices than what we have been considering (up to 7 choices), creating the opportunity for an even greater improvement in performance.

Table 3. Overall NAS results

	User's choice	SA choice	Best Choice
Geometric Mean of the Turn-Around Time (secs)	1164.70	278.04	253.05
Relative Performance	-----	4.19	4.60

Indeed, consider Fig. 10, which groups the results by the restriction posed by the number of processors a NAS benchmark can use. Note that the maximum improvement is greater for EP than for the other NAS benchmarks. The presence of EP also explains the greater maximum improvement of NAS benchmarks (whose best choice's relative performance equals 4.60) compared to jobs with Downey's speed-up (whose best choice's relative performance equals 2.98). The large number of choices offered by EP makes adaptively selecting the request more attractive. Note also that **SA** is still able remain close to the maximum improvement for EP, which suggests that increasing the number choices doesn't make it harder for **SA** to find a very good request.

Fig. 11 contains the NAS results by N, the relative load of the system. As with the simulations based on Downey's speedup (see Fig. 3), the execution time increases with N. Again, this is because the more jobs there are in the system, the longer an arriving job will probably have to wait in the queue. The relative performance, on the other hand, tends to decrease as N increases, showing however a modest increase for $N \geq 0.2$. Since the relative performance for jobs with Downey's speed stabilizes around the same value, we don't believe this represents a distinct phenomenon.

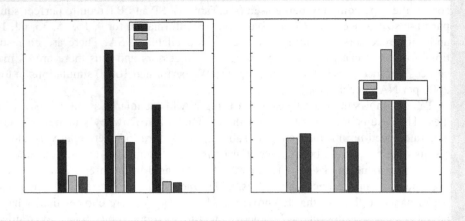

Fig. 10. NAS results by kind of benchmark

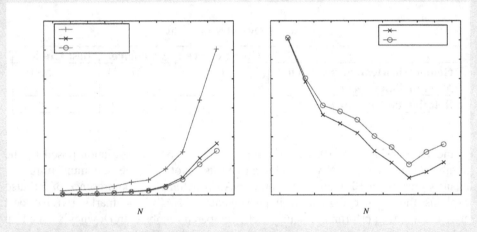

Fig. 11. NAS results by N (number of jobs in the system)

Fig. 12 presents the results by the accuracy of the user's estimates a. Note the similarity to Fig. 8, which displays the results based on Downey's model by accuracy. Again **SA** presents a high tolerance to variance in accuracy a. Only small values of a seem to affect the performance of **SA**.

We therefore believe that the NAS results validate the use of Downey's model in our simulations.

5   Future Work

As with any research, this answers some questions but raises others. To follow up this work, there are four research topics we intend to pursue. First, we would like to develop **SA** into a tool for production jobs. For some sites, the supercomputer scheduler allows for arriving jobs to affect existing ones, increasing the uncertainty **SA** has to cope with. It would be important to evaluate the impact of this added uncertainty on **SA**.

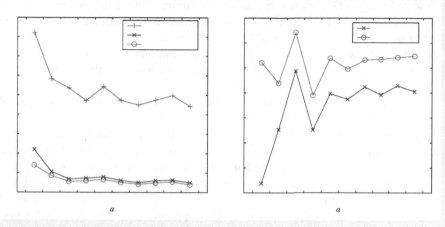

Fig. 12. NAS results by *a* (accuracy of the requests)

Second, we intend to investigate the effect multiple instances of **SA** have on each other, a question that has been called the *Bushel of AppLeS* [3]. We expect the improvements to the performance of an individual job to be smaller when many jobs have their requests crafted by **SA**, because the system as whole becomes more efficient, making it harder for **SA** to find very good "slots" in the supercomputer schedule. We want to investigate whether this is really the case and, if so, to what extent. Also, it might be that different mixtures of jobs produce different Bushel of AppLeS effects. This also needs to be understood.

Third, we plan to extend **SA** to target multiple supercomputers, instead of only one. In principle, **SA** could be used to submit the same job to all available supercomputers. While this guarantees a turn-around time that is at least no worse than selecting one supercomputer, it increases the load on all supercomputers, and thus might produce a bad Bushel of AppLeS effect. If this indeed happens, it is natural to ask what policies can supercomputer schedulers implement to discourage such a submit-to-all strategy. For example, charge for submission as well as execution might be a promising approach.

Fourth, we aim to enable **SA** to better deal with priorities. Real-life supercomputer schedulers enable users to specify a priority to the jobs they submit. **SA** could deal with priorities at the cost of spending more time scheduling. However, it is very plausible that some users don't want to optimize for turn-around time *at any cost*. How we enable the user to express an optimization goal that includes cost and how **SA** pursues such a goal are also intriguing research questions.

6   Related Work

There has been great interest in supercomputer scheduling in recent years. Some of the research in this area allow for the scheduler to choose the number of processors allocated to a job [8] or even to change this number during the execution of the job [6] [17]. Such schedulers therefore try to improve the performance of the system in the same way **SA** aims to improve the performance of the job. The main distinction is exactly that these efforts take the system-wide viewpoint. Alternatively, we approach the problem by scheduling one job at a time and use a user-centric performance metric.

The very fact the **SA** works at the application level, makes it potentially useful for *Grid Computing* [12]. Computational Grids consist of resources that are geographically scattered and/or under control of multiple entities, but can be combined as execution platform for some application. In this scenario, one needs an application scheduler to select the resources of interest, determine what piece of work is to be assigned to each to them, and then craft requests to have each piece of work carried out. This applicability of **SA** to Grid Computing is no accident. In fact, it was instrumental in deciding for the application-level approach (in opposition to the system-level one). As mentioned in the previous Section, we plan to extend **SA** to deal with multiple supercomputers, potentially by selecting which machine to submit the job to.

The current research in Grid scheduling that involves supercomputers seems to target jobs that spread across multiple machines. *Advance reservations* are the basic service to support application scheduling for such jobs [5] [13]. They have been shown to provide better system-wide utilization compared to dedicating supercomputer time for the jobs that spread across multiple supercomputers [21]. Interestingly enough, the availability list is touted in this context as providing the information that enables one to decide on which reservation to request [5] [13] [18]. Our research complements this work in that it explores the availability list to improve the performance of jobs that use a single supercomputer, a far more common case.

An alternative approach was adopted by the GTOMO, a Grid application that simultaneously uses supercomputer nodes and workstations [20]. GTOMO relies on a simplified version of the availability list to craft a request that can start running immediately. GTOMO can use this strategy because it schedules an embarrassingly parallel application, which can always start running immediately on the workstations. The supercomputer processors that happen to be available simply add more resources to the poll of workstations, boosting therefore the performance of the application.

7   Conclusions

This paper demonstrates that adaptively selecting the partition size of a supercomputer request can substantially improve the job's turn-around time. Here we introduce **SA**, an AppLeS application scheduler, and evaluate how it performs with four different real-world workloads. **SA** schedules moldable jobs, i.e. jobs that have flexibility regarding the size of the partition on which they execute. It decides which partition size should be requested considering the current state of the system, and consistently improves the turn-around time compared to the user's choice.

We simulate **SA** with four different workloads to evaluate how it performs under a variety of scenarios. We found **SA** to consistently improve the turn-around time of the job it schedules, but by different degrees depending on the scenario. In summary, the performance improvement attained by **SA** improves with the increase in the amount of parallelism in the job, the number of choices **SA** has available to choose from, and the range over which such choices are spread. On the other hand, **SA**'s performance decreases with the system's load. The size of the job doesn't appear to have a linear correlation to the performance of **SA**: **SA** does better for medium sized jobs than for small or large jobs. Finally, the slope of the job's speed-up and the accuracy of the user's estimates seem to have surprisingly little effect on **SA**.

We also investigate how close **SA** gets to the turn-around time obtained by the best choice offered to it. Always finding the best choice is impossible in practice due to the lack of perfect information about the jobs' execution times. Nevertheless, we found **SA**'s performance to be close to (above 90% of) the performance achieved by the best choice.

Acknowledgments

We thank our supporters: CAPES grant DBE2428/95-4, DoD Modernization contract 9720733-00, NPACI/NSF award ASC-9619020, and NSF grant ASC-9701333. We also want to express our gratitude to Victor Hazlewood, Dror Feitelson and the people who made their workloads available at the Parallel Workloads Archive (http://www.cs.huji.ac.il/labs/parallel/workload/). Finally, thanks to the members of the AppLeS group, Rich Wolski, Allen Downey, and Warren Smith for the insightful discussions and valuable suggestions.

References

[1]   Kento Aida, Hironori Kasahara, and Seinosuke Narita. *Job Scheduling Scheme for Pure Space Sharing among Rigid Jobs*. In Job Scheduling Strategies for Parallel Processing, Springer-Verlag, Lecture Notes in Computer Science Vol. 1459.

[2]   Fran Berman, Richard Wolski, Silvia Figueira, Jennifer Schopf, and Gary Shao. *Application-Level Scheduling on Distributed Heterogeneous Networks*. Supercomputing'96. http://www-cse.ucsd.edu/groups/hpcl/apples/hetpubs.html

[3]   Fran Berman and Rich Wolski. *The AppLeS Project: A Status Report*. In Proceedings of the 8th NEC Research Symposium, Berlin, Germany, May 1997. http://www.cs.ucsd.edu/groups/hpcl/apples/hetpubs.html

[4]   Walfredo Cirne and Fran Berman. *Application Scheduling over Supercomputers: A Proposal*. UCSD-CS99-631 Technical Report, October 1999. http://www.cs.ucsd.edu/Research/TechReports/dienst.html

[5] Steve *J.* Chapin, Dimitrios Katramatos, and John Karpovich. *The Legion Resource Management System.* IPPS Workshop on Job Scheduling Strategies for Parallel Processing, pp. 105-114, San Juan, Puerto Rico, 1999.
http://www.cs.virginia.edu/~chapin/papers/allpub.html

[6] Su-Hui Chiang and Mary K. Vernon. *Dynamic vs. Static Quantum-Based Parallel Processor Allocation.* In Job Scheduling Strategies for Parallel Processing, Springer-Verlag, Lectures Notes in Compututer Science vol. 1162, pp. 200-223, 1996.
http://www.cs.wisc.edu/~suhui/suhui.html

[7] Allen B. Downey. *A model for speedup of parallel programs.* U.C. Berkeley Technical Report CSD-97-933. http://www.sdsc.edu/~downey/model/

[8] Allen B. Downey. *Using Queue Time Predictions for Processor Allocation.* In Job Scheduling Strategies for Parallel Processing, Springer-Verlag, Lect. Notes Comput. Sci. vol. 1162, 1997. http://www.sdsc.edu/~downey/predalloc/

[9] A. B. Downey and D. G. Feitelson. *The elusive goal of workload characterization.* Perf. Eval. Rev. 26(4), pp. 14-29, Mar 1999. http://www.cs.huji.ac.il/~feit/pub.html

[10] D. G. Feitelson and A. Mu'alem Weil. *Utilization and predictability in scheduling the IBM SP2 with backfilling.* In 12th Intl. Parallel Processing Symp., pp. 542-546, April 1998. http://www.cs.huji.ac.il/~feit/pub.html

[11] D. G. Feitelson and *L.* Rudolph. *Metrics and benchmarking for parallel job scheduling.* In Job Scheduling Strategies for Parallel Processing, pp. 1-24, Springer-Verlag, 1998. Lecture Notes in Computer Science Vol. 1459. http://www.cs.huji.ac.il/~feit/pub.html

[12] Ian Foster and Carl Kesselman (editors). *The Grid: Blueprint for a New Computing Infrastructure.* Morgan Kaufmann Publishers. 1999.

[13] I. Foster, C. Kesselman, C. Lee, R. Lindell, K. Nahrstedt, A. Roy. *A Distributed Resource Management Architecture that Supports Advance Reservations and Co-Allocation.* International Workshop on Quality of Service, 1999.
http://www-fp.globus.org/documentation/papers.html

[14] Jochen Krallmann, Uwe Schwiegelshohn, and Ramin Yahyapour. *On the Design and Evaluation of Job Scheduling Algorithms.* In Job Scheduling Strategies for Parallel Processing, Springer-Verlag, Lectures Notes in Compututer Science vol. 1659, 1999.

[15] David Lifka. *The ANL/IBM SP Scheduling System.* In Job Scheduling Strategies for Parallel Processing, D. G. Feitelson and *L.* Rudolph (Eds.), Springer-Verlag, Lecture Notes in Computer Science Vol. 949, 1995.
http://www.tc.cornell.edu/UserDoc/SP/Batch/what.html

[16] Maui High Performance Computing Center. *The Maui Scheduler Web Page.*
http://wailea.mhpcc.edu/maui/

[17] Thu D. Nguyen, Raj Vaswani and John Zahorjan. *Parallel Application Characterization for Multiprocessor Scheduling Policy Design.* In Job Scheduling Strategies for Parallel Processing, Springer-Verlag, Lectures Notes in Computure Science vol. 1162, pp. 175-199, 1996. http://bauhaus.cs.washington.edu/homes/thu/papers/list.html

[18] Bill Nitzberg. *Advance Reservations and Co-Scheduling Workshop Web Page.* May 11, 1999. http://www.nas.nasa.gov/~nitzberg/sched-g/AdvRes_May99/index.html

[19] Platform Computing Corp. *Load Sharing Facility Web Page.*
http://www.platform.com/platform/platform.nsf/webpage/LSF?OpenDocument

[20] Shava Smallen, Walfredo Cirne, Jaime Frey, Fran Berman, Rich Wolski, Mei-Hui Su, Carl Kesselman, Steve Young, and Mark Ellisman. *Combining Workstations and Supercomputers to Support Grid Applications: The Parallel Tomography Experience.* 9th Heterogeneous Computing Workshop, held in conjunction with IPDPS'2000, Cancun, Mexico, May 2000. http://www-cse.ucsd.edu/users/walfredo/resume.html#publications

[21] Quinn Snell, Mark Clement, David Jackson, and Chad Grogory. *The Performance Impact of Advance Reservation Meta-scheduling*. 6th Workshop on Job Scheduling Strateties for Parallel Processing. In Conjunction with IPDPS 2000, Cancun, Mexico, May 1 2000.
[22] The SPEC (Standard Performance Evaluation Corporation) web page. http://www.spec.org/
[23] D. Zotkin and P. Keleher. *Job-Length Estimation and Performance in Backfilling Schedulers*. 8th International Symposium on High Performance Distributed Computing (HPDC'99), Redondo Beach, California, USA, 3-6 Aug 1999.

Author Index